AF564611

THE COMPANIES ACT, 2013

New Challenges in Contemporary Indian Economy

THE COMPANIES ACT, 2013

New Challenges in Contemporary Indian Economy

Editor

Partha Pratim Mitra

Foreword by

Professor Autar Krishen Koul

Formerly Vice Chancellor, National University of Study & Research in Law, Ranchi,
Formerly Vice Chancellor, National Law University, Jodhpur,
Formerly Dean, Faculty of Law, The University of Delhi

REGAL PUBLICATIONS
New Delhi - 110 027

DECLARATION

This book has been published only for academic and educational purpose. All the views, comments and expressions are individual author's own of the respective chapter where Editor and Publisher are no way responsible.

THE COMPANIES ACT, 2013: New Challenges in Contemporary Indian Economy

ISBN 978-81-8484-562-4 [HB]

Typeset by
THE LASER PRINTERS
8/15, 3rd Floor, Subhash Nagar, New Delhi-110027

Printed in India at
NEW ELEGANT PRINTERS
A-49/1, Mayapuri Phase-I, New Delhi-110064

Published by
REGAL PUBLICATIONS
F-159, Rajouri Garden, New Delhi - 110 027
Phone: 45546396, 25435369
E-mail: regalbookspub@yahoo.com, regaldeepbooks@yahoo.com

Contents

Foreword

This book is devoted to underpin the importance of the Companies Act, 2013 to achieve the economic growth of India in the context of it being liberalized and globalised after 1980s'and in terms of the avowed objectives of the present policy framework to facilitate the doing of business in India and beyond in a less cumbersome way than it used to be prior to liberalization. As all of us know how business and business people used to be throttled by laws and policies of the erstwhile policy makers as a consequence all sorts of corruption and mismanagement were ruling the roost and the Companies Act of 1956 was used as an instrument of state controls allowing hardly any freedom and choice with the business people. The company law became so obtuse that hardly any economic growth was possible and often times business people could do and manage business only when they could get state and political patronage. India was the only country in the world where limits on production were imposed as a result the average national growth rose by 2-3%. After the economic liberalization, globalization and privatization the policy makers kept on changing the law and legal trajectory and finally the Companies Act of 2013, was passed to make substantial changes in the company and corporate laws so that not only doing of business in India is made easy and competitive but also new strategies are introduced keeping in view the fast changes happening in international and domestic financial markets. Economics teaches us that economic growth of a country is possible if the law and legal framework allows full freedom to investors where and when to invest and to withdraw their investments with less of hassles and the policy makers have realized it although very late and after so many scams notably Satyam, Sahara, Sharda *et al.* Therefore, the Companies Act, 2013 have introduced new norms in the Companies Act as well as revamp of the SEBI and other securities laws.

This book is a collection of twenty three articles written by authors from different law universities and faculties spread across the country and is divided into ten chapters ranging from one person company, insider trading, class action, special courts, cross border merger and amalgamation, corporate social responsibility, independent directors, women directors, fund raising and new challenges such as uniform financial system, shareholders oppression and statutory remedies. Thus the canvas of this volume is important and wide reflecting on almost all major changes introduced by the 2013 enactment. All these articles comprising this volume are well researched articles and are testimony of the labor, hard work and understanding which these authors have demonstrated in their respective articles.

The topic of One Man Company illustrates the good and bad of the effects of one man company notwithstanding the fact that that one man company is a necessity and not a luxury. Insider Trading is a contentious issue and the 2013 Act tries to plug the loopholes by providing an exhaustive definition and correspondingly SEBI has further tightened its noose on the insider trades, with a code of fair dealing and monitoring. Class Action have been introduced in 2013 Act with the dual purpose of allowing one or more plaintiff to prosecute and file a case on behalf of group of person who have a common cause of grievances against the defendant/respondents; the objective is to protect the shareholders in the eventuality of defendant committing acts which are either in violation of the company or company laws and thus is very salutary in protecting the interest of shareholders and others. The most tantalizing topic from the point of avoiding tax by companies of indulging in cross border mergers and amalgamations and at the time realizing the importance of allowing Indian companies to expand beyond the shores of India in the globalised world, the 2013 Act allows cross border amalgamation of Indian companies with the rest of the world with fair amount of checks and balances and is a salutary innovation. Corporate social responsibility is a concept which imposes obligations on company of means having certain amount of turnover, to indulge in causes which are well defined in terms of the existing social dysfunctions, which do not need justifications as these social causes require some immediate attention by providing economic palliatives and as such the 2013 Act is very progressive. Equally the role of directors and their responsibilities and obligations in the 2013 dispensations have been not only elaborated but equally made stricter. Further the concept of independent directors a novel concept has been introduced in the new companies Act. The introduction of women directors in 2013 enactment striving to achieve some elements of gender justice is laudable.

The book exhibits a good understanding of the subjects dealt by the respective scholars. Indeed it is a worthy edition to the literature of the company and corporate law and I feel proud to write a foreword to this collection of essays. Finally I appreciate the efforts of Professor Mitra for publishing this volume. The well researched articles in this volume should find a place in the library of lawyers and students practicing company and corporate laws.

PROFESSOR AUTAR KRISHEN KOUL

Preface

The main purpose of this book is to simplify the understandings about functions of companies within the ambit of economic laws of the country. Recent generation of students in different law schools are very much passionate about corporate laws and business laws to expertise their skill.

The present approach to company legislation in India is very atypical because of the co-existence of the Companies Act, 1956 and the Companies Act, 2013. In the academic world, students, teachers, examiners or question setters all are eager to pacify this co-existence of old and new laws. In common parlance the word 'company' is normally reserved for those associated for economic purposes, i.e. to carry on business for gain. But company law provides vehicles in addition to the company in which people can associate for gainful business and companies incorporated under the Companies Act may be used for carrying on not-for-profit business or for purposes which can be only doubtfully characterized as business at all.[1] From the days of the joint trading companies which built up the merchant empires of England and Holland in the 17th century, the quasi-public corporation has been well known. Its entrance into the field of industry, however, dates from early 19th century. In 1800, the corporate form was used in America mainly for undertaking involving a direct public interest: the construction of turnpikes, bridges and canals, the operation of banks and insurance companies and the creation of fire brigades.[2] Recently after the 2008 crisis, governments and law-makers worldwide desire regulatory strategies to resolve systemic crises. The new company law of India was the demand of rapid changes in socio-economic climate of the nation with the rhythm of international economic growth. The need of

1. Principles of Modern Company Law, Gower and Davies, Thomson Sweet & Maxwell, 8th edition, 2008, p. 4.
2. Adolf A. Berle and Gardiner C. Means, *The Modern Corporation and Private Property*, Transaction Publishers, 11th printing, 2010, p. 11.

independent directors was realized from Satyam scam for auditing default. The prohibition to company on acceptance of deposits and several repayment mechanisms are the outcome of series of debates from the Amendment of 1974, 1988, 1996, 2000 and 143rd report of Law Commission in 1991. We have realized the struggle of jurisdiction between Ministry of Corporate Affairs and SEBI on private placement or convertible debenture issue in *Sahara* case. The nation was witness to the suffering of small investors due to legislative shortsightedness and inadequacy in forum relating to chit fund issue in *Sharda* scam throughout eastern part of country. Impact of globalised business can be seen in the insertion of Cross-border merger, Global Depository Receipts, Indian Depository Receipts in the company law though RBI also entering in the jurisdiction fund raising from foreign market. The Companies Act, 2013 is the backbone of corporate laws and it is the fountainhead of Corporate Finance, Corporate Governance, Merger & Amalgamation, Investment & Securities Laws, Foreign Investment Laws, Competition Laws and other allied subjects which are being generated time to time for minute study of company laws. It has become very much necessary to know every nook and corner of the new statute for sake of legal practice as well as to understand new theories and concepts introduced in consistent with globalised market for better economy. It is company law that provides the basic features that makes the company an especially attractive organizational form for the channeling of finance to business.[3] This book has many chapters particularly related to company form business by government and public as well as public-private partnership also in India. The entire book is divided in Ten Sections comprising of 21 Chapters selected carefully on the basis of their contents with the major issues of new company law. All these chapters are written mainly to understand the new law in better way. Here writers include very young students just narrating the principles of company law as lucid as possible and some are serious researchers critically analyzing various legal perspectives in economic standpoint. All these chapters are written in a way that a layman is also able to understand new company law in better way. I hope readers will find this book easy to grasp and it will also be helpful for those readers who want to know major changes of company law within Indian economy. I am also optimistic that the book will serve as reference for the lawyers, academicians, researchers and others.

PARTHA PRATIM MITRA

3. Eilis Ferran, *Principles of Corporate Finance Law*, Oxford University Press, 1st edition, 2008, p. 4.

Acknowledgements

First and foremost I want to express my hearty acknowledgments to all those contributors who have given their thought provoking articles and also waited for a long period for the publication. I should convey my deep sense of appreciation to my colleagues and friends from a number of Law Schools and Faculty of Law from different Universities. I am obliged to all those students who have contributed articles with their unconditional and whole-hearted support. I am highly thankful to all the authors for their precious offerings.

I want to convey my sincere gratitude to our Hon'ble Vice-Chancellor Prof. (Dr.) B.C. Nirmal for his kind support toward such type of academic venture. I am obliged to him for his blessings and well wishes. I am also grateful to my all colleagues of NUSRL, Ranchi and more precisely to young colleague Mainan Roy for his continuance help for collection of articles from teachers and scholars from various parts of country.

I am also thankful to Pratap Kumar Sarkar of S.C. Sarkar & Sons (P.) Ltd., Kolkata who has played very important role to make this venture successful one.

I must extend my full respect and love to my father, Pranab Kumar Mitra and mother, Ila Mitra for their blessing and uninterrupted help during this edition.

For the finishing touch, I am grateful to R.D.S. Bhatia of Regal Publications, New Delhi for his spontaneous support which has inspired this new editor to motivate so many upcoming authors.

This publication is a collective effort but all limitations are mine whereas credit goes to everyone associated with it.

PARTHA PRATIM MITRA

List of Contributors

Dr. Sunitha Abhay Jain, Associate Professor, School of Law, Christ University, Bengaluru.

Aakanksha Mishra, 4th Year student, B.A., LL.B. (Hons.), Gujarat National Law School, Gandhinagar.

Sagar Godbole, 4th Year student, B.A., LL.B. (Hons.), Gujarat National Law School, Gandhinagar.

Nitesh Mathur, 4th Year B.A. LL.B. (Hons.) student of Chanakya National Law University, Patna.

Gurminder Dhami, Company Secretary.

Pratiti Nayak, Assistant Professor of Law, School of Law, KIIT University, Bhubaneswar.

Dr. Preetha S., Assistant Professor, School of Legal Studies, Cochin University of Science and Technology, Cochin-22.

Anindhya Tiwari, Faculty of Law at National Law University, Jodhpur, Rajasthan and he is also a Ph.D. scholar at the same institution.

Amit Agarwal, Associate Company Secretary and a former Postgraduate student of National Law University, Jodhpur.

Rashi Chandhoke, BBA/LLB, 4th Year (Business Law Hons.), KIIT School of Law, KIIT University, Bhubaneswar, Odisha.

Ankit Sahoo, BBA/LLB, 4th Year (Business Law Hons.), KIIT School of Law, KIIT University, Bhubaneswar, Odisha.

Dr. Aparajita Bhatt, Assistant Professor at National Law University, Delhi.

Rukma Roy, 6th Semester student of KIIT Law School, KIIT Univerisity, Bhubaneswar, Odisha.

Dr. Aneesh V. Pillai, Assistant Professor, School of Legal Studies, Cochin University of Science and Technology, Kerala.

Dr. Souvik Chatterji, Assistant Professor of Law, National Law University, Jodhpur.

Subhankar Das, 2nd Year BBA, LLB Student, National Law University, Odisha.

Arpita Sharma, 4th Year, BA, LLB (Hons.) student, College of Legal Studies, University of Petroleum & Energy Studies, Dehradun, Uttarakhand.

Puja Kumari, 4th Year, B.A., LL.B. (Hons.) student, College of Legal Studies, University of Petroleum & Energy Studies, Dehradun, Uttarakhand.

Gunjan Arora, B.A., LL.B. (Hons.), LL.M. (National Law University, Delhi) and currently practising at Delhi High Court and District Courts.

Varun Tandon, B.A., LL.B. (Hons.), Institute of Law, Nirma University, Ahmedabad.

Amit Pande, B.A., LL.B. (Hons) from Institute of Law, Nirma University, Ahmedabad.

Dr. Arundhati Bhattacharyya, Assistant Professor, Department of Political Science, B.G. College, Kolkata-700056.

Rishika Lekhadia, 4th year, B.A., LL.B. (Hons.), WB National University of Juridical Sciences, Kolkata.

Shreyash Shah, Law Student from Jitendra Chauhan College of Law, Mumbai University and a Chartered Accountant.

Navtika Singh, Assistant Professor, Galgotias University, Greater Noida, UP.

Shuchita Agarwal, Assistant Professors, Galgotias University, Greater Noida, UP.

Devarshi Mukhopadhyay, B.A., LL.B. (Hons.), NALSAR University of Law, Hyderabad.

Priyam Ratnam, Practicing Lawyer, Delhi High Court.

Hansa Sinha, A Legal Associate at TPM Solicitors and Consultants, New Delhi.

Introduction

The Companies Act, 2013 is the major piece of legislation in India relating to formation, operation and control of companies and at the same time keeps balance between securities laws for investors and corporate finance for companies. This is a drastic step to regulate corporate sectors after replacing half century old existing statute. It was the demand of existing society on the backdrop of national economic growth and rapid changing international trade and business. This law is totally based to deal with contemporary economic problems of nation. Previously maximum company laws of India were influenced by English law and those were more or less dominated by thoughts of English company laws like Companies Act of 1850 (English Law of 1844) and Act of 1857 (English Law of 1856), Act of 1866 (English Law of 1862), Act of 1913 (English Law of 1908) or Act of 1936 (English Law of 1929). Now this law is purely Indian in nature and very much related to cope with Indian problems of present context on securities irregularities or corporate maladministration. The company incorporated under the successive Companies Acts, is a dominant institution in our society, all the more so with the retreat in recent decades of the government owned or public sector of the economy from a number of areas in which it previously had been a monopoly or near-monopoly provider of services or less often, of goods.[1] In England, the company is the most popular form for modern business of economic significance because it has advantages over other types of business vehicle as an organizational form through which to limit financial risks and to raise large amounts of finance from investors whilst keeping the day-to-day running of business concentrated in the hands of a relatively small group of managers. These special features of company law act as incentives to trade and commerce and can play a critical role in

1. Gower & Davies, *Principles of Modern Company Law*, 8th edition, Thomson Sweet Maxwell, p. 1.

promoting enterprise and investment.[2] In April 1601 the English East India Company sent its first expedition to the East Indies and second expedition by same ships in March 1604. The shareholders in these two voyages made a profit of 95 per cent on their investment. After the first 12 voyages were financed separately, the company sifted to a method of finance that spread risks over a number of voyages and then became a fully fledged joint stock company, with, after 1657, continuous investment unrelated to specific voyages. In 1688 trading in its stocks began on the London Stock Exchange.[3] But the origins of modern global securities market lie in medieval Italy where in the city states of Venice, Genoa and Florence new financial arrangements emerged out of growing trade between East and West and advances included such development as deposit banking, marine insurance, bill of exchange, joint stock companies and transferable securities.[4] The century between the enactment of the Bubble Act, 1720 and its repeal in 1825 was an extremely fertile period for the later development of English company law. Many legal contrivances, generally associated with modern company laws were developed during this apparent 'dark age' for technical innovation. New means and varieties of shareholding and capital raising were developed during this period. Preference shares, debentures and deferred shares were all first introduced during this period of apparent inaction. This was also a period during which considerable refinement occurred in respect of the means by which the liability of shareholders might be limited.[5] Again, the Joint Stock Companies Act, 1844, as per recommendation of the Gladstone Committee, set an important milestone in the development of the corporation in England. The industrial revolution which established the factory as a predominant form of production and separated the worker from control over the instruments of production, the corporate revolution, separating ownership from control over the instruments of production, has come on us gradually. Its beginning in the America can be traced back to the early 19th century. Much had been written on the big corporation and its effect on competition in the free market, particularly after the great merger movement at the

2. Eilis Ferran, *Principles of Corporate Finance Law*, Oxford University Press, 1st published 2008, p. 3.
3. James Fulcher, *Capitalism: A very short introduction*, Oxford University Press, 1st published 2004, pp. 1 and 3.
4. Ranald C. Michie, *The Global Securities Market: A History*, Oxford University Press, 2008, p. 17.
5. Rob McQueen, *A Social History of Company Law: Great Britain and the Australian Colonies, 1854-1920*, Ashgate, p. 17.

turn of the century.[6] The promotion of canal and railway companies in the early 19th century permanently changed the attitudes of many sectors of the English people towards Joint Stock Company[7] and between 1850 and 1900 stock exchanges evolved into central institutions of the capitalist world, providing an essential interface between money and capital markets at the national and international levels.[8] In the thirteenth century, Pope Innocent IV espoused the theory of the legal fiction by saying that corporate bodies could not be ex-communicated because they only exist in abstract. This enunciation is the foundation of the separate entity principle and the common law jurisdictions do invariably impose taxation against a corporation based on the legal principle that the corporation is "a person" that is separate from its members. It is the decision of the House of Lords in *Salomon vs. Salomon* (1897) A.C. 22 that opened the door to the formation of a corporate group.[9] The Companies Act, 2013 has introduced so many radical changes like Corporate Social Responsibility which is purely sociological approach of companies and overlapping of economic and societal functions of company. The prohibition of insider trading is an area of new law on corporate crimes which has come also in the domain of corporate affairs from securities law. The US model of Class Action suit has given a forum for recognition of rights of shareholders and other stakeholders first time in India. Finally, National Company Law Tribunal and National Company Law Appellate Tribunal have got constitutional sanctity under 1956 law[10] as well as 2013 law[11] through successive judgments of the Supreme Court. Now we have to see the workability of present law to improve corporate governance in our contemporary Indian economy.

---

6. Adolf A. Berle and Gardiner C. Means, *The Modern Corporation and Private Property*, Transaction Publishers, 11th printing 2010, p. xliii.
7. Rob McQueen, *A Social History of Company Law: Great Britain and the Australian Colonies, 1854-1920*, Ashgate, p. 24.
8. Ranald C. Michie, *The Global Securities Market: A History*, Oxford University Press, 2008, p. 117.
9. *Vodafone International Holdings B.V.* vs. *Union of India*, Civil Appeal No. 733 of 2012 [Arising out of SLP (C)], No. 26529 of 2010, pp. 32 and 38.
10. *Union of India* vs. *R. Gandhi*, Civil Appeal No. 3067 of 2004, Judgment dated May 11, 2010.
11. *Madras Bar Association* vs. *Union of India*, Writ Petition (c) No. 1072 of 2013, Judgment dated May 14, 2015.

CHAPTER I

One Person Company

1

One Person Company: A Viable Option?

DR. SUNITHA ABHAY JAIN

Introduction

India opened up its economy in 1991, more as a compulsion due to the then prevailing precarious foreign exchange situation, than by choice. More than twenty years on, today the decision has proved to be in the right direction, especially considering the fall of socialist and communist bastions around the world. Unfortunately, Indian laws relating to business remained unchanged for a very long time. The Limited Liability Partnership Act[1] was enacted only in 2008 and the law relating to companies continued to be governed by the archaic Companies Act, 1956, with periodic amendments. Though the new Companies Bill was drafted way back, it could receive the President's assent only on 29th August 2013. In the meanwhile, new corporate trends were emerging in the global order and it was imperative that India enact suitable laws to make it an attractive destination for foreign investors, who were finding it extremely difficult to operate in the existing scheme of things. As a result, India was losing out to countries like China and Singapore which provided a comparative better ease of doing business. It is in this context that the Government constituted an expert committee on Company Law under the Chairmanship of

1. Limited Liability Partnership Act, 2008.

J.J. Irani[2] on 2nd December, 2004 which culminated in the introduction of the Companies Bill on 23rd October, 2008 in the 14th Lok Sabha and eventually the Parliament enacted the Companies Act in 2013 to amend and consolidate the law relating to companies. Some of the salient aspects introduced by the Act are Class Action suits, women on Board of Directors, Corporate Social Responsibility, setting up of National Company Law Tribunal, simplified procedures for mergers and amalgamation, cross-border mergers with the permission of Reserve Bank of India, prohibition on forward dealing and insider trading, increase in number of shareholders, independent directors, rotation of arbitrators, etc. The concept of One Person Company is one of the novel concepts introduced by the Companies Act, 2013.

One Person Company—A Conceptual Analysis

An innovative feature of the Companies Act, 2013 has been the introduction of the concept of 'One Person Company'.[3] Section 2 (62) of the Companies Act, 2013 defines One Person Company, 'as a company which has only one member.' A single natural person can constitute a One Person Company.[4] This concept has opened up new vistas of business opportunities for sole proprietorships and entrepreneurs who can now enjoy the advantages of limited liability and the benefit of separate legal entity as well. The introduction of One Person Company is expected to encourage the corporatization of micro-businesses. The legal regime is now made simpler to save time, energy and resources. It gives an opportunity to the small businessmen to contribute to the economic growth and also help in generating employment opportunities.

Historical Background of Companies Act, 2013

One of the most important legislations for regulating the entire corporate structure and for dealing with various aspects of governance of companies was the Companies Act, 1956. The Act had been amended, from time to time, to bring in more transparency and accountability in

---

2. J.J. Irani, Expert Committee report, India, *available at*: http://www.prime directors. com/pdf/JJ%20Irani%20Report-MCA.pdf (Visited on April 22, 2015).
3. Ministry of Corporate Affairs vide its G.S.R. Notification No. 250(E), dated 31st March, 2014, notified the Companies (Incorporation) Rules, 2014 under the Companies Act, 2013 which provide for formation of One Person Company.
4. Rule 3(1) of the Companies (Incorporation) Rules, 2014.

the corporate sector, but with limited success. For the regulation of the Corporate sector there are various other enactments of importance, some of them being the Securities Contracts (Regulation) Act, 1956, the Securities and Exchange Board of India Act, 1992 and the Depositories Act, 1996 which have been introduced by Securities and Exchange Board of India (SEBI), with a view to protect the interests of investors in the securities markets as well as to maintain standards of corporate governance in the country. The Companies Act, 1956 was enacted with the object to consolidate and amend the law relating to companies and certain other associations. Many changes had taken place in the national and international economic environment since the enactment of the said Act. The economy was changing at a fast pace and had become more complex, dynamic and diverse in nature. Corporate form of business had become a preferred vehicle by many for economic and commercial activities. Indian economy needed to harness its entrepreneurial and economic resources efficiently as there was an increase in international business, trade and capital flow in the companies. The statutory framework also needed to be strong enough to protect the investors.

In a competitive and technology-driven business environment, there was a growing need for greater autonomy of operation and innovation to the corporate sector. To meet the requirement of evolving economic activities and business models, a new framework had to be developed. It was felt that a piece-meal re-engineering of the corporate regulatory framework would not be adequate to enable the systemic changes required. A comprehensive review of the Companies Act, 1956 and the introduction of new Companies Bill were considered necessary for taking the corporate legal framework to the next level. The review of the Companies Act, 1956 and drafting of a new Companies Bill was taken by the Government on the basis of a detailed consultative process. A concept paper on new Company Law was placed on the website of the Ministry on 4th August, 2004 and the inputs received were put to detailed examination in the Ministry. The Government also constituted an expert committee on Company Law under the Chairmanship of Dr. J.J. Irani on 2nd December, 2004 to make recommendation in respect of the new Company Law. The Committee included representatives from concerned departments, trade bodies and individual experts as members or special invitees. The committee deliberated extensively on various issues and submitted its report to the Government on 31st May, 2005. After considering the report of the committee and other inputs received from time to time, the Government took up the exercise of a comprehensive review of the Companies Act, 1956. The main objective of the review was to retain the essential features of the existing framework and segregate the substantive law from the procedural law to enable good corporate governance. Further, the review committee was of the view that that law must be revised in such a manner that it should be easy to understand and interpret. The protection of investors and other stake-holders was also accorded due importance.

Finally a comprehensively revised Bill, the Companies Bill, 2008 was prepared in consultation with the Ministry of Law and was introduced in the Lok Sabha on 23rd October, 2008 in the 14th Lok Sabha and was subsequently referred to the Department-related Parliamentary Standing Committee on Finance for examination and report. However, before the said committee could present its report, the 14th Lok Sabha was dissolved and the Companies Bill, 2008 lapsed. In view of this, it was proposed to introduce the Companies Bill, 2009, which was introduced in the Lok Sabha on 3rd August, 2009. This Bill was referred to the Parliamentary Standing Committee on Finance, which submitted its report on 31st August, 2010 and was withdrawn after the introduction of the Companies Bill, 2011. The Companies Bill, 2011 was also considered by the Parliamentary Standing Committee on Finance which submitted its report on 26th June 2012. Subsequently the Bill was approved by the Lok Sabha on 18th December 2012 as the Companies Bill, 2012. The Bill was later approved by the Rajya Sabha on 8th August, 2013. It received the President's assent on 29th August, 2013 and has now become the Companies Act, 2013. The changes brought about by the Companies Act, 2013 are expected to have far-reaching implications and are set to significantly change the face of corporate India. The concept of One Person Company (OPC), which has been introduced for the first time in India by the enactment of the Companies Act, 2013.

Genesis of One Person Company

The concept of one person companies is already in existence in countries like the US, China, UK, Australia, Singapore, Qatar, Pakistan amongst others. The J.J. Irani Committee has suggested that; "with the increasing use of information technology and computers and the consequent emergence of the service sector, it is time that the entrepreneurial capabilities of the people are given an outlet for participation in economic activity. Such economic activity may take place through the creation of an economic person in the form of a company. Yet it would not be reasonable to expect that every entrepreneur who is capable of developing his ideas and participating in the market place should do it through an association of persons. We feel that it is possible for individuals to operate in the economic domain and contribute effectively. To facilitate this, the Committee recommends that the law should recognize the formation of a person economic entity in the form of 'One Person Company'. Such an entity may be provided with a simpler regime through exemptions so that the single entrepreneur is not compelled to fritter away his time, energy and resources on procedural matters".[5]

Features of a One Person Company under the Companies Act, 2013

A One Person Company is incorporated as a Private Limited Company.[6] It has only one member at any point of time and may have one[7] or more directors. However, it can have directors up to a maximum of 15 which can also be increased by passing a special resolution.[8] Rule 3 of Companies (Incorporation) Rules, 2014 provides for the incorporation of One Person Company and further provides that, only a natural person who is an Indian citizen and resident in India, i.e., a person who has stayed in India for a period of not less than one hundred and eighty-two days during the immediately preceding one calendar year, shall be eligible to incorporate a One Person Company. Further it provides that a person shall not be eligible to incorporate or become a nominee in more than one such company. A minor shall not become a member or nominee of a One Person Company or hold shares with beneficial interest. Such a Company cannot be incorporated or converted into a type of company as stipulated under Section 8 of the Act. Such a Company cannot carry out Non-Banking Financial Investment activities, including investment in securities of any Body Corporate. No One Person Company can convert voluntarily into any kind of company unless two years have expired from the date of incorporation of such Company, except when the threshold limit (paid-up share capital) is increased beyond fifty lakh rupees or its average annual turnover during the relevant period exceeds two crore rupees. A One Person Company also loses its status if the paid up capital exceeds Rs. 50 lakhs or the average annual turnover is more than 2 crores in three immediate preceding consecutive years.[9] An existing Private Company other than a company registered under Section 8 of the Act

5. One Person Company, available at: www.icsi.edu/Docs/Webmodules/ONE%20PERSON%20COMPANY.pdf (Visited on April 24, 2015).
6. Section 3 (1)(c) of the Companies Act, 2013.
7. Section 149(1)(a) of the Companies Act, 2013.
8. Section 149(1)(b) of the Companies Act, 2013.
9. Rule 6(1) of the Companies (Incorporation) Rules, 2014.

which has paid up share capital of Rs. 50 Lakhs or less or where the average annual turnover during the relevant period is Rs. 2 crores or less, may convert itself into one Person Company by passing a special resolution in a general meeting.[10] A distinct advantageous feature which a One Person Company enjoys over a proprietorship concern is of limited liability. At the same time, unlike the Private Limited or Public Limited companies, the incorporation and running of a One Person Company requires far less compliances and financial resources. It can raise capital through venture capital financial institution and later graduate into a private limited company. Mandatory rotation of auditor after expiry of a maximum term is not applicable to it. The annual return of the One Person Company is required to be signed by the company secretary, or in his absence, by the director of the company.[11] The provisions of Section 98 and Sections 100 to 111 (both inclusive) relating to holding of general meetings, do not apply to a One Person Company.[12] For the purposes of holding Board meetings, it is sufficient compliance if all resolutions required to be passed by such a company at a board meeting are entered in the Minutes book, signed and dated by the member and such date shall be deemed to be the date of the Board Meeting.[13] At least one board meeting is required to be held in each half of the calendar year and the gap between the two meetings should not be less than 90 days.[14] The financial statement of One Person Company can be signed by one director alone.[15] Cash Flow Statements are not a mandatory part of the financial statement for a One Person Company.[16] It has to be filed with the Registrar after they are duly adopted by the member within 180 days of closure of financial year, along with all necessary documents.[17] Board's report has to be annexed to the financial statements and it can also contain explanation or comments by the Board on every qualification, reservation or adverse remark or disclaimer made by the auditor in his report.[18] The other exemptions available to a One Person Company under the Companies Act, 2013 are:

10. Rule 7(1) of the Companies (Incorporation) Rules, 2014.
11. Proviso to Section 92 (1) of the Companies Act, 2013.
12. Section 122 (1) of the Companies Act, 2013.
13. Section 122 (3) of the Companies Act, 2013.
14. Section 173 (5) of the Companies Act, 2013.
15. Section 134 (1) of the Companies Act, 2013.
16. Section 2 (40) of the Companies Act, 2013.
17. Proviso to Section 137 (1) of the Companies Act, 2013.
18. Section 134 (4) of the Companies Act, 2013.

- Section 96—Option to dispense with the requirement of holding an AGM;
- Section 98—Power of Tribunal to call meetings of members;
- Section 100—Calling of extraordinary general meeting;
- Section 101—Notice of meeting;
- Section 102—Statement to be annexed to notice;
- Section 103—Quorum for meetings;
- Section 104—Chairman of meetings;
- Section 105—Proxies;
- Section 106—Restriction on voting rights;
- Section 107—Voting by show of hands;
- Section 108—Voting through electronic means;
- Section 109—Demand for poll;
- Section 110—Postal ballot; and
- Section 111—Circulation of members' resolution.

In the light of the above features and exemptions accorded to a One Person Company, it may be deduced that the government is keen on encouraging more participation from small and medium entrepreneurs in the economic activities through corporatisation of their business. This is sought to ostensibly bring about transparency in small business, which is usually absent in a proprietorship concern. Further, it may be seen as a first step towards the creation of Private and later Public Limited Companies.

One Person Company vis-à-vis Sole Proprietorship

Proprietorship is the simplest, oldest and the most common form of conducting business. In a sole proprietorship, the owner is solely responsible for all the losses and enjoys the benefit of retaining all the profits. It is easy to set-up and there are minimal procedural requirements to start one, with registration being optional. A distinct disadvantage of a sole proprietorship is that the liability is unlimited and it ceases to exist upon the death or incapacity to contract of the proprietor. Also, it is difficult for a proprietor to raise capital from venture capitalists and other financial institutions, thereby making it heavily dependent upon personal resources and debts to operate its business.

On the other hand, in a One Person Company there is limited liability on the part of the owner. It enjoys perpetual succession and is a separate legal entity in the eyes of law. Since a One Person Company requires to be registered, it creates transparency in its working thereby making it feasible for venture capitalists and other institutions to invest in such companies.

Conversion of One Person Company into Public or Private Company

A One Person Company can convert itself into a Public Company or a Private Company in certain cases. Firstly, where the paid up share capital of One Person Company exceeds fifty lakh rupees or its average turnover during the relevant period exceeds two crore rupees, it shall cease to be entitled to continue as a One Person Company. Further, One Person Company shall be required to convert itself, within six months of the date on which its paid up share capital is increased beyond fifty lakh rupees or the last day of the relevant period during which its average annual turnover exceeds two crore rupees as the case may be, into either a private company with a minimum of two members and two directors or public company with at least seven members and three directors in accordance with the provisions of Section 18 of the Act. An One Person Company shall alter its memorandum and articles by passing a resolution in accordance with Section 122 (3) of the Act to give effect to the conversion and to make necessary changes incidental thereto. A notice to the Registrar has to be given by the company within a period of sixty days informing that it has ceased to be a One Person Company and is required to convert itself into a Private or Public Limited Company as the case may be. One Person Company or any officer of such company shall be punishable with a fine which may extend to ten thousand rupees and with a further fine which may extend to one thousand rupees for every day during which such contravention continues.

Conversion of Private Company into One Person Company

A Private Company other than a company registered under Section 8 of the Act having a paid up share capital of fifty lakh rupees or less or average annual turnover during the relevant period is two crore rupees or less may convert itself into One Person Company by passing special resolution in the general meeting. Before passing such a resolution the company shall obtain 'No Objection' in writing from members and creditors. It has to file the copy of the special resolution with the Registrar of Companies within thirty days from the date of passing of such resolution. Further, it has to file an application for its conversion along with the fees as prescribed in the Companies (Registration offices and fees) Rules, 2014, by attaching the declaration of the Directors, along with an affidavit duly sworn in confirming that all members and creditors have given their consent for conversion and the paid up share capital of the company is fifty lakhs rupees or less, or the average annual turnover is less than two crore rupees, as the case may be. The list of members, list of creditors, the latest Audited balance sheet, Profit and Loss Account, copy of the 'No objection' letter of the secured creditors has to be filed along with the application for conversion. On being satisfied with the compliances stated therein, the Registrar shall issue the required certificate.

Nomination/Withdrawal or Death of Nominee or Member of OPC

An essential feature of any corporate entity is perpetual succession, since a company is an unnatural person and is a creation of statute. Rule 4 of the Companies (Incorporation) Rules, 2014 mandates that the subscriber or member nominates a person who shall step into his shoes in case of his death or incapacity to contract. The person so nominated by the subscriber or member of One Person Company may withdraw his consent by giving a notice in writing to such sole member and to the One Person Company. The sole member shall nominate another person as nominee within 15 days of the receipt of notice of withdrawal and the same has to be intimated to the Registrar of Companies along with the written consent of the person so nominated. Further, where the sole member of the One Person Company ceases to be the member due to his death or incapacity to contract, his nominee becomes the member of such One Person Company. Such new member can nominate within 15 days a person to be his nominee.

One Person Company—The way forward

In view of the above, it can be concluded that a One Person Company can prove to be an effective method of carrying on business activities. It gives a boost to spirited entrepreneurs who can concentrate on carrying on their businesses without being unduly worried about unlimited liability. However, one needs to take into consideration the following aspects in order to make the concept of One Person Company more effective. Firstly, the waiving of several statutory compliances for the creation and working of the One Person Company has placed much information regarding it working outside the purview of third parties—especially business creditors and banks, who are entitled to such information. This opacity may work against One Person Companies with creditors and banks preferring to extend credit to proprietorship concerns, where they can attach the personal assets of the proprietor in case of default. The absence of a credit-rating system adds to the problem of ascertaining the credit-worthiness of One Person Companies. In view of the above, it is suggested that banks should treat One Person Company at par with Proprietorship Concern with relation to the ease of opening and operating an account or extending credit facilities. A credible credit-rating system could be created for the purpose. Till then, the CIBIL scores of the Sole Member may be taken into consideration to ascertain the credit-worthiness of the One Person Company. Further, in its present form, the One Person Company is treated at par with other companies for the purpose of income tax. This essentially means that the One Person Company shall be charged a flat rate of 30% tax on its net. Income, while for a proprietorship concern the income tax chargeable is as same as it prevails for an individual, with the benefit of a slab system. It is suggested that the One Person Company may be treated as an individual for the purpose of ascertaining Income Tax liability by clubbing all other personal incomes of the Sole Member. Though the concept of separate legal entity will be diluted to a certain extent by this step, it is required to encourage and enable more people to adopt this mode of conducting business.

Though the Act provides for ease of starting and running a One Person Company, the winding up procedure for a One Person Company is on the same footing as any other company, which makes it an unattractive proposition. Moreover, the Act is silent on the manner in which a One Person Company by default becomes a Proprietorship Concern.

To ensure perpetual succession, Rule 4 of the Companies (Incorporation) Rules, 2014 stipulates that a person is to be nominated to be the director in case of the death of the subscriber or member. It further stipulates that the nominee may within 30 days of registration withdraw his consent by issuing a notice in writing to the subscriber or member and to the Company. Thereafter, the subscriber or member is required to submit the name of another nominee within 15 (fifteen) days of receipt of such notice, amend the memorandum of the company and communicate it to the jurisdictional Registrar of Companies. Further, it provides that in case of death or incapacity to contract of the subscriber or member, the nominee who steps into the shoes of the subscriber or member is obligated to appoint a nominee. This in effect would transfer the control of the One Person Company into the hands of persons which the subscriber or member would not have desired. This is in sharp contrast to the proprietorship mode, where upon the death or incapacity of the proprietor, the control of the proprietorship concern automatically passes on to his legal heirs in accordance with his personal laws. In view of the above, the winding up procedures for a One Person Company may be simplified on lines with the procedures laid down for the winding-up of a Limited Liability Partnership. Moreover, in case of death or incapacity to contract of the subscriber or member, the One Person Company should be deemed to have become a proprietorship concern and the control of the One Person Company should automatically move into the hands of his legal heirs instead of his nominee.

Conclusion

One of the arguments put forth in favour of a One Person Company is that it shall reduce the role of middlemen and bring about more transparency, especially in businesses like those involving craftsmen and small farmers. This is just one side of the story, since such craftsmen and small farmers are usually neither educated nor tech-savvy to conduct the business in the One Person Company mode without the assistance of professionals, who could exploit their ignorance and could be difficult to handle than the middle-men who are usually from the same village and known to them since generations. It is suggested that the procedures for incorporation, running of and winding-up of a One Person Company may be simplified by permitting the use of vernacular languages in all matters pertaining to the One Person Company. Things may be made easier for persons contemplating setting up a One Person Company by establishing help-desks of the Registrar of Companies at Taluk levels to enable the registration and legal compliances without going to the Office of the Registrar of Companies which is usually situated in the capital city of the state, located probably hundreds of kilometres away. However, with some systemic changes the concept of One Person Company is indeed a viable option, and is here to stay!

2

One Person Companies: An Empty Promise without Effective Regulatory Framework

AAKANKSHA MISHRA AND SAGAR GODBOLE

Introduction

Notwithstanding that Indians have a long experience with Company law, incorporating a company is still not the most preferred mode of doing business in India for an entrepreneur starting his own venture. Instead a sole proprietorship model has been favoured because of its perceived simplicity in comparison to a company. However, the global emergence and increasing legal recognition of Single Member Company or One Man Company or Single Person Company or One Person Company or Single Shareholder Company (different jurisdictions employ different terms) having a strong political, economic and legal theoretical basis[1] prompted Indian legislators to give a serious thought to this new business model. Borrowing from the experience of other countries and based on the suggestions of the J.J. Irani Committee, One Person Companies (OPCs) were recognized by the Company law framework in India in 2013. The committee emphasizing the need for

1. Beihui Miao, A Comparative Study of Legal Framework for Single Member Company in European Union and China, 5 JPL (2012).

recognition of OPCs, gave the rationale for it; 'With increasing use of information technology and computers, emergence of the service sector, it is time that the entrepreneurial capabilities of the people are given an outlet for participation in economic activity. Such economic activity may take place through the creation of an economic person in the form of a company. Yet it would not be reasonable to expect that every entrepreneur who is capable of developing his ideas and participating in the market place should do it through an association of persons. We feel that it is possible for individuals to operate in the economic domain and contribute effectively. To facilitate this, the Committee recommends that the law should recognize the formation of a single person economic entity in the form of 'One Person Company'. Such an entity may be provided with a simpler regime through exemptions so that the single entrepreneur is not compelled to fritter away his time, energy and resources on procedural matters.'[2]

Legal Position of One Person Company

In the Companies Act, 2013 a 'One Person Company' has been defined as a company which has only one member[3] and like a private company, it can be incorporated with a minimum paid-up share capital of Rs.1 lakh.[4] The single member of an OPC also has to nominate another person who shall become the member of the OPC in case the original single person dies or suffers any disability.[5] The nominee is required to give his written consent to become a nominee and the nominee may also withdraw his consent at anytime and similarly, the member is also permitted to change the nominee at any time.[6] The words 'One Person Company' must be mentioned below the name of the company, wherever the name is affixed, used or engraved.[7] The Companies (Incorporation) Rules, 2014 have clarified the position that sole member must be a natural person who is not only an India citizen but is also resident in India.[8] Furthermore, the rules have clarified that if the paid-up share capital of an OPC exceeds Rs. 50 lakhs or its average annual turn-over during the relevant period of time exceeds Rs. 2 crores,

---

2. Expert Committee on Company Law, Report on Company Law (Ministry of Corporate Affairs, 2005).
3. Section 2(62), the Companies Act, 2013 (Act 18 of 2013).
4. Section 2(68), the Companies Act, 2013 (Act 18 of 2013).
5. Section 2(68), the Companies Act, 2013 (Act 18 of 2013).
6. Rule 4(5), the Companies (Incorporation) Rules, 2014.
7. Second Proviso to Section 12(3), the Companies Act, 2013 (Act 18 of 2013).
8. Rule 3(1), the Companies (Incorporation) Rules, 2014.

then it ceases to be entitled to continue as an OPC and must convert into a private or public company within 6 months.[9] The incorporation of an OPC is relatively easy due to certain privileges and relaxations from corporate compliances given to it. Section 122(1) of the Companies Act, 2013, provides that the provisions of Section 98 and Section 100 to Section 111 relating to General Meetings, Extra Ordinary General Meeting and Notice Convening to General Meeting are not applicable to any One Person Company. However, for fulfilling the purposes of Section 114 of the Companies Act, 2013, where any business is required to be transacted at an Annual General Meeting, or other General Meeting of the company by means of an ordinary or special resolution, it shall be sufficient if the resolution is communicated by the member of the company and entered in the minutes book which is required to be maintained under Section 118 and signed and dated by the member and such date shall be deemed to be the date of meeting under the purposes of Companies Act, 2013.[10]

The single member naturally becomes the sole director of the company upon the incorporation and does not need to conduct board meetings but the Act also empowers the company to have more than one director if the sole member so desires.[11] However, it is compulsory for the OPC to conduct two Board meetings an year if more than one director is appointed.[12] Though a One Person Company is required to file a copy of its financial statements duly adopted by its member to the Registrar of Companies like any other company,[13] the financial statements of the OPC need not necessarily be signed by a Company Secretary and it is enough if just one director signs it.[14] Similarly, for an OPC, the annual return also need not necessarily be signed by a Company Secretary and the signature of one director suffices.[15] The 2013 Act also contains a mandate that all contracts between the sole shareholder and the company must be recorded in writing and the Registrar of Companies shall be informed about it.[16] While the Act and the rules framed thereunder, have granted exemption from several compliance requirements to the OPCs, it has also laid down certain

---

9. Rule 6, the Companies (Incorporation) Rules, 2014.
10. Section 122(3), The Companies Act, 2013 (Act 18 of 2013).
11. Section 149, The Companies Act, 2013 (Act 18 of 2013).
12. Section 173, The Companies Act, 2013 (Act 18 of 2013).
13. Section 137, The Companies Act, 2013 (Act 18 of 2013).
14. Section 134, The Companies Act, 2013 (Act 18 of 2013).
15. Proviso to Section 92(1), The Companies Act, 2013 (Act 18 of 2013).
16. Section 193, The Companies Act, 2013 (Act 18 of 2013).

requirements particularly for the OPCs to follow, owing to its peculiar features.

Reason for Development of One Person Company

It is a common phenomenon that across jurisdiction incorporation of business in form of company is made possible by the use of "straw men" in order to merely satisfy the registration formalities requiring two or more subscribers to the Memorandum of Association. If one analyzes this artificial participation of other members, contributing in reality nothing to the company and gaining no benefits therefrom, *quid juris*?[17] President Elliot of Harvard University regarded limited liability as "the corporation's most precious characteristic" and "by far the most effective legal invention made in the nineteenth century".[18] The concepts of separate legal personality and limited liability have been the motivating factors behind incorporation of companies for a long time now. Over the past century, many individuals wishing to take advantage of the separate legal personality provided by a corporation have incorporated multi-member companies which were *de-facto* one person companies with the other members holding miniscule portion of the shares and being related to the *de-facto* owner. In fact, even in the celebrated company law case of *Saloman v. Saloman & Co*[19] a company was incorporated by a sole proprietor mainly to take advantage of the separate legal status that can be availed by incorporating a company. The term "One Person Company" is an oxymoron for the term 'company' implies a plurality of persons. However it is neither legally or morally wrong to seek for oneself the privilege of limited liability by the formation of OPCs. The introduction of OPCs as a new model to carry out business in India is perhaps an attempt to address the practical exigencies of current times. What is the rationale behind introducing OPCs and how are the main objectives defined? Regarding the experience based on the *Solomon* case, the first goal was to limit the only one owner's liability. The second goal is to allow genuine individual entrepreneur to limit his liability by guaranteeing him the right of freedom of companies' establishment.[20]

---

17. Mario Rotondi, Limited Liability of The Individual Trader: One Man Company or Commercial Foundation?, 48 Tul. L. Rev. 989 (1973-74).
18. Bernard F. Cataldo, Limited Liability with One Man Companies and Subsidiary Corporations, 18 L & CP 473-504 (1953).
19. *Salomon* vs. *Salomon* [1897] AC 22 (HL).
20. Dragana Radenkovic Jocić, A Single Member Company—Convenient or Not For the Founders, UDC 347.72 (4-672).

Sole Proprietorship *vis-a-vis* One Person Company

One of the reasons why most entrepreneurs decide to start their businesses as sole proprietorships is because sole proprietorships seem to be easier and hassle free as compared to companies. However, in reality, it is not the case that a sole proprietorship involves no paperwork at all. Even after two decades of alleged dismantling of License Raj, significant number of licenses and permits are required irrespective of the business model to start certain kind of businesses. While it is not disputed that there shall be more procedural requirements to be followed when a business is run as an incorporated company instead of a sole proprietorship, the new Act has relaxed a great deal of requirements for OPCs and thus reduced the compliance hassle to a bare minimum. In fact, the benefits to the businesses such as limited liability distinct legal personality and perpetual existence may outweigh the costs of compliance. Also, the perpetual existence and distinct legal personality of an OPC allows for easy transfer of business with comparatively lower costs. This is evident in two ways. Firstly, no fresh licenses will be required by the new member to whom the membership of the OPC has been transferred as any license to carry on a particular business previously granted shall be in the name of the OPC rather than in the name of the previous sole member. Secondly, upon the transfer of an OPC business involving holdings of immovable property, there is no actual conveyance of property from the previous sole shareholder to the new sole shareholder as the property continues to belong to the OPC and therefore there is no need to pay stamp duty, thereby reducing the costs paid as duties. The word 'company' itself has a certain sense of credit that would inspire more trust in lenders and creditors.[21] Since an OPC is a separate legal entity, it is easier for the lender to keep track of the finances of the company and in events of default the banks simply have to file for winding up of the company to recover the debt to the greatest extent possible without worrying about any inheritance dispute or attaching the property of any member. Most of the new companies require additional capital beyond what the entrepreneur brings in at the time of incorporation. Getting incorporated as an OPC leaves the entrepreneur with borrowings as the only effective way of raising capital (if the paid-up capital of the company is not much, lenders also may not be willing to lend significant amounts to the OPC). Capital cannot be raised by selling a part of the equity in the business because an OPC can

21. "One person Company: From concept to reality", http://www.arkayandarkay.com/one-person-company-from-concept-to-reality/, (last visited April 9, 2014).

have only one member. This, rules out the possibility of raising money from angel investors and venture capitalists which has become an increasingly popular mode of raising capital in India.[22] As per the Companies (Incorporation) Rules, 2014, an OPC having paid up share capital of more than fifty lakh rupees or turnover exceeding two crore rupees is no longer entitled to operate as an OPC and must compulsorily convert to a private or a public company. In the Micro, Small and Medium Enterprises (MSME) Development Act, 2006, a micro enterprise has been defined as a company in which the investment in plant and machinery does not exceed twenty-five lakh rupees and a small enterprise is one in which investment is more than twenty-five lakh rupees but not exceeding five crore rupees and a medium enterprise is one requiring an investment between five crore rupees and ten crore rupees. It is apparent that the maximum capital limit of fifty lakh rupees imposed by the OPC business structure is too little to even be enough to operate as a small enterprise, let alone a medium sized one. The limit therefore needs to be revised to at least maximum 1 crore rupees capital and at least 5 to 10 crore turnover considering the global standards. That way there will be greater number of proprietors opting for OPC. Conversion of existing proprietary businesses to OPC can create complexities relating to tax matters. Generally any profits or gains arising out of the transfer of a capital asset will be chargeable to Income tax under the head of capital gains. However, where a sole proprietary concern is succeeded by a company in the business carried on by it as a result of which the sole proprietary concern sells or otherwise transfers any capital asset or intangible asset to the company, then profits and gains made out of such transfer will not be chargeable to income tax under the head of capital gains. Thus, section 47(xiv) of Income-tax Act, 1961 shall help the sole proprietor in availing relief from capital gains arising out of conversion of his Sole Proprietorship into an OPC although the section wasn't originally framed with an OPC in mind. However, after conversion, an OPC as far as taxation under the Income Tax Act, 1961 is concerned will be put in the same bracket of taxation as other private companies. According to Income Tax Act, 1961 a private limited company is under the bracket of 30% tax on total income with an additional surcharge of 5% if the income exceeds 10 million with an addition to 3% of education cess along with other applicable taxes like

22. Anirban Sen, Five Indian Start-ups Get Funding from Venture Capital Companies, MINT, Aug. 27, 2013 at http://www.livemint.com/ Companies/ BhRGYEC7XviztaBKdu09VO/Five-Indian-startups-get-funding-from-venture-capital-compa.html?ref=also_read (last visited Feb. 13, 2015).

minimum alternative tax (base tax rate 18.5%), dividend distribution tax (base tax rate 15%) and others. Thus, the tax implications of OPC are much higher than of sole proprietorship. But this deterrence could be offset by adopting necessary corresponding amendments in the taxing statutes by making specific provisions for taxation of One Person Companies.

Misuse of Limited Liability and Separate Corporate Identity

It is most doubtful whether the concept of corporate enterprise was ever intended or designed to embrace this institution of One Person Companies.[23] Nevertheless the one-person company and the family corporation have become familiar modes of business enterprise and have started receiving legislative as well as judicial approval globally. Limited liability is a privilege held out by the company law of the state; one who organizes a one-man or family company, in compliance with the formalities of that law, for the purpose of attaining limited liability in a commercial venture, is merely taking advantage of a privilege conferred by law.[24] The fact that almost all the shares of a corporation are owned by one individual is not sufficient ground for disregarding corporate personality. Accordingly the distinction between the corporate property and the individual property of the sole shareholder is carefully preserved for legal purposes. The rule is quite elementary that a corporation is an entity separate and distinct from its shareholders, with separate and distinct rights and liabilities; and this is true even though a single individual may own all, or nearly all, of the shares.[25] The same is true of the distinction between corporate obligations and the personal obligations of the sole shareholder. Corporate creditors cannot obtain satisfaction from the sole shareholder and his individual property[26]; creditors of the sole shareholder cannot obtain satisfaction from the corporation and corporate assets.[27] The sole shareholder may lend money to the business and share as a corporate creditor upon the subsequent insolvency of the venture. The sole or principal shareholder may become a secured corporate creditor and thus acquire priority over the unsecured corporate creditors. This position was sustained by the

23. Rutledge, Significant Trends in Modern Incorporation Statutes, 22 WASH. U.L.Q. 305 (1937).
24. *Salomon* vs. *Saloman & Co. Ltd.*, [1897] A.C. 22; *Inland Revenue Commissioners* vs. *Sansom*, [1921] 2 K. B. 492.
25. *In re John Koke Co.*, 38 F. 2d 232, 233 (9th Cir. 1930).
26. *Louisville Banking Co.* vs. *Eisenman*, 21 S.W. 531 (1893).
27. *In re John Koke Co.*, 38 F. 2d 232, 233 (9th Cir. 1930).

eminent authority of the English House of Lords a half century ago in *Salomon vs. Salomon & Co. Ltd.*,[28]—a decision which haunts every discussion of corporate entity and limited liability. Lord Herschel in his famous dicta laid down; "It is said that the respondent company is a 'one man' company, and that in this respect it differs from such companies as those to which I have alluded. But it has often happened that a business transferred to a joint stock company has been the property of three or four persons only, and that the other subscribers of the memorandum have been clerks or other persons who possessed little or no interest in the concern. I am unable to see how it can be lawful for three or four or six persons to form a company for the purpose of employing their capital in trading, with the benefit of limited liability, and not for one person to do so, provided, in each case, the requirements of the statute have been complied with and the company has been validly constituted. How does it concern the creditor whether the capital of the company is owned by seven persons in equal shares, with the right to an equal share of the profits, or whether it is almost entirely owned by one person, who practically takes the whole of the profits?" However, some thirty years later the Maryland court, faced with the same issue, reached a different conclusion and drily remarked; "This court does not think the law contemplates that one may incorporate an established business of his own, continue to own and control it as before, and at the same time, for his personal benefit, put beyond the reach of prospective creditors all the assets of the corporation."[29] The opportunity to enjoy the benefits of limited liability and the notion of corporateness must not be used as a weapon of fraud: it should be a shield and not a sword'.[30] The concept of corporate personality will be sustained only so long as it is invoked and employed for legitimate purposes. Courts will not sanction a perversion of the concept for improper uses and dishonest ends. There is a marked tendency to disregard corporate personality in those cases where adherence to the concept of corporateness will result in inequity or will prevent a full settlement of the dispute between the real parties in interest in a given situation. These sentiments have special significance with respect to one-man companies. Here the sole shareholder has complete dominion and superior knowledge and carries the

28. *Salomon* vs. *Saloman & Co. Ltd.*, [1897] A.C. 22.
29. *Dollar Cleaners & Dyers, Inc.* vs. *MacGregor*, 163 Md. 105.
30. Power, "Twelfth European Company Directive", I.C.C.L.R., p. 45, 1990.

opportunities for manipulation and manoeuvring.[31] Accordingly his privilege of limited liability is conditioned on compliance with two requirements—first, he must conduct the business on a corporate footing and thereby maintain and preserve the separate identity of the venture[32]; second, he must establish the corporate venture on an adequate financial basis.[33] Piercing the corporate veil has produced a lot of questions and different solutions. Should the sole member be responsible in any case or should the law define the situations of liability? Who will be responsible to creditors—the sole member or somebody else? Definitely, piercing the veil is a concept made in order to protect all creditors.[34] Assuming that corporate personality is to be disregarded, the formal consequence is that "the corporation" vanishes and a sole proprietorship occupies the entire scene. The particular practical results would be:

(1) The erstwhile sole shareholder will not enjoy limited liability;
(2) He will not be permitted to share as a corporate creditor and will be denied reimbursement for loans advanced to the business; and
(3) All the assets remaining after secured or lien creditors have exhausted their security will constitute a common fund for the satisfaction of the unsecured claims held by the business and the personal creditors alike. There could be no quarrel with the first two results, but the third result may be open to question. When insolvency has overtaken the business venture, or the shareholder, or both, the competing equities of the personal and the business creditors may justify or require a marshalling of assets.[35] One possible solution, which might lead to quixotic results if indiscriminately applied, is to lump together the assets of both the company and the personal asset of the sole shareholder and permit the creditors of both units to share this common fund pro rata.[36] Another solution, which would better accord with prevailing concepts in other legal areas (like

---

31. *Pepper* vs. *Litton*, 308 U.S. 295, 313 (1939).
32. *In re Looschen Piano Case Co.*, 261 Fed. 93 (D.N.J. 1919).
33. *Pepper* vs. *Litton*, 308 U.S. 295, 313 (1939).
34. Dragana Radenkovic Jocić, A Single Member Company—Convenient or Not For the Founders, UDC 347.72 (4-672).
35. Bernard F. Cataldo, Limited Liability with One Man Companies and Subsidiary Corporations, 18 L&CP 473-504 (1953).
36. Elvin R. Latty, Subsidiaries and Affiliated Corporations—A Study in Stockholder's Liability (Chi. Found. Press, 1936).

partnerships), is to assemble the respective assets of the company and sole shareholder in his personal capacity into two separate funds and give each set of creditors priority in its particular fund – business creditors in the company's asset and personal creditors in the personal asset of the sole shareholder.[37] Future action in this arena of legal controversy will, therefore, depend more upon judicial sensitivity to the equities of a case than upon the verbal sweep of general rules.[38]

Role of Judiciary on Corporate Personality

Courts in India have taken an extremely calibrated approach towards disregard of the corporate personality. A decision by corporate law to allow shareholders limited liability is a decision to allow them, as investors, to allocate some of the risks of doing business to third parties. Piercing the veil rules are one of the traditional ways that courts have supervised that risk allocation decision.[39] It is impossible to ascertain all the factors which operate to break down the corporate insulation.[40] The matter is largely in the discretion of the courts and will depend upon the underlying social, economic and moral factors as they operate in and through the corporation.[41] In general, there are three elements that the complainant must prove in order to pierce the corporate veil: (1) control and domination, (2) improper purpose or use, and (3) resulting damage or harm.[42] A non-exhaustive list of commonly relied upon circumstances used to establish the requisite degree of control includes failure to follow corporate formalities, inadequate capitalization or undercapitalization, identity of directors and officers, sole or majority stock control, commingling of funds, diversion of funds or assets for non-corporate purposes, etc. The second inquiry focuses on the relationship between the plaintiff and the corporation whereby the plaintiff must establish that some improper conduct has occurred beyond establishing that the

37. The Deep Rock Doctrine: Inexorable Command or Equitable Remedy?, 47 COL. L. Rev. 8oo, 811 (1947).
38. *Comstock* vs. *Group of Institutional Investors*, 335 U.S. 211, 238 (1948).
39. Robert B. Thompson, Piercing the Corporate Veil: Is the Common Law the Problem?, 37 CONN. L. REV. 619, 622 (2005).
40. Warner Fuller, *The Incorporated Individual: A Study of One-man Company*, (1938) 51 Harv LR 1373, 1377.
41. *Tata Engineering Locomotive Co.* vs. *State of Bihar*, AIR 1965 SC 40.
42. *Morris* vs. *Department of Taxation & Fin.*, 623 N.E.2d 1157, 1160-61 (N.Y. Ct. App. 1993); *Belvedere Condominium Owners' Ass'n* vs. *R.E. Roark Cos.*, 617 N.E.2d 1075, 1086 (Ohio 1993).

corporation was controlled and dominated. There are no straitjacket rules with respect to the improper purpose element. However, the requisite morally culpable conduct has been found in a variety of circumstances where piercing claims have succeeded, including the commission of torts,[43] undercapitalization with the intent to defraud creditors,[44] and violations and evasion of statutes. Thirdly, the plaintiff must prove that, unless the corporate veil is pierced, it will have been treated unjustly by the defendant's exercise of control and improper use of the corporate form and, thereby, suffer damages. So far as Indian cases are concerned, there are some important decisions which must be discussed to underline the fact that the fear of abuse of OPC structure can be remedied by a vigilant court that is willing to pierce the corporate veil in such circumstances. The first of such cases is *Life Insurance Corporation of India vs. Escorts Ltd.*[45] where Justice Chinappa Reddy did not find it necessary or desirable to enumerate the classes of cases where lifting the veil is permissible, "since that must necessarily depend on the relevant statutory or other provisions, the object sought to be achieved, the impugned conduct, the involvement of the element of public interest and the effect on the parties who may be affected." The next important case is *State of U.P. vs. Renusagar Power Company*[46] where the willingness of Indian courts to apply this doctrine to combat the real exigencies of the circumstances is reflected. The court declared; "In the expanding horizon of modern jurisprudence, lifting of corporate veil is permissible. Its frontiers are unlimited. It must, however, depend primarily on the realities of the situation. The aim of legislation is to do justice to all the parties. The horizon of the doctrine of lifting corporate veil is expanding." In *Tata Engineering Locomotive Co. vs. State of Bihar*,[47] the court emphasized that the exceptions to the distinct personality of a corporation may expand to mitigate economic realities. The court noted:

> "...in the course of time, the doctrine that the corporation or a company has a legal and separate entity of its own has been subjected to certain exceptions by the application of the fiction that the veil of the corporation can be lifted and its face examined in substance. The doctrine of the lifting of the veil thus marks a

43. *Kincaid* vs. *Landing Dev. Co.*, 344 S.E. 2d 869, 872.
44. *Grote Meat Co.* vs. *Goldenberg*, 735 S.W. 2d 379, 387.
45. *Life Insurance Corporation of India* vs. *Escorts Ltd.*, AIR 1986 SC 1370.
46. *State of U.P.* vs. *Renusagar Power Company*, AIR 1988 SC 1737.
47. *Tata Engineering Locomotive Co.* vs. *State of Bihar*, AIR 1965 SC 40.

change in the attitude that law had originally adopted towards the concept of the separate entity or personality of the corporation. As a result of the impact of the complexity of economic factors, judicial decisions have sometimes recognized exceptions to the rule about the juristic personality of the corporation. It may be that in course of time these exceptions may grow in number and to meet the requirements of different economic problems, the theory about the personality of the corporation may be confined more and more." In the case of *T.R. Pratt (Bombay) Ltd. vs. E.D. Sassoon And Co. Ltd*[48], Justice Kania recognized that, "although all the shares may be practically controlled by one person, in law a company is a distinct entity and it is not permissible or relevant to inquire whether the directors belonged to the same family or whether it is, as compendiously described, a one man company." Similarly, in *Vodafone International Holdings BV vs. Union of India,*[49] the court noted that "a company is a separate legal persona and the fact that all its shares are owned by one person or by the parent company has nothing to do with its separate legal existence." Perhaps the most important Indian case law on piercing of corporate veil that would assume great importance in case of One Person Companies is the observations of the court in *Spencer & Co. Ltd., Madras vs. the Commissioner of Wealth Tax.*[50] The Court noted; "It is well settled that an incorporated company is a legal person and it cannot be equated to its shareholders. The position continues to be the same even if the number of the shareholders is reduced to one by accident or otherwise. The act of the company cannot, therefore, be regarded as that of any of the shareholder and *vice versa*. It is true that occasionally the corporate veil of a company is pierced through in order to find out the substance but that is only where it is permitted by a statute or in exceptional cases of fraud."

The observation of the Division Bench of Madras High Court in the aforementioned case not only contemplates the possibility of a single shareholder company either by accident or otherwise (the use of the word 'otherwise' could be interpreted to cover the new legislation permitting incorporation of OPCs), but also allows disregard of its'

48. *T.R. Pratt (Bombay) Ltd.* vs. *E.D. Sassoon & Co. Ltd*, AIR 1936 Bom 62.
49. *Vodafone International Holdings BV* vs. *Union of India*, (2012) 6 SCC 613.
50. *Spencer & Co. Ltd., Madras* vs. *The Commissioner of Wealth Tax*, AIR 1969 Mad 359.

corporateness in case it is incorporated with a view to perpetuate fraud. The Court's dicta in *Delhi Development Authority vs. Skipper Construction*[51] emphasizes the Indian judiciary's readiness to lift the corporate veil to check fraud perpetrated by companies on its creditors. The court noted:

> "The concept of corporate entity was evolved to encourage and promote trade and commerce but not to commit illegalities or to defraud people. Where, therefore, the corporate character is employed for the purpose of committing illegality or for defrauding others, the court would ignore the corporate character and will look at the reality behind the corporate veil so as to enable it to pass appropriate orders to do justice between the parties concerned. The fact that Tejwant Singh and members of his family have created several corporate bodies does not prevent this Court from treating all of them as one entity belonging to and controlled by Tejwant Singh and Family if it is found that these corporate bodies are merely cloaks behind which lurks Tejwant Singh and/or members of his family and that the device of incorporation was really a ploy adopted for committing illegalities and/or to defraud people." Thus, it is apparent that Indian courts have matured enough in the application of doctrine of 'lifting the corporate veil' and will not shy away from using it to check the abuse of OPCs.

Corporate Governance for One Person Company

Traditionally, the core value of the shareholders meeting is to protect their legitimate rights and interests through the exercise of the right of shareholders to control the board of directors. However, there is no need to set-up shareholders meeting for one-man company because of the following reasons: the shareholder is only one, the company is completely controlled by the sole shareholder, the company's major decision-making power belongs to the sole shareholder, and the shareholder's interests are the company's interests. Secondly, the function of the company's board of directors is to supervise the internal directors, managers and staff to execute business; externally, it is to protect creditors and safety of the transactions with relative third part. In an OPC, it is hard for the Board of Directors to be independent because the Board usually consists of just the sole shareholder himself. Because of these peculiarities in the structural set-up of OPCs, the usual method of

51. *Delhi Development Authority* vs. *Skipper Construction*, AIR 1996 SC 2005.

checks and balances vide AGMs, Board meetings, etc. becomes infructuous. Thus the challenge is to strictly control one-man company by improving its governance structure. The crux of corporate governance lies in the balanced relationship amongst various stakeholders. Stakeholders are defined as 'all those who contribute dedicated assets to the enterprise, and the persons or groups who make some risky investment to the enterprise as a result'. Companies should be for all the interests of stakeholders, not just to the interests of shareholders. The shareholders only have limited liability and the remaining part of the risk is transferred to the creditors and other stakeholders.[52] From the point of view of risk exposure, the shareholders can effectively decentralize the risks according to limited liability, however, other stakeholders like creditors, etc. are charged with greater risks. In order to incentive the stakeholders to invest into the enterprise, some rights to control the business must be endowed to the stakeholders and hence stakeholders must participate in the corporate governance. In context of an OPC the participation of stakeholders in corporate governance would compensate for the imbalance caused by sole shareholder.[53] The shareholder in a One Person Company may lack the consciousness to protect the interests of creditors in the process of business. Allowing the creditors to monitor the company's operation is, to some extent, to take the initiative to protect the interests of creditors. The main function of the board of directors in One Person Company should not concentrate on ensuring the interests of sole shareholder but rather must be focussed on guaranteeing that the creditors' interests are not violated by the sole shareholder. A single director (i.e. the sole member himself) cannot achieve this objective. Hence, the presence of a Board of Directors must be made mandatory (currently there is an option of having up to 15 directors) and must have a proper proportion of the staff/employee representatives and creditors' union representatives who should be elected democratically.[54] One Person Company

---

52. Margaret M. Blair, *Ownership and Control: Rethinking Corporate Governance for the Twenty-first Century*, (Brookings Institution Press, Washington, D.C., 1994).
53. BAI Xiaojun, SU Zhenhong, "Corporate Governance for One-man Company in View of the Theory of Stakeholders" (Unpublished, School of Economics and Management, Shenyang Ligong University, China), http://www.seiofbluemountain.com/upload/product/201002/1265779897wzf1roe9.pdf (last visited Feb. 13, 2015).
54. BAI Xiaojun, SU Zhenhong, "Corporate Governance for One-man Company in View of the Theory of Stakeholders" (Unpublished, School of Economics

emphasizes on the separation of the shareholder's personal property and his business property, i.e. the property belonging to the OPC. If this distinction is not maintained strictly, problems occur. To encounter these risks and prevent investors from abusing this form of company, a 'personal property disclosure system' should be established by following the lead of foreign countries like Germany, requiring that the sole shareholder of the single member company registers and discloses his personal property.[55] Liechtenstein, where the one person company was first legally recognized in 1925, provided creditors the right to go beyond the limited liability company and access personal assets of the promoter if there is gross negligence in management. In addition, where they suspect gross negligence, creditors can ask for dissolution of the company or inspect the company accounts.[56] The only mandate that the Indian Company Act, 2013 contains with a view to protecting creditors is a record in writing of all contracts between the sole shareholder and the company. Perhaps, a new condition could be imposed wherein third party liabilities—consisting of creditors, loans and provisions—must be restricted to the capital. If this liability exceeds the capital infused, one person companies would stand to automatically lose their limited liability. Such a provision would exclusively protect the small creditors and employees who have less bargaining power, in contrast to lenders who can and do seek personal guarantee of shareholders to overcome limited liability.[57]

Conclusion

The OPC model in its present form with its myriad lacunae doesn't attract its intended target audience. Perhaps the following suggestions could be implemented to boost this new business model:

(1) The right of incorporating an OPC should be extended to both natural as well as juristic persons. This would be a major incentive for foreign players to enter into the national economy by easily establishing wholly owned subsidiaries.

---

and Management, Shenyang Ligong University, China), http://www.seiofbluemountain. com/upload/product/201002/1265779897wzf1roe9.pdf (last visited Feb. 13, 2015).

55. Beihui Miao, A Comparative Study of Legal Framework for Single Member Company in European Union and China, 5 JPL (2012).

56. Cui Zafei, "A Comparative Analysis of One-man Company", http://www.szcourt.gov.cn/ArticleInfo.aspx?id=523 (last visited Feb. 13, 2015).

57. Shankar Jaganadhan, "One Person Companies: Speed without effective brakes?", *India Together*, 10 October 2013.

(2) A substantial minimum amount of capital definitely not lower than that prevailing for small and medium-term enterprises under the current laws should be established for OPCs.

(3) Suitable amendments must be made in taxing statutes (particularly Income Tax), so that the high rates applicable to Companies with several members is not blindly applied to company with a single member. This will incentivize more entrepreneurs to form OPCs.

(4) The sole shareholder must be made personally liable in cases of fraud or in cases where the creditor is harmed due to gross negligence on part of the sole shareholder in carrying out the OPC business.

(5) Third party liabilities, consisting of creditors, loans and provisions—must be restricted to the amount of capital infused into the OPC. If this liability exceeds the capital, the OPC should automatically lose their limited liability. This would protect small creditors and employees who have less bargaining power and cannot seek the personal guarantee of shareholders to overcome limited liability unlike the bigger and more influential creditors.

(6) The complete dominion and superior knowledge of a sole shareholder gives him an opportunity to manipulate and manoeuvre the business of OPC for his personal benefit. Thus, the privilege of a distinct corporate personality and limited liability must be extended only as long the sole shareholder preserves the separate identity of the corporate venture without mixing it with his proprietary interests. The Courts must not hesitate to disregard the corporate personality by lifting the corporate veil where there are strong indications of fraud and abuse of the OPC structure for personal gains.

Thus, the perceived advantages of an OPC in form of singular shareholder, distinct legal personality and limited liability could easily become the ghost impeding the growth of such a model if the corporate governance model of an OPC is not strengthened. Presently, the Indian laws on OPC fall acutely short of answering the pressing concerns of the abuse of OPC structure by the greedy human minds. If legislative developments are not made swiftly, OPC will fail to be a practical substitute to sole proprietors in its current form.

3

One Person Company under the Companies Act, 2013: A Critical Study

NITESH MATHUR

Introduction

In common parlance a Company means a voluntary association of two or more persons formed and organized to carry out business activities. The newly adopted scheme of "One Person Company" is an exception to this general rule. The Companies Act, 2013 now attributes legal personality to an individual person and creates a distinct legal position as a company. It is an exception to the principle of Democratic Company. This concept is not new in the global context. Countries like Australia, China, USA and Pakistan have already legally recognized this kind of artificial person in their legal system. In India, the concept of One Person Company was first introduced by the J.J. Irani Committee, constituted on 2nd December 2004. It provided as follows: "With increasing use of information technology and computers, emergence of the service sector, it is time that the entrepreneurial capabilities of the people are given an outlet for participation in economic activity. Such economic activity may take place through the creation of an economic person in the Form of a company..."[1] Introduction of One Person Company into the legal system would certainly encourage sole proprietors and entrepreneurs to enter into a systematic business activity which would not only provide better business security but would also result into development of economic growth of the country. The Act has

1. http://www.primedirectors.com/pdf/JJ%20Irani%20Report-MCA.pdf

several provisions of simpler governance and legal regime for One Person Company. It also provides a number of compliance exemptions for the new kind of company by which the burden of legal compliance would undoubtedly decrease. Being a One Person Company, such company can only be of a private nature and can be formed as a company limited by shares or company limited by guarantee or an unlimited company. Statutory requirement into Memorandum of Association during incorporation including name of one other person who on the event of death or incompetency of the sole member takes his place, ensures perpetual succession of the Company.

One Person Company Concept in Other Countries

Legal concept of One Person Company is new for Indian legal regime but not at global level. The concept exists in United Kingdom, China, USA, Australia, Singapore, Qatar and Pakistan. Section 7 of the United Kingdom Companies Act, 2006 provides that a company may be formed by one or more persons. In United States of America several States permit formation of a single member Limited Liability Company (LLC). The Tennessee Revised Limited Liability Company Act, 2005 which came into effect from January 1st, 2006 is a recent example of it. In Pakistan, the scheme of Single Member Company was introduced by Single Member Companies Rules, 2003 and Section 2(g) of the legislation defines "single member company" (SMC) as a private company which has only one member.

One Person Company in India

Incorporation: The new legislation of 2013 and the Companies (Incorporation) Rules 2014 include provision of One Person Company in detail. Section 2(62) of the Act defines "one person company means a company which has only one person as a member." Section 3(1)(c) of the Act provides that one person can form a company for any lawful purpose. Such company may only be of a private nature. The requirements of subscribing the name of such person to a Memorandum and complying with such other requirements of the Act in respect of registration are of similar nature. The salient features of One Person Company are easy to establish and not subject of stringent statutory provisions of the Act.

Position of 'the other person': The Act of 2013 ensures the One Person Company to be of a perpetual nature for which the provision further provides that in addition to the requirement of subscription of shares, indication of name of the other person is mandatory by filing Form No. INC-2. Name of such other person who is none other than a nominee, is to be mandatorily provided, who shall in event of the subscriber's death or his incapacity to contract becomes the member of the company.[2] A Written Consent of such nominee has to be filled mandatorily in Form No. INC-3 in a written form along with the Article at the time of incorporation of the company. Withdrawal of consent may also be done by such nominee by sending notice to the subscriber in this regard. Where such withdrawal of consent is done by the other person, the sole member shall nominate another nominee within fifteen days of receipt of withdrawal.[3]

Name of One Person Company: Application for reservation of name of the company shall be filed by Form No. INC-1. Further INC-2 shall be filled for incorporation of name of the One Person Company within sixty days of filing Form INC-1. Wherever the name the company is printed, affixed or engraved the One Person Company is statutorily required to mention the words "One Person Company" in brackets below the name of the company.[4] The Company may also change its name at any time after its incorporation by giving notice to the Registrar of Companies (ROC). Further the Act imposes statutory obligation upon the member to intimate the ROC where change in name of the company or change in name of the nominee has been done, within 30 days to receipt of change by filing Form INC-4. The proviso also states that such change in the name of the nominee shall not be deemed to be an alteration of the memorandum.

Registered office of One Person Company: The Act of 2013 provides no exemption to One Person Company with regard to registered office. Section 12 of the Act is silent in relation to One Person Company. Thus, statutory requirement of having a registered office on and from the fifteenth day of its incorporation and at all times is to be complied by such company.

Eligibility of Member

Rule 3 of the Companies (Incorporation) Rules, 2014 provides eligibility for the member and the other person for forming one person company. Both of such persons shall be 'natural' persons means company or any other artificial legal entity cannot form a One Person Company. It thus creates an exception to the fundamental characteristic of corporate law, i.e. artificial personality. It can be asserted that a One Person Company can neither be a wholly owned subsidiary not it can be

2. Section 4(1)(f) of the Companies Act, 2013.
3. Rule 4(3) of Companies (Incorporation) Rules, 2014.
4. Section 12(3) proviso of the Companies Act, 2013.

converted into a wholly owned subsidiary. The Rule also provides that such person shall adhere to the requirement of being a citizen of India and Resident of India. A person can be called 'Resident of India' only when he has stayed in India for a period of not less than 182 days during the immediate preceding financial year. The Rule also provides, 'No person shall be eligible to incorporate more than a One Person Company or become nominee in more than one such company'. Where such sole person is a member or the other person in such other company, he has to mandatorily withdraw such membership or position of the other person in a One Person Company. In such a case notice of withdrawal of consent and name of another person so nominated shall be filed to the Registrar in Form No. INC-4 within thirty days of receipt of withdrawal of consent.

Conversion of One Person Company

Mandatory Conversion: The Companies (Incorporation) Rules, 2014 imposes a threshold limit upon One Person Company, crossing of which would lead to mandatory conversion of such Company into a private company or a public company and it ceases to be a One Person Company. Where the paid up share capital of an One Person Company exceeds fifty lakh rupees or its average annual turnover during the relevant period exceeds two crore rupees, the One Person Company is mandatorily required to convert itself into a private or a public company within six months from the date of such excess of threshold limit so prescribed. The One Person Company shall intimate the Registrar about such cessation of the Company by notifying in Form No. INC-5 within sixty days from the date of exceeding of the threshold limit. The Act does not specifically provide minimum capital requirement for a One Person Company. However, being a private company, it is required to have minimum capital of one lakh.

Voluntary Conversion: In situation where the One member has achieved his dream business, he may apply for apply for further conversion into a private or public company. This conversion may give certain advantages in order to expand the company such as listing of securities on a recognized stock exchange, increase in share capital of company, raising funds through foreign direct investment and recognition of company at national and international level, etc. For purpose of such wilful conversion Form No. INC-6 shall be filed by a One Person Company where it is willing to convert itself into a private or public company. The Form is required to be filed within thirty days with fees as provided in the Companies (Registration offices and fees) Rules,

2014, by attaching the prescribed documents, of such voluntary conversion. However, no such voluntary conversion by a One Person Company into any of the companies can take place unless two years have expired from the date of incorporation of the company, except threshold limit prescribed as mandatory conversion. Further, the Rules imposes express restriction that an One Person Company cannot be incorporated or converted into a company formed with charitable objects under section 8 of the Act of 2013. In case where a private company is willing to convert itself into a One Person Company, the same procedural requirements has to be complied with such as filling of the Form and paymen of prescribed fees. In addition to such procedural requirements, in order to become a One P1erson Company legal requirement such as appointment of one 'other person', etc. is required to fulfill.

Exemptions and Benefits of One Person Company

Section 92 read with section 134 and section 137 of the Act states that every company incorporated under the Act must prepare annual return of income which shall be duly signed by a director and the company secretary. Where the company is not having a company secretary, a practicing Company Secretary can duly sign such annual return. However, exemption to One Person Company has been granted by the Act in this regard. It is provided that where there is no such Company Secretary in the One Person Company, a director of company may also sign the annual return. Thus, the provision exempts a One Person Company form hiring a Company Secretary or practicing company secretary for the above purpose. Section 96 of the Act provides that every company except a One Person Company shall hold an annual general meeting. The company is also exempted from provisions of section 98 and sections 100 to 111 of the Act. Therefore, provisions relating to calling of extraordinary general meeting, Quorum, Proxies, Restriction on voting rights, voting by show of hands, demand for poll and Postal ballot does not apply to such One Person Company. A One Person Company may run by appointing a minimum of only one director. The Act nowhere states that such a company shall only consist of one director. There is no restriction on having more than one Director up to fifteen in number. Where any business which is required to be transacted at an annual general meeting or other general meeting of a company by means of an ordinary or special resolution, the Act provides under section 122(3) that it would be sufficient if the sole director communicates the resolution to the company and enter it in the minutes-book with signature and date. Therefore, the requirement of passing of a special or ordinary resolution wherever required is done away for One Person Company. However maintaining the minutes-book is mandatory under section 118. Relaxation regarding conducting Board meeting has also been provided under section 173 of the Act whereby a meeting held by a One Person Company would be deemed to valid if at least one meeting of the Board of Directors has been conducted in each half of a calendar year and the gap between the two meetings is not less than ninety days. Further the provisions of section 174 shall not apply to a One Person Company as there is only one Director on its Board. Provisions relating to appointment of Woman Director, Independent Director and small shareholder director do not apply on a One Person Company. A One Person Company is not required to form an audit committee under Rule 5 of the Companies (Accounts and Audit Rules) 2014). The requirement of not appointing or reappointing of an individual as an auditor of company for more than one term of five consecutive years; and an audit firm as auditor for more than two terms of five consecutive years does not apply to an One Person Company with effect of Rule 5 of the Companies (Accounts and Audit Rules) 2014. The Act reduces the burden of compliance by exempting the One Person Company from preparing cash flow statement while preparing financial statements of company under section 2(40) of the Act. A One Person Company shall not contribute part of its profits for activates related to corporate social responsibility as its average annual turnover during the relevant period cannot exceed two crore rupees.

Disadvantages of One Person Company

The Act provides the requirement of being a person resident in India for both sole member and for the nominee. Thus, a non-resident person cannot be a part of the company in any manner. No such person can incorporate more than a One Person Company or become nominee in more than one such company. Thus another One Person Company cannot be opened with a view to expand the business by its sole member. In such a case the only option left is to voluntary convert the company into a private or public company. A One Person Company can neither be incorporated under section 8 of the Act nor can be converted into a company formed with charitable objects, etc. No minor can be a part of One Person Company in any manner. Though as its main feature the One Person Company protects the sole proprietor by limited liability. However, no specific Income Tax rate has been provided for One Person Company. The company is required to pay annual tax returns at the rate of 30.9% of the taxable income against the slab rate of tax provided for an individual proprietor. Further such a company is not entitled to avail benefit of tax deduction under Section 80C of Income Tax Act, 1961 like an individual. The Company may be misused as a tool for unscrupulous transactions and to evade tax liability. However, the Act under section 139 mandatorily requires appointment of an auditor for the purpose of putting a check on the transactions of the One Person Company. The One Person Company cannot be a part of Non-banking financing activities. Thus, such a company cannot involve itself in activity relating to lending or investment.

Conclusion and Suggestions

The recognition of One Person Company structure by the Companies Act, 2013 will certainly help the entrepreneurs to take a risk of doing business, with a limited liability and in a systematic manner. It ensures expansion of business by converting a sole proprietor or LLP into a company. The new concept allows personal freedom, which opens up the way for a professionally skilled person to adopt the business of his choice and avail the benefit of limited liability. It is expected to benefit those who are engaged into self-employment business and small scale business. However, absence of a democratic system, there seems to be a possibility of mutualizing the privileges conferred on the One Person Company. It is strongly recommended that there lies a need to bring down the level of compliance as it is more than that of a LLP or Sole Proprietorship. The threshold limit of paid up share capital of 50 lakh is very less and it should be increased. Further, the threshold limit, i.e. average annual turnover of two crore rupees is too low to be achieved as it would be highly unfair to mandatorily convert an One Person Company if its average annual turnover reaches to five crore rupees in one year of its incorporation. It is also recommended to done away the requirement of 'one *natural* person, one company' as well as the threshold limit. There lies a need to provide a separate tax structure for One Person Company which may grant several privileges to it. The Act of 2013 exempts One Person Company from conducting an Annual general meeting. In absence of any specific provision, it is difficult to ascertain the time within which the annual return must be filled. As the scheme of One Person Company is included for the first time in India legal regime, it is worthwhile to mention that relevant aspects like appointment of auditor, minutes of One Person Company, articles of One Person Company, minimum capital requirement of the One Person Company require further substantial clarifications which we can expect with the passage of time.

CHAPTER II

Insider Trading

4

Insider Trading: The White Collar Crime

GURMINDER DHAMI

Introduction

Corporate frauds and scandals are committed by the insiders and not the ones who are outside the organization. The concept of insider trading was first recognized in law by United States of America in the year 1934. The provisions dealing with insider trading were incorporated in the Securities Exchange Act, 1934. USA is the first country which came up with such law as back as five decades ago but India did not have a specific piece of legislation rather relying on Securities Exchange Board general provisions and judicial opinions. Simply put insider trading means trading by an insider. Insider here means one in possession of special information whether by virtue of being within an organization or otherwise. Trading on basis of this special information by the insider is in violation of the principle of access of information to everyone in the market and is also in breach of the fiduciary duties of the insiders. This is clearly dealing in company securities with a view of making a profit or avoiding a loss while in possession of information that, if generally known, would affect their price. It is asymmetric information which makes insider trading possible. By late nineties majority of the countries over the world had put in place laws to curb insider trading.[1] However, the effectiveness of these laws is still an area of debate.

1. Utpal Bhattacharya & Hazem Daouk, "The World Price of Insider Trading", 57, *The Journal of Finance* (Feb. 2002).

Indian Historical Background

In India, Thomas Committee of 1948 was the first to study insider trading which examined the provisions of Securities Exchange Act, 1934 of USA. Thereafter, sections 306 and 307 of the Companies Act, 1956 also required the Directors to disclose their shareholding in the Company. In 1979, Sachar Committee was constituted followed by the Patel Committee in 1986 and the Abid Hussain Committee in 1989 which were of recommendation that a separate statute regulating insider trading should be in place. Securities and Exchange Board of India (SEBI) came out with SEBI (Insider Trading) Regulations in the year 1992, the very year in which it came into existence. These regulations were further amended in the year 2002 and the regulations were renamed as SEBI (Prohibition of Insider Trading) Regulations, 1992. Later on SEBI came out with various amendments with time to pluck the loopholes. On January 15th, 2015, SEBI (Prohibition of Insider Trading) Regulations, 2015 were notified to replace the 23 year old set of regulations. The J.J. Irani Committee on Company law was of view that measures should also be there in Company law to prohibit insider trading.[2] Accordingly, provisions pertaining to prohibition of insider trading and forward dealing of securities were introduced in Companies Act, 2013 ('Act') as well.

Provisions of the Companies Act, 2013

It is Section 195 of the Act which prohibits that any person including Director or Key Managerial Personnel (KMP) of a Company from entering into insider trading. As per the provision subscribing, buying, selling, dealing in securities or agreeing to do so by a Director, KMP or an officer of the Company when he/she is reasonably expected to have access to non-public price sensitive information is insider trading. Also procuring or communicating directly or indirectly any non-public price-sensitive information constitutes insider trading. Therefore, it can be concluded that insider trading is communicating any information which is price sensitive and at the same time not available to public or trading in securities of the company while in possession of such information. However, if the communication of such information is required in the ordinary course of business, profession or employment or under any law then it would not amount to insider trading. Now, the question that arises is, what is non-public price-

2. Government of India, Report: Report on Company Law (Ministry of Corporate Affairs, 2005).

sensitive information, it is defined as any information which relates directly or indirectly to a company and which if published is likely to materially affect the price of securities of the company. The person contravening these provisions shall be liable to imprisonment for a term up to five years or with minimum fine of Rupees Five lakhs which may extend to Rupees Twenty-five crores or thrice the amount of profit made out of insider trading, whichever is higher, or with both imprisonment and fine. The duties of Director as envisaged under section 166 also indirectly casts a duty that he/she shall not enter into insider trading. The provisions of section 194 of the Companies Act, 2013 also prohibits forward dealings in securities by Director or KMP. According to the said section they cannot deal in futures or options of shares or debentures of the company, its associate, holding or subsidiary. If a Director or KMP acts in contravention of the foregoing provisions then he/she shall be liable to imprisonment up to 2 years or minimum fine of Rupees One lakh which may extend to Rupees Five lakhs or with both. The power to prosecute insider trading or forward dealing in securities, in case of listed companies and companies which intend to get its securities listed is conferred upon SEBI by virtue of section 458 of the Companies Act, 2013. It can be inferred from above that although Companies Act, 2013 has put in place provisions to curb insider trading but they are more of prohibitive and punitive nature and no preventive measures are there which could actually ensure that the shareholder/debenture holders' rights in case of unlisted companies are protected. In case of listed Companies, the SEBI (Prohibition of Insider Trading) Regulations, 2015 is an optimum mix which strives to prevent, prohibit and penalize insider trading. Unlisted Companies can voluntarily adopt practices and procedures to prevent insider trading for example laying a code of conduct for senior management while entering into a restructuring deal.

Role of SEBI to Prohibit Insider Trading

SEBI was formed in the year 1992 with one of its objective to protect the interest of investor in securities and as per section 11(2)(g) and (2A) of the SEBI Act, 1992, it is the duty of SEBI to prohibit insider trading in listed companies or companies which intend to get its securities listed. Further section 12A says that no person shall directly or indirectly engage in insider trading and penalty for such offence is given under section 15G of the Act. In 2013, SEBI had set-up a high level committee to review the SEBI (Prohibition of Insider Trading) Regulations, 1992 under the chairmanship of N.K. Sodhi, former Chief

Justice after which the SEBI (Prohibition of Insider Trading) Regulations, 2015 has come into existence. The provisions of the regulations are discussed below.

Major Concepts Relating to Insider Trading

(a) Insider means any person who is a connected person or in possession of or having access to unpublished price sensitive information.[3]

(b) Connected person means any person who is or has during the six months prior to the concerned act been associated with a company, directly or indirectly, in any capacity including by reason of frequent communication with its officers or by being in any contractual, fiduciary or employment relationship or by being a director, officer or an employee of the company or holds any position including a professional or business relationship between himself and the company whether temporary or permanent, that allows such person, directly or indirectly, access to unpublished price sensitive information or is reasonably expected to allow such access.[4] Without prejudice to the generality of the foregoing, the persons falling within the following categories shall be deemed to be connected persons unless the contrary is established:

(i) an immediate relative of connected persons specified,
(ii) a holding, associate or subsidiary company,
(iii) an intermediary defined under section 12 of the SEBI Act and its Director/employees,
(iv) an investment, trustee or asset management company or an employee or director thereof,
(v) an official of a stock exchange or of clearing house or corporation,
(vi) a member of board of trustees of a mutual fund or a member of the board of directors of the asset management company of a mutual fund or is an employee thereof,
(vii) a member of the board of directors or an employee, of a public financial institution as defined in section 2(72) of the Companies Act, 2013,
(viii) an official or an employee of a self-regulatory organization authorized by the Board,
(ix) a banker of the company, and

3. Reg. 2(1)(g).
4. Reg. 2(1)(d).

(x) a concern, firm, trust, Hindu undivided family, company or association of persons wherein a director of a company or his immediate relative or banker of the company, has more than ten per cent of the holding or interest,

(c) Immediate relative means a spouse of a person, and includes parent, sibling, and child of such person or of the spouse, any of whom is either dependent financially on such person, or consults such person in taking decisions relating to trading in securities.

(d) Unpublished price[5] sensitive information: means any information, relating to a company or its securities, directly or indirectly, that is not generally available which upon becoming generally available, is likely to materially affect the price of the securities and shall, ordinarily including but not restricted to, information relating to the following;
   (i) financial results;
   (ii) dividends;
   (iii) change in capital structure;
   (iv) mergers, de-mergers, acquisitions, delisting, disposal and expansion of business and such other transactions;
   (v) changes in key managerial personnel; and
   (vi) material events in accordance with the listing agreement.

(e) Generally available information means information that is accessible to the public on a non-discriminatory basis.[6]

(f) Trading means and includes subscribing, buying, selling, dealing, or agreeing to subscribe, buy, sell, deal in any securities, and "trade" shall be construed accordingly.[7]

Communication Restrictions

According to the said regulations no insider shall communicate or allow access to Unpublished Price Sensitive Information (UPSI), relating to a company or securities,[8] to any person including others insiders and likewise no person shall procure an UPSI from any insider. Communication or procurement in furtherance of legitimate purposes, performance of duties or discharge of legal obligations is exception to this rule. UPSI may also be communicated or procured in connection with a transaction, which in the opinion of Board of Directors is in the

5. Reg. 2(1)(n).
6. Reg. 2(1)(e).
7. Reg. 2(1)(l).
8. The Securities Contract Regulation Act, 1956 (42 of 1956).

best interest of the company and triggers open offer under the SEBI takeover code. In case the transaction is such which does not attract making of open offer, the UPSI pursuant to proposed transaction should be made generally available at least two trading days prior to the proposed transaction being effected. However, an agreement for confidentiality and non-disclosure shall be entered to the effect that the UPSI communicated or procured shall only be used for the purpose of transaction referred to above and not for otherwise dealing in securities. It is mere Communication or procurement of UPSI which is prohibited, irrespective of the fact that any trade on basis of such information has been entered into or not. However, exceptions have been carved out such that these provisions do not restrain persons from performing their duties and obligations or do not put a restraint on commercial prudence by barring flow of information when the transaction pursuant to which information is being shared is in the best interest of the company.

Trading Restrictions

An insider shall not trade in securities when in possession of UPSI. In case of connected persons the onus of establishing that while trading in securities he/she was not in possession of UPSI shall be on him/her only. Insider may prove his innocence in following cases:

(i) The transaction is an off-market *inter-se* transfer between promoters who were in possession of the same unpublished price sensitive information and both parties had made a conscious and informed trade decision.

(ii) In case of non-individual insiders, the individuals who were in possession of such unpublished price sensitive information were different from the individuals taking trading decisions and appropriate and adequate arrangements were in place to ensure that these regulations are not violated.

(iii) The trades were pursuant to a trading plan set-up in accordance with the regulations.

The regulations put restrictions on trading therefore it is important to understand the term trade the definition of which has already been reproduced above. The expert committee was of view that instead of dealing the word trading should be used as dealing is very wide in its scope when compared to trading and may at times outlaw routine *bona-fide* transactions that have no nexus with the objective of the regulations, for instance pledging of securities or dematerialization. However, the definition proposed by the committee was not accepted by SEBI and dealing or agreeing to deal is also covered under the definition. The practical feasibility of this will be known after few years from now.

Trading plan

Like USA the concept of trading plans allowing a perpetual insider the opportunity to trade in securities of company in a predetermined fashion is first time introduced in India. An insider can prepare a trading plan following which he/she can trade in securities of the Company. The plan shall be presented to compliance officer (to be designated by the Board of Company) for approval and public disclosure and shall contain information pertaining to number of securities or value of trades to be effected, nature of trade (i.e. acquisition/disposal) and dates on or intervals at which such trades shall be effected. The trading plan cannot:

(i) commence trading earlier than six months from the public disclosure of the trade plan;
(ii) before a period of less than 12 months;
(iii) entitle trading during period commencing Twenty trading days before last day of period for which results are to be announced and ending on Second trading day after disclosure of results;
(iv) overlap with any other trading plan for the same period;
(v) allow trading in securities for market abuse; and
(vi) be revoked and the insider shall mandatorily implement the plan without any deviation.

The compliance officer shall review the trading plan to assess whether the plan would have any potential for violation of these regulations and shall be entitled to seek such express undertakings as may be necessary to enable such assessment and to approve and monitor the implementation of the plan. After approval of the plan compliance officer shall notify it to the stock exchanges where the securities are listed. In case the UPSI which was in possession of insider at the time of making of trading plan has not become generally available at the time of commencement of the trading plan, the plan shall not be commenced and the compliance officer shall ensure that plan is deferred until the UPSI becomes generally available. This requirement makes it clear that although a carve out has been created from general rule that trading while in possession of UPSI is not allowed, through introduction of concept of trading plan but to protect the interest of investors it is has been specifically stated that before the trading plan is commenced the UPSI which was with the insider at the time of its formulation should have been disseminated in public domain. It is the maiden effort to introduce the concept of trading plan but it is doubtful whether the industry is going to use this provision. The insider for taking benefit of these regulations has to make a definitive plan giving quantified details for a minimum period of a year which will commence only after 6 months of disclosure of plan to public, where he strictly cannot deviate from it. It has put in too much upon the far sightedness and prudence of the persons who want to get benefited from this provision.

Disclosures

To ensure effective monitoring of the regulations, disclosures are required to be taken from certain persons both initial when he/she gets associated with the company and continual when the trading exceeds the specified limit. The Disclosures are to be preserved for a period of 5 years. Initial disclosures are to be made by Promoter, KMP and Director of his/her holdings within Thirty days of these regulations coming into effect and within Seven becoming promoter, KMP and Director as the case may be. Continual disclosure of number of securities acquired or disposed is required from every promoter, employee and director within Two trading days of transaction if the value of the securities traded, whether in one transaction or a series of transactions over any calendar quarter, aggregates to a traded value in excess of Rupees Ten lakhs. The particulars of such trading shall be notified to SEBI within Two trading days of receiving disclosure or becoming aware of such information. This means suppose if company gets information that a Promoter, Director or an employee has breached the reporting point and has not yet after 7 days of doing so informed the company, then in spite of this fact it would be duty of company to inform SEBI about the particulars of trades executed. The Continual Disclosures made shall be a clubbed one including disclosure pertaining to trading by immediate relatives, and by any other person for whom the promoter, Director or employee takes trading decisions. Moreover, disclosures of trading in securities shall also include trading in derivatives of securities but now the Companies Act, 2013 has put a bar that a Director or KMP is prohibited from dealing in future and options of shares or debentures of the Company. The regulations also contain provision to the effect that a company may in its discretion seek disclosures of holding and trading in its securities from other connected persons other than mentioned above to monitor compliance with the regulations at such frequency as it may deem fit.

Code for Fair Disclosure of UPSI

The regulations mandates to have a code of practices and procedures for fair disclosure of UPSI to public in order to avoid speculative and selective disclosure which will be more detrimental as it would have a bearing on the price discovery process. It is the Board of the Company who shall formulate the code without diluting the provisions of the regulations which shall be published on the website of the company and also be promptly intimated to the stock exchange where the securities are listed. The principles to be adhered to while formulating such code are spelt out in Schedule-A to the regulations which broadly are uniform and universal dissemination in non-selective manner, designation chief investor relations officer to deal with disclosures, appropriate responses to queries by regulators, sharing of UPSI on need to know basis and making of transcripts of investor relations conferences.

Code of Conduct to Regulate, Monitor and Report Trading by Insiders

There should be a code of conduct to regulate, monitor and report trading by insiders as required by the regulations. The code of conduct should observe minimum standards as envisaged under Schedule-B to the regulations. The minimum standards are:

(i) reporting to chairman of audit committee or board,
(ii) adopting Chinese wall procedures while dealing with information,
(iii) disciplinary actions for contravention of the code,
(iv) reporting to SEBI in case of violation of regulations,
(v) governing persons designated on the basis of their functional role and their immediate relatives by internal code of conduct,
(vi) setting up notional trading windows only during which they can trade,
(vii) pre-clearance of every trade subject to declarations as the compliance officer may require,
(viii) execution of trade within maximum 7 (Seven) days from pre-clearance,
(ix) restriction on contra trade for a minimum period of 6 (Six) months which may be relaxed by the compliance officer after recording the reasons in writing, and
(x) formulating formats for reporting trades, seeking pre-clearance, etc.

Conclusion

The protection of interest of investors and establishing information parity is at the heart of the intention of the Government and the Regulator, therefore, the Companies Act, 2013 and the SEBI (Prohibition of Insider Trading) Regulations, 2015 have been brought into force to curb insider trading by unlisted and listed companies respectively. The new SEBI regulations have tried to overcome the loopholes and widened its reach in comparison to the erstwhile regulations like expanding the scope of definition of connected person, making it practical to communicate UPSI for investment due-diligence before but at the same time it is at certain places quite impractical to adhere to such as mere communication of UPSI amounting to insider trading, stringent norms for trading plans which would make it unfeasible for the perpetual insiders to use this provision and Departure from definition of trading as recommended by expert committee and including "dealing" in the definition which would even cover pledging securities whenin possession of UPSI within ambit of insider trading.

5

Insider Trading: An Insight into the New Norms of SEBI

PRATITI NAYAK

Introduction

A transparent, efficient and liquid secondary market is indispensable to ensure the confidence of the investors. Over the past few years, the primary aim of SEBI (Securities Exchange Board of India) has been the improvement and strengthening of the market infrastructure, improvement in the quality of intermediation and intermediaries, structural framework within the stock exchanges and the functions of their member. The SEBI's regulation on insider trading has facilitated in laying down a legal framework to protect the investors against the insider trading and the so-called price rigging. India, over the past decade, has simultaneously witnessed a phenomenal growth in the structure of securities market (i.e. number, volume, size of stock exchange, number of listed companies, etc.) as well as in the number of malpractices and unfair methods of which 'insider trading' is widely used for personal gains. The term 'insider trading' summons many legal and moral repercussions in the mind of an onlooker. The erstwhile conviction of and subsequent $ 13.9 million penalty imposed on ex-Goldman Sachs Inc. Rajat Gupta[1] in early 2014 had brought into foray

1. http://www.reuters.co/article/2014/03/25/us-usa-crime-insidertrading-gupta-idUSBREA2O11M2014325 (Visited on May 16, 2015).

one of the most gruesome offences circumventing the upper rungs of corporate crime and the echoes can be felt across the Atlantic in Europe and India. Consequently, much has been debated[2] in respect of Insider Trading regulations in capital markets around the world and their efficacy in tackling the menace of such corporate crimes. The government's historic crackdown on insider trading, wherein more than 80 individuals have been charged in the aftermath of the Rajat Gupta is more of an event that shook the very guts of Wall Street[3]. Similarly, Mark Cuban, owner of the Dallas Mavericks basketball team and co-host of television show 'Shark Tank', was pursued by the Securities and Exchange Commission on insider trading charges for more than six years and spent around $20 million on defending himself and thereby criticizing the government's defence of broader insider trading prohibitions as part of a closely watched case before a U.S. Appellate Court.[4] In India the situation is all too stern. Despite the presence of Insider Trading Regulations since the inception of SEBI as a statutory body in 1992, it is a case of chasing a ghost with a stick. While lacking clarity, deterrence, predictability the current regulations have not been successful to uphold the idea and framework of fairness in dealings and efficacy of markets and this is precisely where the investor confidence and the forthrightness of price discovery mechanism erodes due to the malady of insider trading.[5]

Understanding the Phenomenon of Insider Trading

The global expansion of business world has led to a continuous increase in trading in shares, bonds, derivatives and other instruments. Amongst all, insider trading has evolved as one of the forms of trading

---

2. In a debate conducted by the Economist as to whether the crackdown on insider trading has gone too far, Harvey L. Pitt representing the side denying the statement argued that over the past decade, crimes affecting our financial and capital markets have seriously eroded the public's confidence in those markets. Thus, the detection and prosecution of insider trading violations is one of the prime enforcement priorities of the concerned regulator.
3. Jason M. Breslow, Should Insider Trading be Legal?, available at: http://www.pbs.org/wgbh/pages/frontline/business-economy-financial-crisis/to-catch-a-trader/should-insider-trading-be-legal/ (Visited on May 18, 2015).
4. Emily Glazer, "Mark Cuban Steps Back into Insider Trading Debate", available at: http://www.blogs.wsj.com/moneybeat/2015/02/19/mark-cuban-steps-back-into-insider-trading-debate/ (Visited on May 18, 2015).
5. Siddharth Sankar, "Insider Trading Regulations, 2013: Greater Clarity", available at: http://businesstoday.intoday.in/story/insider-trading-regulations-2013-greater-clarity/1/204642.html (Visited on May 18, 2015).

that has been of much interest in the recent years. When there is a buying or selling of stock of a corporation by persons having potential access to non-public information about that corporation, it leads to what we call insider trading. The trading becomes illegal with the involvement of substantial and non-public information is and in such cases, there is breach of a fiduciary or other position of trust because the individuals are aware of non-public information gained through the performance of their duties.[6] On the other hand, the trading is permissible if it is done without taking the advantage of non-public information. Insider trading is a term that most investors have heard and it commonly indicates an illegal conduct. But the term actually associates with both legal and illegal conduct. It refers generally to breach of a fiduciary or other relationship of trust and confidence, while in possession of material, non-public information about the security through buying or selling a security.[7] Thus, it involves transactions in a company's securities, such as stocks or options, by corporate insiders or their associates based on information originating within the firm that would, once publicly disclosed, affect the prices of such securities. [8] The term 'Insider' is used here to refer to those persons who gain advantages through information about imminent mergers, by purchasing shares of that company before the news of the merger becomes public by gaining the advantage through their access to the confidential information relating to their company. This generally leads to the increase of the share's price, in consequence to which the insider makes a quick profit by selling the total shares purchased. The studies conducted in USA with regard to the rate of return, shows that businesses based on insider trading obtain a rate that is on an average 3% point more than the average of all stocks.[9] Simply put, insider trading is an act of buying or selling of securities by a person having access to privileged information (to which no one else in the market has access to), usually done with the motive of earning

6. James H. Thompson, "A Global Comparison of Insider Trading Regulations", Vol. 3, No. 1, *International Journal of Accounting and Financial Reporting*, 2 (2013), available at: http://www.macrothink.org/journal/ index.php/ ijafr/ article/viewFile/3269/2976 (Visited on May 18, 2015).
7. Insider Trading, available at: http://www.sec.gov/answers/insider.htm (Visited on May 18, 2015).
8. http://www.econlib.org/library/Enc/InsiderTrading.html
9. Sugato Chakravarty and John J. McConnell, "Does Insider Trading Really Move Stock Prices?" Vol. 34, No. 2, *Journal of Financial and Quantitative Analysis*, 191-209 (1999), available at: http://www.jstor.org/stable/ 2676278 (Visited on May 21, 2015).

profits or doing away with the losses.[10] An insider depending on whether the information, once made public will drive the share price up or down, can either make a profit or avoid a loss.[11] There is a difference between legalised share trading by insiders and prohibitive insider trading. The law puts restrictions only to those insiders, who directly or indirectly use price sensitive information that they are in possession of, to the exclusion of the shareholders before arriving at trading decisions. However, there is no restriction on a trade by an insider, if they don't suppress any price sensitive information from the people. Furthermore, insider trading can equally occur in the market for government bonds and is not only confined to securities issued by companies. Thus, insider trading can be regarded properly as a matter of capital markets law.[12] Insider trading is probably one of the most common offences in the stock market. It is a regular phenomenon in the market. Such instances rarely come to the limelight as it takes place either in small quantities or remain low profile. Insider trading need not always be driven by information pertaining to a company. Information on the activities of the market regulator is enough. Insider trading is trading done by the insider or at the instance of an insider who has in his possession some secret price sensitive information before it is made public and by using such information, he makes private gains at the cost of innocent investors.[13] Insider trading undermines the confidence of investors in the fairness and integrity of the securities markets. Moreover, it also affects market professionals, liquidity traders, small and large shareholders, analysts, etc. in every aspect of their participation in the security market transactions. Security analysts and brokers are those who have acquired private information regarding the firm's prospects by spending their own resources and who do not have any fiduciary relationship with the firm.[14] Similarly, liquidity traders are short-term stock market participants who have some, usually negligible,[15] holdings of the firm's shares

10. Sanjiv Agarwal, Guide to Indian Capital Market, 375 (Bharat Publication, New Delhi, 1st edition, 2000).
11. Clearly, the insider buys in the former case and sells in the latter.
12. Gower and Davies, Principles of Modern Company Law, 1084 (Sweer and Maxwell, London, 8th edn., 2008).
13. *Supra* note 10, p. 376.
14. Kee H. Chung, "Security Analysis and Market Making", *Journal of Financial Intermediation*, 14 (2005), available at: http://www.acsu.buffalo.edu/~keechung/MGF743/Redings/M9.pdf , (visited on May 23, 2015).
15. Gur Huberman, "Optimal Liquidity Trading", Springer (2005), available at: https://www.gsb.columbia.edu/faculty/ghuberman/optimal%20liquidity%20trading.pdf

and trade in order to hedge risk or balance their portfolios without consideration of a firm's prospects. Insider trading can be observed everywhere in Indian markets whenever there is sudden buying or selling of shares, external factors remaining the same. It could be resorted to by persons having secret information of the company's results or achievements, which is one of the most important factors responsible for any sudden buying or selling spree.[16] Every insider would like to seize the opportunity of making quick gains by using the unpublished news about bonus, rights issues, dividend, good export orders, takeovers, mergers, etc. As soon as an insider places an order to buy or sell the share with his broker, he suspects insider trading and while executing the order, does some work for himself and passes on the information to others. An insider takes advantage of his influence at the time of the announcement of price sensitive information to the public. Thus, insider trading is highly objectionable and must be checked on ethical and moral grounds. Insider trading is a worldwide phenomenon and is being curbed in other countries. Different countries have adopted different legislations, all aiming at curbing this detrimental practice. India is one of the few countries to propose strict insider trading regulations, after the formation of SEBI in 1992. But, in reality it was observed that SEBI was merely a paper tiger with insufficient powers to book the offenders. The New Insider Trading Regulation, 2015 have been enacted in pursuance to the N.K. Sodhi Committee Report, incorporating key changes in various definitions as well as introducing some new concepts, thereby renovating the entire landscape of insider trading.

Regulations on Insider Trading

The regulations on insider trading is based on the proposition that if an insider or corporate entity possesses special information but has a business reason for keeping it secret, it may withhold that information from the market place. The law builds on this premise that 'silence is golden' in its instruction to 'disclose-or-abstain'. In the absence of disclosure, an insider may not trade on the basis of the withheld information and must also refrain from tipping.[17] If the insider wishes to trade in securities that are affected by the secret to which he is privy, he

16. *Ibid.*
17. Tipping is essentially trading by an individual who has learnt of price sensitive information from someone who has access to such price sensitive information and thereby has an equal consequential effect on prices in the securities market.

must first disclose the information and continue to abstain from trading until it has disseminated.[18] The definition of 'insiders' is, in legal practice, very wide. The vital add-on to the definition lies on the concept of fiduciary duty and misappropriation of information. Any trading based on the confidential information obtained, when the directors, officers and key employees of a firm who owes a fiduciary duty to the firm perform their corporate duties may be viewed as either breaching their fiduciary duties or misappropriating information that belongs to the firm.[19] Thus, agents who are not directors, officers or key employees of a firm but who bear fiduciary duties to the firm such as firm's contracted lawyers, consultants and investment bankers, would also be banned from trading on any information about the firm they have obtained when performing their duties in order to ban insider trading.[20] India is one of the countries, which recognised the imminent danger that insider trading could inflict upon the shareholders, financial markets and corporate governance. In pursuance to the report of the Thomas Committee, 1948, India incorporated in the Sections 307 and 308 of the Companies Act, 1956 which made it mandatory for the directors and managers to disclose their trading activities in the public.[21] Although these provisions were brought into force with a good intention, they proved to be insufficient for the purpose of tackling the menace of this market abuse and the need for a separate legislation on this matter was deeply felt. Therefore, after the establishment of SEBI, an all embracing regulation known as the SEBI (Prohibition of Insider Trading) Regulations was enacted in the year 1992.[22] The Regulations of 1992, which was designed to curb the insider trading prescribed for two types of insider. *Firstly*, the persons who are 'connected' or 'deemed to be connected' with the company and who are reasonably expected to have access to the unpublished price sensitive information on account of

---

18. *SEC* vs. *Texas Gulf Sulphur Co.*, 401 (2d Cir. 1968)
19. Jie Hu, The Insider Trading Debate, available at: www.frbatlanta.org/frbatlanta/filelegacydocs/Noe-Hu.pdf (Visited on May 23, 2015).
20. Yulong Ma and Huey-Lian Sun, "Where Should be the Line Drawn on Insider Trading Ehics?" Vol. 17, No. 1, *Journal of Business Ethics,* 67-75 (1998), available at: http://www.jstor.org/stable/25073056 (Visited on May 23, 2015).
21. Jonathan Macey, "Getting the Word About Fraud: A Theoretical Analysis of Whistleblowing and Insider Trading", *Michigan Law Review*, 1899-1940 (2007).
22. Ian Tonks, "Discussion of To Trade or Not To Trade: The Strategic Trading of Insiders around News Announcements", 37, *Journal of Business Finance and Accounting,* 408-21 (2010).

their connection, and *Secondly*, the persons who are not connected or deemed to be connected with the company but have actually received or had access to the unpublished price sensitive information.[23] The directors and officers or employees of the company or persons having professional or business relationship with the company and who may be reasonably expected to have an access to unpublished price sensitive information in relation to that company are classified as the 'connected persons'.[24] The moment a person becomes a connected person in possession of unpublished price sensitive information such person shall immediately be deemed as an insider without having to fulfil any other conditions.[25] The definition of 'insider' under the Insider Trading Regulations has three elements: (i) the person should be a natural person or a legal entity, (ii) he should be a natural person or a deemed connected person, and (iii) acquisition of the unpublished price sensitive information should be by virtue of such connection.[26] Further, the regulation provides for two-fold prohibitions on the actions of insiders: *Firstly*, an insider cannot pass on the unpublished price sensitive information in any manner or deal in securities of the company on his own behalf or on behalf of any other person,[27] and *secondly*, no company shall deal in the securities of another company or associate of that other company while in possession of any unpublished price sensitive information.[28] The regulation also mandated that the contravention of Regulation 3 and 3A by any insider would render him/her guilty of the act of insider trading. The Amendment to the Regulations in the year 2002, replaced the word 'the' with the letter 'a' in the second part of Regulation 2(e)(i), which effectively meant that a person would be an insider if on account of his office in one company, he could have access to the unpublished price sensitive information in respect of securities of another company. The most important aspect, unpublished price sensitive information has been described by Regulation 2(ha), as any information which relate to the company and have the capacity to materially alter the price of the securities of that company when disclosed to the public.[29] Any 'price sensitive information' will remain

23. Regulation 2(c) of SEBI (Prohibition Insider Trading) Regulations, 1992.
24. *Ibid.*
25. Regulation 2(e) of SEBI (Prohibition Insider Trading) Regulations, 1992.
26. *Supra* note 10, pp. 381.
27. Regulation 3 of SEBI (Prohibition Insider Trading) Regulations, 1992.
28. Regulation 3A of SEBI (Prohibition Insider Trading) Regulations, 1992.
29. Susan Pulian and Rob Rarry, "Dark Markets: Executives' Good Luck in Trading Own Stock", *Wall Street Journal* (2012).

unpublished for the purposes of insider trading, if such information was not published by the company, its agents and is not specific in nature.[30] SEBI has further clarified that 'unpublished' means which is not published by the company or its agents or which is not made public in print or electronic media and is not specific in nature.[31] According to Justice P.N. Bhagwati, the definition of 'insider' lacks clarity and it ultimately depends on the interpretation of the law to determine whether or not a company, in its capacity as a principal party can be termed as an 'insider'.[32] Only if the insider has dealt in the securities of a listed company, directly or indirectly when in possession of unpublished price sensitive information, then only the offence of insider trading can happen. The phrase 'dealing in securities' was widely worded by the SEBI (Prohibition of Insider Trading) Regulations, 1992 to include all form of dealings relating to the securities including any act of subscribing, buying, selling or agreeing to subscribe, buy, sell or deal in securities by any person either as principal or agent.[33] The SEBI (Prohibition of Insider Trading) Regulations, 1992 though comprehensive in its scope and nature, yet it did not provide SEBI with wide powers to strictly regulate the insider trading regime, prevalent in the securities market. Thus, a need for a revamped piece of legislation was felt, in order to empower SEBI and make the security trading rules reverberate with the modern times. A committee under the Chairmanship of N.K. Sodhi was constituted by SEBI to recommend on the matters relating to the security markets. The report submitted by the committee has led to the enactment of the new set of insider trading norms.[34]

Overview of Sodhi Committee Report

India has been governed by at least a two decades old legal regime as regards insider trading. Amongst the few regulations that were initially prescribed by SEBI upon its establishment, one was the SEBI (Prohibition of Insider Trading) Regulations, 1992. Nevertheless, the execution of the legal system on insider trading has faced its own set of substantial impediments. Though in the due course of time SEBI has

30. Regulation 2(k) of SEBI (Prohibition Insider Trading) Regulations, 1992.
31. Naval Chowdhury v. SEBI, (2004) 49 SCL 351 SAT.
32. *Ibid.*, pp. 380.
33. Regulation 2(d) of SEBI (Prohibition Insider Trading) Regulations, 1992.
34. Utpal Bhattacharya and Hazem Daouk, "The World Price of Insider Trading", Vol. LVII, No. 1, *Journal of Finance* (2002).

initiated various actions in this regard, but its statistics shows that it has not been successful in achieving its goal. Keeping that in mind, various supplemental alterations have been to the Regulations in 2002 majorly due to the experience learnt until then.[35] Although these efforts were beneficial in curbing some of the apparent lacunas in the Regulations, but at a more recent time SEBI realized the need for a complete rebuild of the regulations which would provide an systematic and structured means to restrain the unacceptable practice of insider trading and to intensify equitableness and information uniformity in the securities markets. Accordingly, the Securities Exchange Board of India (SEBI) appointed an 18 member committee under the chairmanship of Justice N.K. Sodhi, former Chief Justice of the High Court of Kerela and Karnataka and former Presiding Officer of the Securities Appellate Tribunal (SAT). One of the major concerns in respect of the insider trading issues was that due to lack of evidence, SAT has overturned several orders of SEBI. The procedural and evidentiary aspects of the regulations are the areas where the difficulty lies to fulfil in insider trading and not with the substantive part which is anyway quite strong. As far as the issue of price sensitive information is concerned, the real question is as to at what stage would information become price sensitive, i.e. is it involved only at an initial stage or only when details are available. In most of the cases of insider trading, it is found that it reveals only circumstantial evidence[36] and very rarely any direct evidence is involved which compounds the evidentiary burden. However, the insider trading regulations currently do not require *mens rea* but there is very less clarity on this point through the judicial interpretation.[37] In respect to the recent debate emanating from the US which has stressed upon powers of wire-tap,[38] etc., the committee has focused its recommendations on the various ways to enhance the investigative powers of SEBI. The Sodhi Committee, after months of discussions,

35. The incident in respect of Hindustan Lever was a major focal point of 2002 Amendment where-in a high profile action initiated by SEBI against Hindustan Lever was overturned by the appellate authority.
36. Andrew Sunter and Joanne Luu, "The Use of Circumstantial Evidence in Enforcement Cases before Securities Commissions: Two Perspectives", (2013), available at: www.bdplaw.com/content/uploads/2013/09/Circumstantial-Evidence-10-Sept-2013.pdf (visited on May 26, 2015).
37. *SEC* vs. *Garcia*, US District Court Ruling, 10-CV-O5268, 2011 BL 327296 (N.D. III. Dec. 28, 2011).
38. Nate Raymond, U.S. Court Studies Wiretaps in Rajat Gupta, Insider Trading Case, available at: http://in.reuters.com/article/2013/05/21/goldman-gupta-appeal-idINDEE94K0C420130521 (visited on May 26, 2015).

consultations and deliberations, issued its report[39] accompanied by the suggested draft of the SEBI (Prohibition of Insider Trading) Regulations, 2013.[40] The Report presented by the committee identified the loopholes and insufficiencies of the current regulation and seeks at dealing with them not just through additional changes, but by reassessing the governing attitude.[41] It aims at streamlining the regulatory approach, simplifying the regulations and reducing the ambiguity and vagueness that was apparent in the pre-existing regulations. The committee has adopted a somewhat unique and modernistic approach of aiding the proper interpretation of the legislations by providing notes and explanations to the specific regulations which would further helps in minimizing their ambiguity.[42]

SEBI's the Regulations, 2015 vis-à-vis the Regulations, 1992

The recommendations of the Sodhi Committee formed the basis for SEBI to notify the Prohibition of Insider Trading Regulations, 2015 which replaces the two-decade framework on the same. The new regulation broadens the ambit of the word insider to include two categories of persons: firstly, the connected persons, and secondly, those persons that have unpublished price sensitive information. The second category includes a company under the same management group or a subsidiary, intermediates, member or board of directors or an employee of a public financial institution, officers or employees of a self-regulatory organisation, relatives of the aforementioned persons, bankers of the company, relatives of connected persons, etc. Further, the new regulation intends at defining a 'connected person' as one who has a connection with the company that is expected to put him in possession of unpublished price sensitive information. The definition further aims at including persons who apparently do not occupy any position in a company but are in some or other way constantly related with the

39. SEBI, Report: High Level Committee to Review the SEBI (Prohibition of Insider Trading) Regulations, 1992, available at: http://www.sebi.gov.in/ cms/ sebi_data/attachdocs/1386758945803.pdf (visited on May 26, 2015).
40. Available at: http://www.sebi.gov.in/cms/sebi_data/boardmeeting/14175145 15705-a.pdf (visited on May 26, 2015).
41. Sandeep Parekh, "Overhauling Insider Trading Laws" *The Financial Express*, Dec. 19, 2013, available at: http://archive.financialexpress.com/news/column-overhauling-insider-trading-laws/1209226/0
42. Tejes Chitlangi, "Insider Beaware", *The Hindu*, Dec. 15, 2013, available at: http://www.thehindu.com/business/markets/insiders-beware/article5460166.ece (visited on May 26, 2015).

company and its officers and are involved in the company's operations.[43] It also intends to include within its scope such persons who would have access to or could access unpublished price sensitive information about any company or class of companies by the reason of any connection that would put them in possession of unpublished price sensitive information.[44] The 2015 Regulations, in addition to broadening the definitions of connected persons, unpublished price sensitive information (UPSI) and insider, also provides for the legal perspective which suggests graver consequences for company officials involved in selective exchange of information.[45] The Regulation has come into force on May 15, 2015, i.e., on the 120th day from the date of its publication in the official gazette. The applicability of the insider trading regulation extends to listed companies or those which are proposed to be listed on any of the recognised stock exchange. The expression 'company' includes other type of entities that are eligible to access the capital markets. There is as such no difficulty when it comes to the application of law, by SEBI, against insider trading to such companies as SEBI is empowered to exercise jurisdiction over the listed companies or those that are to be listed. However, an issue relating to applicability arises when the insider trading law is to be applied against the public unlisted companies and private companies as it is not within the purview of SEBI. However, in contrast to this, Section 195 contains a restriction regarding insider trading as applicable to public unlisted companies and to private companies.[46] This would definitely lead to serious roadblocks in interpreting the laws. Here, it is noteworthy to mention that, the 1992 regulations were clear in its applicability to listed companies only. With regard to the types of instruments to which the prohibition would apply, the Committee opined that it would apply to all types of securities, a term that has been defined under Section 2(h) of the Securities Contracts (Regulations) Act, 1956. The 2015 Regulations have accepted the recommendations by which the purview of the regulations would include both simple instruments such as shares,

---

43. Note to Reg. 2(d) of SEBI (Prohibition of Insider Trading) Regulations, 2015.
44. *Ibid.*
45. BS Reporter, "SEBI notifies new insider trading regulations", *Business Standard*, Jan. 15, 2015, available at: http://www.business-standard.com/article/markets/sebi-notifies-new-insider-trading-regulations-115011500944_1.html (visited on May 26, 2015).
46. Sec. 195 of Companies Act, 2013 prohibits insider trading of securities. It consists of explanatory provisions in respect of insider trading and price sensitive information along with penal provisions.

debentures and bonds as well as more complex one's such as hybrids and derivatives. Further with regard to unpublished price sensitive information, the regulations make clearer what constitutes UPSI by defining it to mean any information relating to a company or its securities, directly or indirectly, that is not generally available which upon becoming available is likely to materially affect the price of securities and shall include; financial results; dividends; change in capital structure; mergers, demergers, acquisitions, de-listings, disposals and expansion of business and such other transactions; changes in key managerial personnel; and material events in accordance with the Listing Agreement.[47] However, under the 1992 regulations, price sensitive information would remain 'unpublished' if the information remains unpublished by the company or its agents. Thus, that concept has been done away with in the new regulations. The new Regulation defines 'trading' to mean and include 'subscribing, buying, selling, dealing, or agreeing to subscribe, buy, sell, deal in any securities'.[48] The scope of the term has been widened in order to include 'dealing' in securities within its purview, keeping in mind the principal legislation, i.e. SEBI (Prohibition of Insider Trading) Regulations, 1992 which prohibits 'dealing' in securities on the basis of material non-public information, amongst other things. Further, in order to facilitate compliant trading by insiders constantly in possession of UPSI, the 2015 Regulations have introduced the novel concept of 'trading plans',[49] whereby every insider is entitled to execute trades in pursuance of predetermined trading plan which has been approved by the compliance officer and has been disclosed in the public six months prior to the commencement of such trading.[50] This concept of trading plan facilitates consistent trading and legitimizing of securities by insiders on a regular basis who may otherwise be deprived from transacting in the securities of the company and thereby is proved to be necessary in bringing about some validity to the insiders who wish to trade. Again, the 2015 Regulations mandate every listed company to formulate and publish a code of practices and procedures which are to be followed for a fair disclosure of UPSI.[51] However, it also sets out certain minimum standards such as equal accessibility to information, proclamation of policies such as those on

---

47. Regulation 2(n) of SEBI (Prohibition of Insider Trading) Regulations, 2015.
48. Regulation 2(l) of SEBI (Prohibition of Insider Trading) Regulations, 2015.
49. Regulation 5 of SEBI (Prohibition of Insider Trading) Regulations, 2015.
50. This is quite similar to Rule 10b5-1 plans in the US.
51. Regulation 8 of SEBI (Prohibition of Insider Trading) Regulations, 2015.

dividend, relative growth pursuits, calls and meetings with analysts, proclamation of manuscripts of such calls and meetings, etc.[52] Still in furtherance to it, every listed company and market intermediary requires its directors to design a framework in order to control, supervise and report trading by its employees and other connected persons.[53]

Conclusion

Inside information is a valuable commodity in the securities market. To have inside information is to have an insight into future stock performance. Insider trading rules are designed to limit the advantages that insiders naturally have in the market so that outsiders feel free to participate.[54] Nonetheless, a certain amount of insider abuse appears to be a constant feature of the marketplace. And because of this, the confidence of the investors in the fairness and integrity of the securities market is being eroded by the act/phenomenon of 'insider trading'. This places the thrust upon the regulating agencies to include the identification and prosecution of insider trading violations, as one of their prime administrative concern. The primary regulating authority of the securities market in India, SEBI has given new and improved form to the entire structure governing the insider trading phenomenon in the country with an aim of plugging in the loopholes and insufficiencies of the 1992 Regulations. The legislative notes interspersed within provisions of the New Regulations, 2015 acts as a unique and effective tool in interpreting the regulations as we move forward. However, it is of equal importance to take into notice that certain changes proposed by the Sodhi Committee, such as introduction of the definition of 'company', inclusion of public servants or persons occupying statutory positions within the definition of 'connected persons' and certain other valid defences have not been incorporated in the Regulations, 2015. Notwithstanding the above mentioned things, the new regulations provides for the much needed validity and coherence in the concerned legal regime. But as far as its efficacy is concerned, it depends upon the way in which it is to be implemented by the regulator and its interpretation by the appellate authority. Taking into account the high

---

52. Schedule A of SEBI (Prohibition of Insider Trading) Regulations, 2015.
53. As per the Schedule B of SEBI (Prohibition of Insider Trading) Regulations, 2015.
54. Nancy Reichman, "Beyond the Law: Crime in Complex Organizations", Vol. 18, *Crime and Justice, Chicago Journals,* 89 (2003), available at: http://www.jstor.org/stable/1147654 (visited on May 27, 2015).

prevalence of misuse of UPSI in India and SEBI's low track record of prosecution of such offences, the new Regulations propounds for a much needed change by providing for much devised, simple and clear-cut provisions based on the principled approach of curbing down the practice of insider trading in India.

CHAPTER III

Class Action

6

Class Action and Shareholder's Activism

DR. PREETHA S.

Introduction

Companies pool capital from investors in the domestic and international securities markets. The investor contributes to the capital of the company and they elect a Board of Directors to monitor the management of the company. The Board of Directors appoints the managers to manage the business of the company. The allocation of power between boards and shareholders is such that shareholders of large companies have little control over their directors and managers.[1] Major corporate decisions are taken by the board of directors and not by the shareholders. Shareholders do not have the power to direct the board of directors to follow a particular policy of action. Where the internal rules of governance of a company has conferred the control of the company's affairs on the board of directors, then the shareholders cannot impose its will upon the directors nor can they usurp the powers vested in the directors.[2] The voting power of shareholders is limited only to those instances where in shareholder approval is mandated by the statute.[3]

---

1. Stephen M. Bainbridge, "Director Primacy and Shareholder Disempowerment", 119, Harv. L.R. 1735 (2006).
2. *John Shaw & Sons Ltd.* vs. *Peter Shaw & John Shaw*, [1935] All E.R. 456 (C.A.); *Scott* vs. *Scott*, [1943]1 All E.R. 582 (Ch.D); *M.P.& Works* vs. *Muruka*, A.I.R. 1961 Cal. 251; *Suburban Bank Ltd.* vs. *Thariath*, A.I.R.1968 Ker. 206.
3. The Companies Act, 2013, Sections 180 and 181 mandates that the powers provided thereunder can be exercised by the board only with the consent of the

Shareholder passivity and the legal rules governing voting makes shareholder monitoring harder. Control of corporate directors by the shareholders is a myth.[4] Shareholders can definitely bring about a change in corporate policy by replacing the existing board. But practically, in closely held companies shareholders have very limited power to replace the directors.[5] Corporate democracy demands increase in shareholder's power with respect to business decisions of substantial importance. The new Companies Act, 2013 has introduced many novel provisions with a view to enhance the corporate governance standards in India. The requirement of independent directors, independent audit, small shareholders' director and women directors are some among the new measures brought in to enhance investor protection. Class action suits attain significance in the light of the limited shareholder participation in corporate governance.

Class Action Suit

A class action suit is a procedural device enabling one or more plaintiffs to file and prosecute a case on behalf of a group of persons having common grievances and rights. It provides a means to enforce claims which would otherwise never be litigated on account of the claim being too small to cover the cost of litigation. It is a well developed concept in countries like UK and USA. In United States, class actions are governed by Rule 23 of the Federal Rules of Civil Procedure. There are four prerequisites to any class action which are referred to as numerosity of members, commonality of question of law or fact, typicality of claim and adequacy of representation.[6] Securities class action, consumers' class action and employees' class action are being filed in large numbers in United States of America.[7] The class action device saves the resources of both the courts and the parties by permitting an issue potentially affecting every member to be litigated in

---

company in general meeting. This includes sale or lease of company's undertaking, borrowing of money beyond paid up capital, investment of compensation received on compulsory acquisition in securities, contributions to any charitable institutions beyond fifty thousand rupees.

4. Adolph A. Berle, Jr. & Gardiner C. Means, The Modern Corporation and Private Property, Brace & World Inc., New York (1932), p. 277.
5. Lucian Arye Bebchuk, "The Case for Increasing Shareholder Power", 118, Harv. L.R. 833 at p. 856 (2005).
6. US Federal Rules of Civil Procedure, Rule 23(a).
7. Eric Helland, Reputational Penalties and the Merits of Class-Action Securities Litigation, 49, *Journal of Law and Economics,* 365 (2006) at p. 397.

an economical fashion.[8] Recently, number of frauds and mis-management reports such as *Satyam* has been on the increase in India.[9] It points out the need for mechanisms to protect the rights of shareholders and to address their grievances. The concept of a class action by shareholders was recommended by the J.J. Irani Committee Report, 2005 which suggested that representative action may be initiated by one shareholder on behalf of one or more of the shareholders. Class action introduced under the new Companies Act, 2013 would pave way for a new era of shareholder activism and corporate democracy in India. The concept has been introduced in India in the aftermath of the Satyam corporate scandal wherein numerous small investors of Satyam Group in India were unable to seek effective relief against Satyam's management.

Class Action in India

Class action is one kind of representative suit filed by shareholders who are aggrieved by acts of oppression or mismanagement by people who control the company. Though representative suits by shareholders have been entertained by courts under the umbrella of public interest litigation, the right was not statutorily recognised until a separate provision was incorporated under section 245 of the Companies Act, 2013. Shareholders who have common grievances and who cannot afford to engage high profile lawyers to litigate small claims against corporate giants can sue together as a group by filing a class action.

Reliefs that can be Granted

The Companies Act, 2013 specifies the reliefs for which class action may be filed.[10] It may be invoked to restrain the company from

---

8. *United States Parole Comm'n* vs. *Geraghty*, 445 U.S. 388 (1980).
9. The Satyam scam involved a fraudulent scheme wherein the revenues of Satyam Computers Services Ltd. were materially overstated based on falsified invoices for hundreds of millions of dollars in consumer products that did not actually exist. In 2011 Satyam Computers and its auditor PwC agreed to pay US$ 125 million and US$ 25.5 million to settle claims filed by shareholders by way of a class action in US. However, due to the absence of any statutory provision for class action under the (Indian) Companies Act, 1956 no similar proceedings could be initiated by the affected shareholders of Satyam in India.
10. The Companies Act, 2013, Section 245: Such number of member or members, depositor or depositors or any class of them, as the case may be, as are indicated in sub-section (2) may, if they are of the opinion that the management or conduct of the affairs of the company are being conducted in a manner prejudicial to the interests of the company or its members or depositors, file an

committing an act which is *ultra vires* the articles or memorandum of the company, to restrain the company from committing breach of any provision of the company's memorandum or articles, to declare a resolution altering the memorandum or articles of the company as void if the resolution was passed by suppression of material facts or obtained by mis-statement to the members or depositors, to restrain the company and its directors from acting on such resolution, to restrain the company from doing an act which is contrary to the provisions of this Act or any other law for the time being in force and to restrain the company from taking action contrary to any resolution passed by the members. Class action can be filed for claiming damages against the company or its directors for any fraudulent, unlawful or wrongful act or omission or conduct. The auditors can also be sued for any improper or misleading statement of particulars made in his audit report or for any fraudulent, unlawful or wrongful act or conduct. Class action can be filed to seek any other remedy as the Tribunal may deem fit. Though the provision has been incorporated under chapter XVI of the Act which deals with

---

application before the Tribunal on behalf of the members or depositors for seeking all or any of the following orders, namely:

(a) to restrain the company from committing an act which is *ultra vires* the articles or memorandum of the company;

(b) to restrain the company from committing breach of any provision of the company's memorandum or articles;

(c) to declare a resolution altering the memorandum or articles of the company as void if the resolution was passed by suppression of material facts or obtained by mis-statement to the members or depositors;

(d) to restrain the company and its directors from acting on such resolution;

(e) to restrain the company from doing an act which is contrary to the provisions of this Act or any other law for the time being in force;

(f) to restrain the company from taking action contrary to any resolution passed by the members;

(g) to claim damages or compensation or demand any other suitable action from or against—

 (i) the company or its directors for any fraudulent, unlawful or wrongful act or omission or conduct or any likely act or omission or conduct on its or their part;

 (ii) the auditor including audit firm of the company for any improper or misleading statement of particulars made in his audit report or for any fraudulent, unlawful or wrongful act or conduct; or

 (iii) any expert or advisor or consultant or any other person for any incorrect or misleading statement made to the company or for any fraudulent, unlawful or wrongful act or conduct or any likely act or on his part;

(h) to seek any other remedy as the Tribunal may deem fit.

prevention of oppression and mismanagement, the kind of reliefs that could be sought is wider in scope ensuring shareholder participation in the conduct of company affairs. So far, filing a case of oppression and mismanagement was the only recourse available to the aggrieved shareholders. Class action suit gives them additional rights and grounds to fight for their rights and sue against any abuse of powers by the directors.

Persons Who Can be Sued

Class action can also be used to claim damages or compensation against the company or its directors for any fraudulent, unlawful or wrongful act or omission or conduct. Relief can also be claimed against the auditor including audit firm of the company for any improper or misleading statement of particulars made in his audit report or for any fraudulent, unlawful or wrongful act or conduct. Any expert or advisor or consultant or any other person can be sued through class action suit for any incorrect or misleading statement made to the company or for any fraudulent, unlawful or wrongful act or conduct or any likely act or conduct on his part. Any order passed by the Tribunal shall be binding on the company and all its members, depositors and auditor including audit firm or expert or consultant or advisor or any other person associated with the company. Any company which fails to comply with an order passed by the Tribunal shall be punishable with fine which shall not be less than five lakh rupees but which may extend to twenty-five lakh rupees and every officer of the company who is in default shall be punishable with imprisonment for a term which may extend to three years and with fine.[11]

Minimum Number of Persons Required

In the case of a company having a share capital, not less than one hundred members of the company or not less than such percentage of the total number of its members as may be prescribed, whichever is less, or any member or members holding not less than such percentage of the issued share capital of the company as may be prescribed are required to file class action suit.[12] This is subject to the condition that the applicants have paid all calls and other sums due on their shares. In the case of a company not having a share capital, the requisite number of members required for filing class action shall be not less than one-fifth of the total

11. The Companies Act, 2013, S. 245(7).
12. The Companies Act, 2013, S. 245(3).

number of its members. The number of depositors required to institute a class action is one hundred depositors or not less than such percentage of the total number of depositors as may be prescribed, whichever is less, or any depositor or depositors to whom the company owes such percentage of total deposits of the company as may be prescribed. Class action suit can be filed by shareholders and deposit holders. The Act provides that an application may be filed or any other action may be taken by any person, group of persons or any association of persons representing the persons affected by any act or omission.[13] This facility to file suit through any person, group of person or associations can motivate NGOs and other activists to take up causes for the affected investors. Investor associations recognised by SEBI can also initiate class action and the SEBI (Investor Education and Protection Fund Regulations), 2009 provides for aiding such investor associations.

Procedural Requirements

The class action suit shall be filed before the National Company Law Tribunal. Several in-built mechanisms are provided in the Act to avoid improper use of class actions because such actions are open for misuse by unscrupulous minority shareholders in furtherance of their vested interest thereby hampering the efficacy of the entire corporate system. There are specified conditions to be taken into account by the Tribunal before considering applications under class suit.[14] The Tribunal shall take into account as to whether the member or depositor is acting in good faith in making the application and whether there is any evidence before it as to the involvement of any person other than directors or officers of the company on any of the alleged matters. It shall consider any evidence before it as to the views of the members or depositors of the company who have no personal interest in the matter being proceeded against under the class suit. Where the cause of action is an act or omission that has already occurred, the tribunal shall consider whether the act or omission would be likely to be ratified by the company. If an application is admitted, then the Tribunal shall issue public notice of the application to all the members or depositors of the class. All similar applications prevalent in any jurisdiction should be consolidated into a single application and the class members or depositors should be allowed to choose the lead applicant and in the event the members or depositors of the class are unable to come to a

13. The Companies Act, 2013, S. 245(10).
14. The Companies Act, 2013, S. 245(4).

consensus, the Tribunal shall have the power to appoint a lead applicant, who shall be in charge of the proceedings from the applicant's side. Two class action applications for the same cause of action shall not be allowed. The cost or expenses connected with the application for class action shall be defrayed by the company or any other person responsible for any oppressive act. Where any application filed before the Tribunal is found to be frivolous or vexatious, it shall, for reasons to be recorded in writing, reject the application and make an order that the applicant shall pay to the opposite party such cost, not exceeding one lakh rupees.[15]

Corporate Governance and Shareholder Activism

The Indian corporate sector is dominated by family businesses and the Indian companies do not have widely dispersed ownership pattern as we see in the UK or US companies. The Indian companies are beset with an inherent problem of conflict of interest between dominant shareholders and minority shareholders. While the corporate governance issue facing US and UK companies is that of disciplining the management and making them accountable to the shareholders, the governance issue facing Indian corporate sector is that of disciplining the dominant shareholders and protecting the minority shareholders. In companies dominated by controlling shareholders, activist shareholders would find it difficult to influence the controlling shareholders and to alter the corporate decisions.[16] A shareholder who has been unsuccessful in persuading the management to change its policies can file a class action suit before the Tribunal and seek appropriate remedies. Class action suits can prove to be an effective medium for enhancing shareholder activism thereby promoting corporate democracy in the Indian corporate sector. Class action suits can play a significant role in disciplining dominant shareholders and in protecting the minority shareholders who are prejudicially affected by actions of the dominant shareholders. Professors Stuart Gillian and Laura Starks defines shareholder activists as investors who, dissatisfied with some aspect of a company's management or operations, try to bring about change within the company without a change in control.[17] Shareholder activism refers

15. The Companies Act, 2013, S. 245(8).
16. Varottil Umakanth, 'The Advent of Shareholder Activism in India', 1, *Journal of Governance,* 582 (2012) at p. 626.
17. Stuart L. Gillan & Laura T. Starks, The Evolution of Shareholder Activism in the United States, 19, *Journal of Applied Corporate Finance,* 55 (2007).

to all kinds of efforts taken to change behavior pattern of the company.[18] Shareholders who are desirous of bringing about a change in the governance pattern of the company can use class action as a tool to fight for their rights. Activism from the part of the retail investors and minority shareholders is the need of the hour. Class action gives an opportunity to the shareholders to become active in the Indian capital market. Shareholder activism would keep the management under check and class action would strengthen shareholder participation in corporate governance. The provision for class action would boost investor confidence in capital market and Indian corporate sector would become more attractive to retails investors.[19] Retail investors have more potential to save and invest, but they are reluctant to invest in the capital market. The participation of retail investor in the Indian capital market is much less when compared to that of institutional investors.[20] The major part of the savings is invested in bank, post office deposits, real estate and gold. If we are able to attract the retails investors, investments lying as dead money can be pumped into the capital market for more productive purposes and for better allocation of resources.

Conclusion

In the modern era of globalization and liberalisation, even the government employees are expected to assume responsibility for their own financial security after retirement. Tax exemptions are given for investment in mutual funds and related securities. In such a scenario investment in capital market is no longer an optional activity. The public is constrained to invest in capital market. The investors cannot be forced to invest their hard earned money in markets which they perceive to be unfair and hence the government is obliged to assure that the investors are treated fairly and honestly. It has to take all necessary steps to ensure a level playing field for all the stakeholders so that investor confidence can be boosted. The new provision for class action can be viewed as an earnest attempt from the part of government to restore

---

18. Stephen M. Bainbridge, Shareholder Activism and Institutional Investors, UCLA School of Law, Law & Economics Research Paper Series, available at http://ssrn.com/abstract=796227.
19. SEBI (Issue of Capital and Disclosure Requirements), 2009, Cl. 2 (ze), "retail individual investor" means an investor who applies or bids for specified securities for a value of not more than one lakh rupees.
20. A survey conducted by the National Council for Applied Economic Research in 2011 has found that only 12 percent of the household savings are invested in the capital market.

investor confidence in the capital market. Class action would improve shareholder participation and make managers and auditors more accountable. Small investors can use class action suits to seek justice. It would ensure that companies become more careful in their action. It provides them with a medium to fight as one unit against the errant company or management, thereby reducing multiplicity of suits, costs of ligation and increasing their chances of success in the process. Deposit holders can also take action against any wrongful act by the company or other specified persons. These help in increasing the accountability of a company or its management towards its stakeholders and in containing any likely prejudice against the minority. The threat of class action would definitely enhance sense of responsibility and diligence of the corporate managers towards the interest of stakeholders.

7

Class Action: A Sentinel of Minority Shareholder's Interest

ANINDHYA TIWARI AND AMIT AGARWAL

Introduction

The Companies Act, 2013 have introduced many changes and one of those is called 'Class Action Suit'. After facing scam like Satyam,[1] Government is thinking of class action suit on the line of US laws as the holder of securities are entitled to bring action against the Satyam in United States of America. Dr. Jamshed J. Irani Committee recommended in the report[2] dated 31st May, 2005 that Class Action Suit to be allowed by the courts on the same footing as derivative action if the shareholders have same Locus Standi. Although Representative Suits[3] are allowed under Civil Procedure Code and also Public Interest Litigation[4] is allowed in the interest of public under the Constitution of India, there was no specific provision as to class action by the shareholders in the Companies Act, 1956. Class Action Suit brings shareholder activism as it entitles the shareholder to file suit in case of misconduct of the affairs of the company. The Companies Act, 2013 introduces the much awaited concept to protect the interest of minority

1. India's Enron, 2009.
2. Government of India, Report: *Expert Committee on Company Law* (Ministry of Corporate Affairs, 2005).
3. Order 1, Rule 8 of Code of Civil Procedure, 1908.
4. Article 32 (Supreme Court) and Article 226 (High Court) of the Constitution of India.

shareholders of the company.[5] It acts as check on the exercise of power by the Board of Directors and other managerial personnel. In fine, Class Action Suit is the suit which allows a group of people having common interest to sue the company, auditors and other persons who are involved in frauds before the appropriate authority. Chapter XVI of the Companies Act, 2013 which deals with the Prevention of Oppression and Mismanagement provides about Class Action which can be brought before Tribunal by members and depositors. Only members are entitled to take action for prevention of oppression and mismanagement under sections 241-244 of the Companies Act, 2013, depositors are not allowed to take action.

Historical Perspective

History of Class Action can be traced from the 13th century as group litigation is allowed in England when any act of person which leads to violation of rule affects several people. As it is not possible for every individual to take an action because of transportation and communication availability, group litigation were allowed. It is generally accepted that the origins of the modern class action lie in a procedural device used in the English Chancery courts known as the 'Bill of Peace.' In the Bill of Peace, one could institute a suit in Chancery against a small number of representative persons whose interests were shared by a larger group known as "the multitude." Before the suit could precede as a representative action, the equity court had to determine that the multitude possessed a joint interest in the right or property at issue.[6] The English Civil Procedure Rules ("CPR") have long facilitated the aggregation of claims via the "representative action." Rule 19.6 of the CPR, entitled "Representative parties with same interest. The Group Litigation Order ("GLO") of Part 19.III of the CPR was also introduced in May 2000 to deal with the supposed limitations of the representative action.[7] In the first half of 1800s in the United States of America, this class action suit is backed by Joseph Story.[8] In 1833,

5. Sec. 245 of Companies Act, 2013.
6. Philip Stephen Fuoco & Joseph A. Osefchen, "Leveling the Playing Field in the Garden State: A Guide to New Jersey Class Action Case Law", 37, *Rutgers Law Journal*, 399-400
7. Mark Stiggelbout, "The Recognition in England and Wales of United States Judgments in Class Actions", 52, *Harvard International Law Journal*, 444-451, (Summer 2011)
8. Former Associate Justice of Supreme Court of the United States

Equity Rule 48, the real precursor of today's class-action procedure, was promulgated which allowed for representative suit in cases where there were too many plaintiffs.[9] But modern class actions were given birth in 1938 with the adoption of Rule 23 of the Federal Rules of Civil Procedure (FRCP) and later matured into the powerful tool available today as a result of amendments to that rule adopted in 1966.[10] Under the original version of Rule 23, class members were often required to affirmatively "opt in" to the litigation in order to be bound to any settlement, trial verdict or other resolution of the case, thus placing practical limits on the ultimate sizes of these classes. The 1966 amendments greatly expanded the scope of U.S. class actions by allowing judges to certify certain types of classes in which participation would now be presumed for every potential member unless the individual or entity formally excused themselves out of the class.[11] In USA, there is contingency fees in which lawyer receive as fees an agreed percentage of the recovery. Another crucial element of the class action financing method is the "American rule": Each side to a lawsuit bears its own costs, regardless of who wins.[12] Later the Class Action Fairness Act of 2005 was introduced which expanded federal jurisdiction over many large class-action lawsuits (where amount in controversy exceeds $5 Million) and mass actions taken in the United States.[13] In order to frivolous lawsuits, US Congress passed the Private Securities Litigation Reforms Act in the year 1995. The Reform Act was designed to address a number of perceived abuses in these cases. In large part, its solution was to create a series of procedural hurdles that make it more difficult for plaintiffs' attorneys to bring and maintain non-meritorious securities

9. Wim J.M. Touw, "*Law Street: America's Dysfunctional and Sometimes Corrupt Legal System*", 109 (iUniverse, USA, 2011), ISBN:978-1-4620-0873-5 (pbk).
10. Nicholas M. Pace, "Class Actions in the United States of America: An Overview of the Process and the Empirical Literature", Available at http://globalclassactions.stanford.edu/sites/default/files/documents/USA__National_Report.pdf (Last Visited on April 18, 2015).
11. *Supra* note 11 at 2.
12. Janet Cooper Alexander, "An Introduction to Class Action Procedure in the United States", Available at http://law.duke.edu/grouplit/papers/ class action alexander.pdf (Last Visited on April 18, 2015).
13. Mrs. Parimala V., "An Overview of Progressive Activism—The Class Action Suit", 2, *Indian Journal of Applied Research*, 137, (December 2012), ISSN 2249-555X.

fraud class actions.[14] In India, Class Action is recognised by the Code of Civil Procedure whereby representative suit[15] is allowed to be filed but with the permission of the court and there must be common interest of the parties. Public Interest Litigation is also recognised in India and the seeds of the concept of public interest litigation were initially sown in India by Krishna Iyer J., in 1976 in *Mumbai Kamgar Sabha, Bombay* vs. *Abdulbhai Faizullabhai.*[16] Public Interest Litigation is allowed before the Supreme Court and High Courts in India. It is a litigation in which the public spirited person files the case on behalf of aggrieved party or parties. J.J. Irani Committee was set-up in December 2004 to advise on a new company law while recording that the courts had recognised and upheld class action and derivative action by the shareholders in sections 397 and 398 of the 1956 Act proposed its recognition and inclusion in the statute. At chapter VI, paragraph 10, the committee suggested the class action or derivative suits.[17] The Companies Act, 1956 has provision under sections 397 and 398 whereby a member can apply to the court or tribunal for the prevention of oppression and mismanagement of the affairs of the company. After the effects of **Satyam Scam**, the Government is thinking of class action suit as like USA where the people are filing suit before courts for recovery of monies. Section 245 of the Companies Act, 2013 specifically deals with the class action where certain number of members can apply before a tribunal if they are of the opinion that the affairs of the company are conducted in a manner prejudicial to the interest of company or its members and depositors.

Class Action: Meaning

Class Action basically means that a suit is filed by some persons on behalf of group of people for redressing their grievances. As it is not possible for every individual to file a suit because he/she may be at a very distant place for which it is not possible for him/her to come and file a suit before the court/tribunal, a small number of persons can file suit on behalf of group.

It is a legal action involving a large group or class of people. Without having every member of the class join the action, a few individuals

---

14. Michael A. Perino, "Did the Private Securities Litigation Reform Act Work", 4, *University of Illinois Law Review,* 914 (2003).
15. *Supra* note 3.
16. AIR 1976 SC 1455.
17. A. Ramaiya, "*Guide to Companies Act*", (Lexis Nexis, Gurgaon, 18th edn., 2015), ISBN: 978-93-5143-325-5 (Box-1).

initiate a court case becoming representatives of the group.[18] In Class Action, common interest is there, so the people are filing a suit. As court we know is full of burden, there is lots of case pending before various courts;[19] Class Action is a tool for expedient disposal of cases as it solves the large number of parties' grievances in a single suit. It also reduces the cost of filing the suit before the courts. Courts are usually taking into consideration the interest of various parties involves in the suits before hearing the class action suit as to whether there is an illicit motive behind the suit so as to coerce the company. The broad types of class actions include:

Consumer Rights: The claims are for individuals' economic losses (not for personal injuries) and are too small to justify individual suits.

Securities and Antitrust: Securities class actions are often regarded as small claim cases, but in fact a small number of very large claims usually account for most of the recovery.

Environmental: This could be considered a form of consumer class action, but it is relatively rare for the environmental laws to be enforced through class actions, partly because the desired remedy is usually injunctive in nature rather than money damages.

Mass Torts: The difference in consumer class actions and these class actions are that these are large claims for personal injuries rather than small claims for purely economic losses.

Civil Rights: Civil Rights, for example, school segregation, prisoners' rights, voting rights, and employment rights of public employees.

Class Action in a way is a sword in the hand of members or other persons for protecting their rights being violated by the company, its managerial personnel and others. Courts or Tribunal can pass orders/ directions to protect the rights of above-mentioned persons by which it may direct the company's official and also the company itself not to do something or to do something so as to redress their grievances.

Derivative Action and Class Action

Derivative Action is the action by the shareholders of the company

18. Black Law Dictionary, Available at http://thelawdictionary.org/class-action/(Last Visited on April 19, 2015).
19. More than 3 Crore Cases Pending Across Country, Available at http://www.ndtv.com/india-news/more-than-3-crore-court-cases-pending-across-country-709595(Last Visited on April 21, 2015).

on behalf of the company for the purpose of enforcing and defending a legal right. When the directors are acting in a manner which may prejudice the company, they will not take action for the purpose of protecting the interest of company, but it is the shareholder who will bring action for the same. In US, Federal Rule of Civil Procedure 23.1 governs derivative actions brought in federal court. In *Foss* vs. *Harbottle*[20] case, the directors of the company were selling their lands at a rate which was over and above the value of the land. Shareholders brought the action for enforcing rights and Court held that shareholders are not but the company itself is entitled to enforce the rights. There are certain exceptions to the *Foss* vs. *Harbottle* rule like When the personal rights of the shareholders are infringed or When there is fraud on the minority or Acts which are *ultra-vires* or Illegal or Where transactions require special majority. In Derivative Action, the damages or compensation which the court ordered go to the company and cannot go to the shareholders. The major difference between derivative action and class action is that the derivative actions are taken for the benefit of company but the class actions may be taken against the company itself. In *Darius Rutton Kavasmaneck* vs. *Gharda Chemicals Limited*[21] case, plaintiff filed a derivative action against defendant No. 2 who was the Chairman and Managing Director of Defendant No. 1 (Company), Defendant No. 3 who was the wife of Defendant No. 2 and Defendant Nos. 4 and 5 who were the Directors of Defendant No. 1. Plaintiff grievance was that the patent was applied in the name of defendant No. 2 and not in the name of defendant No. 1. Plaintiff holds 12% of the shares and other minority shareholders are holding 13% shares who are against this action. Bombay High Court held that this action is not in the interest of company because under section 64(1)(b) of the Patent Act, 1970, any person can apply for revocation of patent if application for patent is made by person who is not entitled to make an application. If the patent was cancelled, defendant No. 1 will not be able to use the patent which is now using royalty free which will cause loss to the company. Court did not granted any relief to plaintiff by taking into consideration the interest of company.

Corporate Governance and Class Action

Corporate Governance ensures transparency in the affairs of the company as it requires proper disclosures and compliance of laws.

20. (1843) 2 Hare 461.
21. 2015(2) Bom CR 100.

Corporate governance warrants the ethical conduct of business. It ensures that the affairs of the company are conducted in a manner which benefits the members and the adequate representation of non-executive and independent directors in the board of directors of the company. When the Company are conducting its affairs which affect the members/depositors, Companies Act, 2013 provides right to sue to the members/depositors. Class Action ensures members right by which they can sue the company, or its director, auditors, etc. for the wrong done to the company or to them. It ensures in a way a compliance of corporate and other laws which are applicable to the company. Class Action provides impetus to the corporate governance norm of the company by which it obligates the company to do only such acts which does not in any way affect the members' interest. Clause 49 of the Listing Agreement provides about the corporate governance which is required to be complied by the companies which are listed on the stock exchange. Shareholders are now much more vigilant and files class action suit in order to redress their grievances with regard to their investments in companies. Sahara Case is the example in which the Sahara India Real Estate Corporation Limited (SIRECL) and Sahara Housing Investment Corporation Limited (SHICL) issued optionally fully convertible debentures to public without complying with the norms as to public issue. The Supreme Court held that the securities which is issued by the companies amounts to public issue and the company is required to comply with the Secs. 67 and 73 of Companies Act, 1956 which the company did not comply thereby violated the said provision of Companies Act, 1956.

Companies Act, 2013 and Class Action

The Companies Act, 2013 introduces the concept of Class Action by inserting Sec. 245 in which class action is permitted on certain grounds and by certain members and depositors. It entitles them to take action before National Company Law Tribunal in case management or conducts of the affairs are conducted in a manner which is prejudicial to the interest of the company, its members or its depositors. The Companies Act, 2013 also provides that the legal expenses which incurred for taking class action suit under sections 37 and 245 of Companies Act, 2013 by members, depositors shall be reimbursed to them out of Investor Education and Protection Fund as per sanction of the Tribunal.[22] Tribunal while considering the application must consider

22. Section 125 of Companies Act, 2013.

the acts of members as to whether they are acting in good faith, whether the members can take action individually instead of class action, whether there is an involvement of other persons other than directors and officers of the company in an act which is *ultra-vires* the Memorandum of Association & Article of Association, or to any resolution which is passed by the members and also opinion of the members who are not interested personally as to the matter. In case the acts or omissions which have not yet occurred but may occur, it shall also take into consideration the authorisation by company the act which is yet to occur and ratification that can be given by the company after occurring of the act. But Banking Companies are not covered under class action.

Instances of Filing a Class Action Suit

If the members or depositors are of the view that the affairs are being conducted in a manner which is prejudicial to interest of company or its members or depositors, they can apply before a Tribunal on behalf of members or depositors for following orders:

(a) To restrain the company from committing an act which is *ultra vires* the articles or memorandum of the company;

(b) To restrain the company from committing breach of any provision of the company's memorandum or articles;

(c) To declare a resolution altering the memorandum or articles of the company as void if the resolution was passed by suppression of material facts or obtained by mis-statement to the members or depositors;

(d) To restraint the company and its directors from acting on such resolution;

(e) To restrain the company from doing an act which is contrary to the provisions of this Act or any other law for the time being in force;

(f) To restrain the company from taking action contrary to any resolution passed by the members;

(g) To claim damages or compensation or demand any other suitable action from or against—

(i) The company or its directors for any fraudulent, unlawful or wrongful act or omission or conduct or any likely act or omission or conduct on its or their part;

(ii) The auditor including audit firm of the company for any improper or misleading statement of particulars made in his audit report or for any fraudulent, unlawful or wrongful act or conduct; or

(iii) Any expert or advisor or consultant or any other person for any incorrect or misleading statement made to the company or for any fraudulent, unlawful or wrongful act or conduct or any likely act or conduct on his part;

(h) To seek any other remedy as the Tribunal may deem fit.

Company's Memorandum of Association (MOA) is the constitution of the company and Articles of Association (AOA) contains rules which govern its functioning. These are public documents which can be accessed from the Ministry of Corporate Affairs website. Company can alter its MOA and AOA by taking members approval by way of special or ordinary resolutions. Company's authorities are limited to above mentioned documents and the members/depositors can apply before the tribunal to restraint the company from acting beyond the above said documents. Company in order to pass a resolution by members have to provide adequate notice and provide details as to the resolution in order to keep them informed about the same. In case of special resolution, explanatory statement is also required to be given.[23] Section 245 of Act, entitles the members/depositors to apply before a tribunal for restraining the company from acting according to resolution, if it passed with suppression of material facts. Company cannot act in a way its directors or key managerial personnel want in their interest which is prohibited by law. It has to observe the rules and regulations (norms) which are applicable to the company and its personnel. If the company or its directors, auditors, any expert, advisor or other persons are acting fraudulently or wrongfully, then the members/depositors can claim compensation or damages from the same. In case, if action is against the audit firm, then the audit firm including members who are involved in the making of untrue statement in the audit report are liable.

Another separate provision has also been made for 'Securities Class Action' under section 37 of the Companies Act, 2013. In case, if the prospectus contains a misleading statement, by which a person or group of persons affected therefrom, they can bring a suit for redressing their grievances.

Requirement as to Minimum Number of Members/Depositors

There is also a requirement of minimum number of members/ depositors which have to make an application before tribunal, i.e.

23. Section 102 of Companies Act, 2013.

In case of Members

For a company having share capital, there must be one hundred (100) members or such percentage of the total number of members as may be prescribed, whichever is less, or any other member or members but there must be a minimum requirement of holding of at least such percentage of the issued share capital of the company and members have paid all money towards the share in the company and for a company not having share capital, at least one-fifth of the total number of members.

In case of Depositors

Depositors must not be less than 100 or such percentage of the total number of depositors as may be prescribed, whichever less is; or any depositor or depositors hold not less than such percentage of the total value of outstanding deposits of the company as may be prescribed.

In case of oppression, etc. tribunal have power to waive all or any of the requirements as to minimum number of members which have to make application[24] but there is no such power with tribunal as to waiver in case of class action. There is also a requirement of serving of public notice to all the members and depositors of the company after admission of the application. All similar applications shall be consolidated and lead applicant shall be appointed by members/depositors and if they fails to appoint lead applicant, then Tribunal had power to appoint the lead applicant. There is a bar of two class actions which are on the same cause of action. The order passed by the Tribunal shall have binding force on the company, its members, depositors and auditors including audit firm or expert or consultant or advisor or any other person associated with the company. Non-compliance of the order of the Tribunal is punishable with fine not less than five lakh Rupees (Rs. 500,000) but it can be extended to twenty-five lakh Rupees (Rs. 2,500,000). The officer who is in default shall be punishable with imprisonment for a term which may extend to three years and also fine can be imposed which shall not be less than twenty-five thousand Rupees (Rs. 25,000) but which may extend to one lakh Rupees (Rs. 100,000). In case of fatuous or inane application, Tribunal have power to reject the application and tribunal is required to make an order directing the applicant to pay cost which must not be more than one lakh rupees (Rs. 100,000).

Appeal against Order of Tribunal and Appellate Tribunal

If any person aggrieved by the order of the tribunal, can appeal before the Appellate Tribunal but appeal is not allowed when the order

24. Section 244 of Companies Act, 2013.

is passed by the Tribunal with the consent of the parties. Appeal must be made within 45 days from the date on which the copy of the order of the Tribunal is made available to person aggrieved from the order. Act also allows the appeal after the expiry of the period of 45 days but there must be sufficient cause for not filing the appeal and appeal must be made within a period of 45 days after the expiry of above said period of 45 days.[25] Further appeal is also provided by the Act, 2013 to the Supreme Court from the order of Appellate Tribunal but must be made within a period of 60 days after receipt of the order of the Appellate Tribunal.[26]

Fair Representation of Minority and Class Action

The Companies Act, 1956 under chapter 6 provides for prevention of oppression and mismanagement by which members can apply before Company Law Board/Tribunal for preventing the affairs being conducted in a manner which prejudice the interest of public, company and oppressive to any member and tribunal make such order as it thinks fit.[27] Class Action under the Companies Act, 2013 ensures protection of minority interest by entitling them to file an application in case when the affairs of the company are not properly conducted. This in a way provide sword in the hand of minority against the company, its directors and others, if their rights are infringed. There are provisions in the Companies Act, 2013 which allows the decision can be taken by the members forming majority of the company and which can affect the rights of minority.[28] This is a provision which safeguards the rights of minority and thereby ensures the proper functioning of the company. The Companies Act, 2013 also provides the punishment for fraud which defines in explanation to section 447 of the Companies Act, 2013. Fraud means an act, omission or abuse of position with a purpose to gain undue advantage from shareholders and creditors. It enables the minority to apply before tribunal for redress of grievances in relation to fraud.

SEBI and Class Action

SEBI is formed basically to protect the interest of investor and to

25. Section 421 of Companies Act, 2013.
26. Section 423 of Companies Act, 2013.
27. Section 397-398 of Companies Act, 1956.
28. Like Sec. 230 of the Companies Act, 2013 allows the decision with respect to compromise and arrangement can be taken by three-fourth majority of members of the company.

regulate the stock market and intermediaries in the stock market. SEBI regulates the Investor Protection and Education Fund in order to provide assistance to the investor.[29] The utilisation of fund may be for the purposes of aiding investor association recognised by the Board to undertake legal proceeding in the interest of investors in securities that are listed or proposed to be listed.[30] There are 15 registered Investors' Association recognised by SEBI as on March 03, 2015.[31] Legal proceeding which defines under the SEBI (Investor Protection and Education Fund) Regulations, 2009 provides that it is a proceeding before a court and tribunal and it also required that at least one thousand (1,000) members or more are affected by mis-representation in dealing of securities, when dividend is not paid, fraudulent and unfair trade practices and such other market wrongdoing.[32] From now on, investor association wishing to file class action suits should approach the centre through the Ministry of Corporate Affairs (MCA), according to the minutes of the SEBI board meeting on February 13, 2014.[33]

Class Action under Different Laws

Code of Civil Procedure Code, 1908 allows the representative suit which provides that when large number of persons are involved in a suit and have the same interest, one or more such persons may with the approval of the court, institute the suit or defend the suit. After the permission is granted, the court shall give notice with regard to the suit to all the persons interested in the suit which may be by way of personal service or by way of public advertisement. If the courts finds that the person who is suing and defending in the suit not diligently, the court have power to appoint other person, instead of him/her. When a court passes a decree in this representative suit, it is binding on all the persons on whose behalf, the suit is filed and defended. In order to establish that

---

29. Regulation 3 of the SEBI (Investor Protection and Education Fund), Regulation, 2009.
30. Regulation 5(1)(d) of the SEBI (Investor Protection and Education Fund), Regulation, 2009.
31. Names and contact information of Investors' Associations recognized by SEBI as on March 03, 2015, Available at http://investor.sebi.gov.in/investadd.pdf (Last Visited on April 15, 2015).
32. Regulation 2(1)(g) of the SEBI (Investor Protection and Education Fund) Regulation, 2009.
33. SEBI to exclude class action suits from legal aid fund, Available at http://www.business-standard.com/article/markets/sebi-to-exclude-class-action-suits-from-legal-aid-fund-114030100602_1.html (Last Visited on April 14, 2015).

the person have same interest, it is not necessary that the person must have same cause of action with regard to the person on whose behalf, the suit is filed/defended. There are some difference between class action under section 245 of Companies Act, 2013 and Order 1 Rule 8 of Code of Civil Procedure, 1908 as in class action suit there is a requirement of minimum number of members/depositors for filing an application before the tribunal but in the representative suit, there is no such requirement even one person on behalf of others can sue. In class action suit, there is no requirement of permission of tribunal but in representative suit, necessary approval from the court is required for suing on behalf of others.

Public Interest Litigation (PIL) is the form of litigation which is filed by person or group of persons for the benefit of others whose rights are violated even though there is no violation of his/her rights. Public Interest Litigation is allowed by the Hon'ble Supreme Court and High Courts under Articles 32 and 226 of the Constitution of India. It is a type of representative suit as a person is commencing legal proceeding for the benefit of others. It is generally resorted when there is large scale violation of human rights and when the person or group of persons whose rights are violated, they are unable to pay the fees and file the suit before the court. The courts have power to take *suo-moto* cognizance of the case when the circumstances required. Class action is an action by members for protecting their rights. Public Interest Litigation is different from class action as in case of class action, it cannot be filed against public bodies but PIL can be filed against public bodies.

Consumer Protection Act, 1986 also provides compliant which may be filed with the District Forum in relation to goods sold, services provided or goods agreed to be sold or services agreed to be delivered by recognised consumer association and it is not necessary that the person to whom the goods and services delivered must be a member of consumer association.[34] Complaint may be filed where there are numerous consumers and must have same interest for the advantage of all consumers so concerned but there is requirement of approval from the District Forum.

Criticism and Suggestions for Class Action

Although Class Action under Companies Act, 2013 protects the rights of the members or depositors from the misconduct of the affairs of the company, there are some loopholes which are required to be removed by way of amendment in order to reduce the frivolous

34. Section 12 of Consumer Protection Act, 1986.

litigation in the name of company and its directors. The members may unite in order to take unlawful gain from the company and its directors. When the class action is not successful, then individual cannot file an action with regard to that matter. Class action suit can only be filed by the members and depositors and the other stakeholders like creditors, regulatory bodies, etc. are not entitled to file the class action. There is no mention in the Act as to how the compensation should be distributed amongst claimants. Banking companies are also excluded from the class action suits.

There must be a provision that members/depositors which have personal hatred with the directors or the company must not be entitle to take action and the members/depositors who suing the company and its directors must require to state that they have no such hatredness with them on the affidavit. Like United States America, there must be a concept of contingency fees by which the advocate fees is dependent on the compensation or damages awarded by the court. It will ensure the commitment of the advocate towards the case. Sec. 244 of the Companies Act, 2013 allows Tribunal to waive the requirement of minimum number of members[35] but this is not the case with the Class Action under sec. 245 of the Companies Act, 2013. This is also required in case of class action and if it is introduced in class action, it will lead to a significant effect on the company. The power must be given to the Tribunal so that the condition of minimum number of members/ depositors can be reduced according to the facts and circumstances of the case. This provision also ensures more disclosures and transparency in the functioning of the company. In Canada, there is government fund to advance class action litigation. Those who wish to receive government litigation funding submit applications. At the conclusion of the case, the government fund is repaid with a percentage of the recovery. There must also be a provision in India with respect to the same in order to fund the class action in addition to Investor Education and Protection Fund which is already there. In US, there is a law called

---

35. There is a requirement under sec. 244 of Companies Act, 2013 that there must be minimum number of members for the purposes of applying before tribunal for relief in case of oppression and mismanagement. The requirement for minimum number of members is as follows:
    (a) In case of Company having share capital, one hundred members or one-tenth of the total members whichever is less or members holding not less than one-tenth of issued share capital of the company.
    (b) In case of company not having share capital, one-fifth of the total number of members of company.

Private Securities Litigation Reform Act, 1995 in order to prevent the person from filing the fraudulent class action. On the same footing, there must be law in India by which the non-meritorious class actions are not filed by the members/depositors against the company and others. Role of the investor association and SEBI should be enhanced in order to make investor much more aware about the class action. There must be inclusion of other stakeholders in order to enable them to file class action. There must be proper guidelines as to distribution of compensation amongst claimants. SEBI needs to take a proactive role not just in funding but encouraging investors to be a part of investor associations. The benefits of class action should be a part of the curriculum for Investor education. Investor awareness programmes should not be promotional activities but should enlighten the investors about their rights and obligations.[36] Banking companies must be included in class action suit as the banks are significant player in the economy of the country. It may cause an adverse effect on the interest of shareholders.

Conclusion

Companies Act, 2013 provides a new concept called class action by which the members/depositors can take action in case of misconduct in the affairs of the company. Even though Ministry of Corporate Affairs have not notified the provision, but it is very significant provision in relation to protection of interest of minority. Ministry must take steps in order to notify this provision in order to curtail the misconduct. There are some other laws which provide representative action in order to ensure that the rights of persons are not infringed. It is a cost saving provision as individual member/depositors will not take an action because it is expensive and if group are taking action, it is in a way save the cost of litigation. But like US where there are more and more litigation as to class action, there needs to be appropriate provision to reduce frivolous actions as US does. Class action brings uniformity as in only one action, there are number of defendants and plaintiff. Court hears the infringement of rights of persons and adjudicates which is binding on all parties to the action. This also reduces the burden on the courts to hear separate action by every individual whose rights are violated. Class Action though deals with the rights of members or depositors, but there are some loopholes which required to be done away with in order to effectively protect their rights.

36. *Supra* note 14 at 139.

CHAPTER IV

Special Court

8

Role of Special Courts in New Companies Law

RASHI CHANDHOKE AND ANKIT SAHOO

Introduction

Special Courts are within a judicial system that generally addresses only one area of law with a specifically defined jurisdiction. These are not court of general jurisdiction rather they have a specialized jurisdiction addressing a single area of law. Such kinds of Courts are set-up for some reason i.e. to addresses a specific kind of problem that needs urgent attention. In USA these Courts are also known as the Problem Solving Courts and a considerable percentage of Courts in USA are Special Courts which includes all Courts of limited and specialized jurisdiction. Special Courts in USA handle a vast majority of all the cases that are brought in the United States.[1] The perceptive behind establishment of special courts or problem-solving courts in USA is a broad one as compared to in India. In USA, Special Courts like drug courts, domestic violence courts, homeless courts, teen courts and reentry courts—take a broad and a more complete approach to delinquency and criminality[2]. For further clarity we can say that unlike

1. Problem-Solving Courts Overview, New York State Unified Court System, available at: https://www.nycourts.gov/courts/problem_solving/ (Last Visited on 26th April 2015).
2. Problem-Solving Courts Resource Guide, National Center for State Courts (NCSC), available at: http://www.ncsc.org/Topics/Problem-Solving-Courts/

conventional courts these courts do not focus solely on the crime conducted by the defendant rather attempt to address the underlying social and economic factors that added to the defendant's association in the crime. USA Special Courts try to incorporate the principle of restorative justice. The Special Courts improves the efficiency in decision-making by having experts decide complex cases. It reduces pending case backlogs in general Courts by shifting complex cases to specialized courts. Specialized judges are in a better position to effectively impose, monitor such cases and would require less time to research and reflect on the fundamental issues of the case than a generalist judge. Specialized court judges don't need to be educated by the bar and are much more capable of reducing the scope of the legal framework to the vital issues on which resolution of the case depends. The generalist judges deal with complex legal issues occasionally so they have to refresh their familiarity with them and update themselves on recent developments. A Special Court act as a consistent national body of law which can reduce appeals, forum shopping as it will reduce the conflicts of law between different general courts.[3]

Development of Special Courts in India

The concept of right of speedy trial is achieving significance in Indian Judicial system. Article 21 of the Indian Constitution states that no person shall be deprived of his life or personal liberty except according to the procedure established by law. Krishna Iyer J. held that our justice system even in grave cases, suffers from slow motion syndrome which is lethal to 'fair trial' whatever the ultimate decision. Speedy justice is a component of social justice since the community, as a whole, is concerned in the criminal being condignly and finally punished within a reasonable time and the innocent being absolved from the inordinate ordeal of criminal proceedings.[4] Also speedy trial is finally held to be a fundamental right by the Supreme Court of India.[5] To comply with the right to speedy trial, Special Courts were established in India under the Special Courts Act, 1979 which was enacted by the Parliament on 16th May, 1979. According to the preamble of the Act, the Special Courts are established to provide for the speedy trial of a

---

Problem-Solving-Courts/Resource-Guide.aspx (Last Visited on 26th April, 2015).

3. Markus B. Zimmer, "Overview of Specialized Courts", IJCA, 1-2 (2009).
4. *Babu Singh and Ors.* vs. *The State of UP*, AIR 1978 SC 527.
5. *Sheela Barse and Ors.* vs. *Union of India & Ors.*, 1986 SCALE (2) 230.

certain class of offences and the Central Government has the power to establish Special Courts.[6] It shall consist of a single judge of a High Court, to be notified by that High Court, with occurrence of the Chief Justice of India, within whose jurisdiction the Special Court is established.[7] Based on this principle, many other enactments came into existence consisting of provisions regarding establishment of Special Courts dealing with particular class of offences for speedy trial and the Central Government's power to establish them under section 36 of the Narcotic Drugs and Psychotropic Substances Act, 1985, section 43 of the Prevention of Money Laundering Act, 2002, section 22AA of the Immoral Traffic (Prevention) Act, 1956 and so on. The power for establishment of Special Courts for speedy trials in India is also seen to be embedded with the State Government. The Special Courts established by the State Governments, after consultation of the High Court, have the jurisdiction over that particular local area only and will only deal with those offences that are notified by the State Government itself under a particular Act.[8] The State Governments also have power to set the Special Court through chapter 4 of the Scheduled Castes and Tribes (Prevention of Atrocities) Act, 1989, section 4(1) of the Disturbed Areas (Special Courts) Act, 1976, section 3(1) of the Uttarakhand Special Court's Act, 2011 and some other legislation. Thus, Special Courts in India are established for speedy trial for criminal offences in society or terrorist crimes and also for economic offences. These offences are so serious and grave in nature that a delay in these cases would be denial of justice. It is evident that the concept of speedy trials has been given importance in our country by setting up Special Courts for specific matters. These Courts are still being embedded as new concepts in statutes presently for speedy trials thus making our Indian judicial system grow more and more efficient.

Adjudication System of the Companies Act, 1956

In the initial Company Law, there was absence of establishment of any administrative body or any Tribunal to deal exclusively in the matters of company and the Companies (Amendment) Act, 1988 introduced for establishment of the Company Law Board (CLB) by the Central Government.[9] The CLB was embedded with powers and

6. The Special Court's Act, 1979, s. 3(1).
7. The Special Court's Act, 1979, s. 3(2).
8. The Criminal Procedure Code, 1973 (Act 2 of 1974), s. 11 (Proviso).
9. The Companies Act, 1956 (Act 1 of 1956), s. 10E.

functions of the Central Government specified under the Act and had discretionary powers to regulate on its own procedure but had to follow the principles of natural justice.[10] The orders of this Board were appealable to the High Court on any question of law arising out of such order.[11] CLB was subsequently dissolved by virtue of Companies (Amendment) Act, 2002[12] and the National Company Law Tribunal (NCLT) stepped into the shoes of the CLB[13] which was based on the recommendation of the Justice Eradi Committee on Law Relating to Insolvency and Winding up of Companies[14]. The NCLT has powers and jurisdiction of the Board for Industrial and Financial Reconstruction (BIFR), the Appellate Authority for Industrial and Financial Reconstruction (AAIFR), Company Law Board, High Courts relating to compromises, arrangements, mergers, amalgamations and reconstruction of companies, winding up, etc.[15] Its orders are appealable before the National Company Law Appellate Tribunal (NCLAT)[16] and the orders of NCLAT are appealable to the Supreme Court. The NCLT and NCLAT were basically formed to deal with the matters dealt by the above mentioned authorities. The Companies Act, 1956 barred the civil courts[17] to take up any suit or proceedings which the NCLT or NCLAT is empowered to determine under the Act but did not bar the criminal jurisdiction. The criminal offences were dealt by Presidency Magistrates or Magistrates of first class under section 622 of the 1956 Act. There was no special forum established to deal with criminal offences separately under the Companies Act, 1956.

Adjudicatory Structure under the Companies Act, 2013

The relief seeking mechanism in the new Act can be categorized

---

10. The Companies Act, 1956 (Act 1 of 1956), s. 10E(5).
11. The Companies Act, 1956 (Act 1 of 1956), s. 10F.
12. The Companies Act, 1956 (Act 1 of 1956), s. 10FA.
13. The Companies Act, 1956 (Act 1 of 1956), s. 10FB.
14. Committee headed by Shri Justice V. Balakrishna Eradi, and was formed on 22nd October, 1999 to scrutinize the existing winding up laws of companies in order to re-frame it according to the latest developments in corporate law and governance and to recommend procedures for insolvency proceedings of companies to eliminate delay.
15. National Company Law Tribunal—A Single Window Institution For Corporate Justice, available at: http://www.icsi.edu/ WebModules/ Programmes/PCS/7PCS/BG%20PCS-6-Grover.pdf (Last Visited on 13th April, 2015).
16. The Companies Act, 1956 (Act 1 of 1956), s. 10FQ.
17. The Companies Act, 1956 (Act 1 of 1956), s. 10GB.

under heads of Serious Fraud Investigating office (SFIO), National Company Law Tribunal (NCLT), Special Court, Mediation and Conciliation Panel. The Criminal Court and NCLT were two heads where relief could be sought under the 1956 Act. Presently Serious Fraud Investigating Office, Special Courts and Mediation and Conciliation Panel are new provisions introduced in the 2013 Act. The prosecution structure under the new Act is two-fold; one is through SFIO and other Special Courts.

Serious Fraud Investigation Office

SFIO is a multi-disciplinary organization under the Ministry of Corporate Affairs, headed by a director and a team of experts from the fields of accountancy, taxation, corporate affairs, forensic auditing, law, information technology, capital market, banking, investigation.[18] The SFIO doesn't only detect white-collar crimes and frauds but also prosecute and recommend for prosecution.[19] It was set-up in the year 2003 (2nd July) as an autonomous body in the Ministry of Corporate Affairs by a Resolution issued by the Government.[20] SFIO was established on the basis of the recommendations in the Naresh Chandra Committee on Corporate Audit and Governance.[21] As per the committee there was a need to establish a 'multi-disciplinary team that would not only uncover the fraud, but also able to direct and supervise prosecution under various economic legislations through appropriate agencies'[22] and as per its charter, SFIO normally takes up those cases for investigation which are characterized by[23] complexity and having inter-departmental and multi-disciplinary ramification, substantial involvement of public interest to be judged by size, either in terms of

---

18. The Companies Act, 2013 (18 of 2013), s. 211.
19. Serious Fraud Investigation Office, Government of India, available at: http://www.sfio.nic.in/websitenew/aboutus.asp (Last Visited on 14th April, 2015).
20. Serious Fraud Investigation Office, Government of India, Ministry of Company Affairs, available at: http://www.sfio.nic.in/thesfio.htm (Last Visited on 14th April 2015).
21. This was a high level committee appointed by Ministry of Corporate Affairs in the year 2002 to study the various corporate governance issues and was entrusted to analyse those issues and recommend changes if necessary.
22. Executive Summary, available at: http://finmin.nic.in/reports/chandra.pdf (Last Visited on 14th April, 2015).
23. Serious Fraud Investigation Office, Government of India, available at: http://www.sfio.nic.in/websitenew/charter.asp (Last Visited on 14th April of 2015).

monetary misappropriation or in terms of persons affected and the possibility of investigation leading to or contributing towards a clear improvement in systems, law and procedure. SFIO doesn't have the power to take up cases *suo-moto* for investigation. It can only investigate those cases which are assigned (by order) by the Central Government, i.e. the Ministry of Corporate Affairs. When a case has been assigned by the Central Government to be investigated by SFIO, no other investigating authority or agency of the Central Government or State Government take up the same case or if investigation has already been initiated by some other agency, it cannot further proceed with the investigation and the concerned agency shall transfer all the relevant documents and records of the said case to SFIO.[24]

Position of Special Courts in New Law

The idea of Special Courts is one commendable constitute pioneered in the new Act. The rationale behind this amendment is the technicalities involved in the technical matters can with dealt in ease. The procedure of trails can be concluded with alacrity and would also help in good corporate governance and stricter implementation of the new Act. The Central Government by notification can establish or designate as many Special Courts as it may deems fit for the purpose of providing speedy trial of offences under the Act.[25] The Special Court shall consist of a single judge who shall be appointed by the Central Government in consensus with the Chief Justice of the High Court within whose jurisdiction the appointed judge would be working.[26] Also the judge to be appointed, immediately before such appointment, should be holding an office of a Sessions Judge or Additional Sessions Judge.[27] The Special Court may function like a CBI court. Further, the investigation done by SFIO under section 212 and prosecution of offenders by SFIO in the Special Courts will ensure faster justice delivery system. This Court is an addition to NCLT, the reason being that Special Courts are to take only criminal cases for adjudication. Criminal offences being more graver in nature should be dealt faster and setting up Special Courts for the said matter might serve the purpose of speedier justice delivery. Section 436 of the Companies Act, 2013 provides for jurisdiction and powers of a Special Court but this

---

24. The Companies Act, 2013 (18 of 2013), s. 212(2).
25. The Companies Act, 2013 (18 of 2013), s. 435(1).
26. The Companies Act (18 of 2013), s. 435(2).
27. The Companies Act (18 of 2013), s. 435(3).

provision has not yet been enforced or given effect.

Jurisdiction of Special Court[28]

A Special Court has jurisdiction over all the offences covered under this Act. These provisions are not affected by the provisions of the CrPC, 1973. Any offence committed by a company under this Act shall be triable by the Special Court which is established for that area where the registered office of the company situates. In case there is more than one Special Court for such area, then either of them shall have the jurisdiction as specified by the High Court of that particular jurisdiction. An accused person or a person suspected to have been committed an offence under this Act can be forwarded to a Magistrate under sub-section 2 or 2A of section 167 of CrPC, 1973. Such Magistrate has the power to detain such a person as he deems fit for a period not more than fifteen days in the whole and not more than seven days in the whole in case of an Executive Magistrate. If such Magistrate believes that such detention of a person is unnecessary, then he shall order such person to be forwarded to the special court which will have the jurisdiction over that matter.

Powers of Special Court[29]

A Special Court has discretion to exercise the powers which are embedded with a Magistrate having jurisdiction under section 167 of CrPC, 1973, if an accused person is forwarded to it under section 436(1)(b) of the Act. If the investigation does not get completed within twenty four hours, then the Special Court can authorize detention of the accused, in judicial custody, beyond fifteen days if satisfied that there are adequate grounds exists for doing so; but it cannot extend the detention beyond ninety days for offences punishable with imprisonment not less than 10 years and not beyond sixty days for any other offences.[30] A Special Court under this Act also has the power to take cognizance of an offence on the basis of a police report or on the basis of receiving a complaint, without committing the accused person for trial. This power of a Special Court is unlike the power of court of sessions to take cognizance under section 193 of CrPC, 1973 wherein the court of sessions can only take cognizance of an offence which is committed to it by a magistrate.

---

28. The Companies Act, 2013 (18 of 2013), s. 436 (1) (a) and (b).
29. The Companies Act, 2013 (18 of 2013), s. 436 (1) (c) and (d).
30. The Criminal Procedure Code, 1973 (Act 2 of 1974), s. 167(2).

Special Powers of a Special Court[31]

Other than trying offences under the Companies Act, a Special Court has the power to try any other offences, under the CrPC if the accused person is charged with them at the same trial. A Special Court has the power to conduct summary trials for offences which are punishable with imprisonment for period not more than three years. This provision prevail over the provisions of CrPC, wherein summary trails can be conducted only by Chief Judicial Magistrates or Metropolitan Magistrates or First Class or Second Class Magistrates empowered by the High Court.[32] There are two limitations that are placed on a Special Court. Firstly, a Special Court, while convicting in a summary trial, shall not provide with a sentence for imprisonment exceeding one year. Secondly, if a Special Court is of the opinion that a particular case cannot be tried summarily or sentence for imprisonment exceeding one year has to be passed, then in this case, the Special Court has to record an order after hearing the parties and recall any witnesses who have been examined to hear and rehear the case as per the procedure of a regular trial under CrPC.

Proceedings under Special Court

The proceedings of the Special Court, according to the 2013 Act, shall be in accordance with the CrPC, 1973. The CrPC shall be applicable to the proceedings of the Special Court. The Special Court shall be deemed to be a Court of Session and the person conducting the prosecution shall be deemed to be Public Prosecutor.[33] A Special Court under the Companies Act, by virtue of s. 438 of the said Act, would deem to be a Session Court and follow the procedure laid under chapter XVIII[34] of CrPC. The prosecution conducted before a Special Court, in all trials, has to be done by a Public Prosecutor.[35] The Prosecutor opens his case by unfolding the charge brought against the accused and stating by what substantiation he proposes to prove the guilt of the accused. The Prosecutor does so only when the accused appears or is brought before the Court in pursuance of a commitment of the case under s. 209 of CrPC.[36] If the judge after considering the documents submitted and hearing the submissions of the accused and prosecution, is of the view

31. The Companies Act, 2013 (18 of 2013), s. 436 (2) and (3).
32. The Criminal Procedure Code, 1973 (Act 2 of 1974), s. 20.9
33. The Companies Act, 2013 (18 of 2013), s. 438.
34. Trial by Court of Session.
35. The Criminal Procedure Code, 1973 (2 of 1974), s. 225.
36. The Criminal Procedure Code, 1973 (2 of 1974), s. 226.

that there is no sufficient ground for the proceeding against the accused then he shall discharge the accused and record his reasons for doing so.[37] When the judge is of the opinion that the there is sufficient ground for presuming that the accused has committed the offence then he shall frame in writing a charge against the accused.[38] The accused has two options to pick after the framing of charge to plead guilty of the offence[39]; or refuse to plead guilty.[40] When the accused pleads guilty, the Judge records the plea and may, in his prudence, convict him thereon and when the accused refuses to plead guilty or claims to be tried or not convicted section 229 of CrPC, the Judge shall fix a date for examination of witnesses or on the application of the prosecution issue any process for compelling the attendance of any witness or production of document. The Judge, on the date fixed, shall proceed to take all such evidence as may be produced in support of the prosecution. But, after considering the evidences of the prosecution, examining the accused and hearing the prosecution and the defense on the point, the Judge is convinced that there are no sufficient evidences or no evidence that the accused has committed the offence the he shall record an order of acquittal.[41] In cases where the accused is not acquitted section 232 CrPC, then he can be called upon to enter on his defense and adduce any evidence to support it. The accused can also apply for issue of any process for compelling the attendance of any witness or production of any document and after the examination such witness, the prosecutor shall sum up his case and the accused shall be entitled to reply.[42] Finally after hearing arguments and points of law, the Judge shall give a judgment in the case.[43]

Appeal and Revision

Section 437 of the Companies Act, 2013 provides that orders passed by a Special Court can be appealable before the High Court within local limits of jurisdiction of which that Special Court is situated as if the Special Court were a Court of Sessions.[44] In case of conviction under Companies Act, if a Special Court convicts a person with sentence for

37. The Criminal Procedure Code, 1973 (2 of 1974), s. 227.
38. The Criminal Procedure Code, 1973 (2 of 1974), s. 228.
39. The Criminal Procedure Code, 1973 (2 of 1974), s. 229.
40. The Criminal Procedure Code, 1973 (2 of 1974), s. 230.
41. The Criminal Procedure Code, 1973 (2 of 1974), s. 231 and s. 232.
42. The Criminal Procedure Code, 1973 (2 of 1974), s. 233 and s. 234.
43. The Criminal Procedure Code, 1973 (2 of 1974), s. 235.
44. This provision has not been yet enforced.

imprisonment for more than seven years, then appeal against the same shall lie to the High Court.[45] Similarly, in case of acquittal, appeal can be made before the High Court against the order of a Special Court only upon the leave of the High Court.[46] The High Court has absolute power to re-appreciate and review all the evidences on the basis of which the order of acquittal was given and to reach on its own conclusion on the basis of such evidences.[47] In case of order of acquittal given by a Special Court under Companies Act, the High Court has the power to reverse the order and direct further inquiry or re-trial or find the accused person as guilty and impose sentence on him according to the law. Similarly, in case of order of conviction passed by a Special Court, the High Court has the power to reverse the finding and acquit or discharge the accused; or order to be re-tried in the special court; or alter the findings of the Special Court without affecting the sentence given by it.[48] The High Court under section 397 of CrPC has the power to call for and examine the records of any proceeding before any inferior criminal court, i.e. Special Court under Companies Act, situated within its local jurisdiction. The High Court has the power to satisfy itself as to the correctness, legality or propriety of the findings, sentence or order passed by the Special Court. The High Court, here, also has the suo moto power to exercise the revisional powers under this provision. The High Court as a revisional court, cannot convert the order of acquittal to conviction.[49] The High Court will ensure that the Special Courts function within the well-defined limits of Companies Act. The High Court can set aside the order of Special Courts and by observing the principles of natural justice and fair play can order for re-trial. It cannot re-appreciate or re-assess the evidences on records as a revisional court under s. 401 of CrPC. The High Court exercise revisional powers to rectify the defects in procedure or errors of law made by the Special Court. The High Court has the power to withdraw or transfer revisions in cases where in several accused are been convicted in the same trial and some of them may make revision to the Court of Sessions.[50] Similarly, if High Court decides to dispose of revisions, then it will direct the Special Court under Companies Act, to transfer all the revisions to the High

45. The Criminal Procedure Code, 1973 (Act 2 of 1974), s. 374(2).
46. The Criminal Procedure Code, 1973 (Act 2 of 1974), s. 378.
47. Justice C.K. Thakkar, 'Takwani' and Mrs. M.C. Thakkar, Takwani Criminal Procedure 288 (Lexis Nexis, Gurgaon, 3th Edition, 2011).
48. The Criminal Procedure Code, 1973 (Act 2 of 1974), s. 386.
49. The Criminal Procedure Code, 1973 (Act 2 of 1974), s. 401(3).
50. The Criminal Procedure Code, 1973 (Act 2 of 1974), s. 402.

Court and where High Court decides not to dispose of the revisions then *vice versa*.

Non-Cognizable Offences

Section 439 of the Companies Act, 2013 provides for non-cognizable offences.[51] It states that all the offences under the Companies Act are considered to be non-cognizable, not affected by the CrPC. Unlike the old Act's provision for non-cognizable offences[52], which stated that all offences under the Act are to be non-cognizable, section 439 provides an exception, i.e. of cognizable offences which are listed under section 212 (6) of the Act. There are further more limitations under section 212 (6) wherein it states that no person shall be released on bail unless the Public Prosecutor gives an opportunity to oppose such release; or if the court is satisfied on reasonable grounds that the accused is not guilty of such offence; or if the accused person is below 16 years of age or a women or sick or infirm. The Special Court cannot take cognizance for cognizable offences unless a complaint is made in writing by Director of SFIO or any authorized officer of the Central Government. The court shall take cognizance of any offence committed by a company or any of its officers (excluding liquidators of the company[53]) under this Act only if a complaint in writing is been filed by the Registrar, or a shareholder of the company or by any other person authorized by the Central Government; or in case of offences related to issue and transfer of securities and non-payment of dividend compliant filed by any person authorized by Securities and Exchange Board of India.[54] This sub-provision shall not apply to any prosecution by a company of any of its officers. These provisions do not apply to any action taken by the liquidator of the company with respect to offences of matters under Chapter XX[55] of the Act or anywhere else within the Act relating to winding up of the company.[56] In case the complainant is the Registrar or any person authorized by the Central Government, presence of such person before the concerned Court trying the offences shall not be necessary unless his personal attendance at the trial is required by the Court.[57]

51. Came into force on 12th September, 2013.
52. The Companies Act, 1956 (1 of 1956), s. 624.
53. The Companies Act, 2013 (18 of 2013), s. 439 (Explanation).
54. The Companies Act, 2013 (18 of 2013), s. 439(2).
55. Deals with the Provisions of Winding Up of the Companies.
56. The Companies Act, 2013 (18 of 2013), s. 439(3).
57. The Companies Act, 2013 (18 of 2013), s. 439(4).

Compounding of Offences

Compounding, under the purview of criminal law, means refrain from the prosecution as a result of an agreeable settlement between the parties. Compounding of offences was discussed in a case of *Murray v. The Queen Empress*[58], where the Court stated that, "that the person against whom the offence has been committed has received some gratification, not necessarily of a pecuniary character, to act as an inducement of his desiring to abstain from a prosecution." It refers to a situation where the victim has received certain amount of compensation from the accused and the attitude between them changes. Thus, the criminal law provides for compounding that offence. Whether a particular offence should be compounded or not is a decision of the legislature to make. Generally, offences of serious and grave nature are not permitted to be compoundable. There is no hard and fast rule as to identify the compoundable and non-compoundable offences. Basically, the legislature looks into the nature, magnitude and consequences of an offence.[59] The compoundable offences are listed in the Table under sub-sections (1) and (2) of section 320 of CrPC, 1973. These offences are limited to the offences under IPC. The offences under the Companies Act are not covered under the purview of CrPC. The offences, under the Companies Act, which are punishable with fine only, are compoundable under section 441 of this Act. Powers to compound such offences were vested previously with the Central Government and also to the Court where such prosecution was initiated.[60] But now, under the new Act of 2013, the same powers to compound such offences are vested with the Tribunal or Regional Director and also to the Special Court. All the applications for compounding of offences shall be made to the Registrar, who shall forward the same to the Tribunal or Regional Director or any officer authorized by the Central Government. Wherein an offence is been compounded under this Section, the same should be intimated to the Registrar within seven days from the date of which such offence was compounded by the company. If an offence is compounded before the initiation of any prosecution, then the Registrar or any shareholder of the company or any officer authorized by the Central Government is barred to initiate any prosecution for such offence against the company or its officer. If an offence is compounded after the initiation of any

58. [1894] 21 ILR 103.
59. Law Commission of India, 237th Report on Compounding of (IPC) Offences, (December, 2011).
60. The Companies Act, 1956 (Act 1 of 1956), s. 621A.

prosecution, then compounding shall be brought in by the Registrar in writing to the notice of the court where such prosecution is been taken place. Accordingly, the concerned company or its officer shall be discharged after the offence gets compounded. A Special Court has the power to permit compounding of any offences punishable under this Act with imprisonment or fine; or imprisonment or fine or with both. Such compounding of offence has to be in accordance with the procedure so laid down by this section. Any offence under this Act which is punishable with imprisonment only; or imprisonment and also fine, shall not be compoundable.

Appointment of Company Prosecutors

Section 24 of CrPC, 1973, empowers the Central or State Government to appoint Public Prosecutors for every High Court. But, under s. 443 of Companies Act,[61] the Central Government solely has been given the power to appoint one or more Company Prosecutors for any local area, in general or for any specified case or classes of cases, for conducting prosecution which shall be arising out of this Act before a Special Court, prevailing over the provisions of section 24 CrPC. Every trial before a Special Court shall be conducted by the Company Prosecutor just like every trial before Court of Sessions is conducted by Public Prosecutors.[62] A Company Prosecutor shall also have the power of a Public Prosecutor to withdraw any prosecution, with the consent of Court in certain cases at any time before the judgment is pronounced.[63]

Appeal against Acquittal

Section 378 (1) of CrPC, 1973, empowers a State Government to direct or authorize a Public Prosecutor to present an appeal to the High Court against an order of acquittal passed by any court other than a High Court. But under section 444 of the Companies Act,[64] the above direction or authorization is empowered to be given by the Central Government to a Company Prosecutor, prevailing over the CrPC provision.

Compensation for Accusation without Reasonable Cause

Under section 625 of Companies Act, 1956, the provision was for

61. Corresponding to The Companies Act, 1956 (Act 1 of 1956), s. 624A.
62. The Criminal Procedure Code, 1973 (Act 1 of 1974), s. 225.
63. The Criminal Procedure Code, 1973 (Act 1 of 1974), s. 321.
64. Corresponding to The Companies Act, 1956 (Act 1 of 1956), s. 624B.

payment of compensation in cases of frivolous or vexatious prosecution and the provisions under section 250 of CrPC were exempted from application under this provision. Instead, section 625 provided provisions[65] similar to section 250 of CrPC but with certain changes made under it. S.445 of Companies Act, 2013, removed the provisions of section 625 and placed the provision for compensation for accusation without reasonable cause before a Special Court or a Court of Session. Now, provisions of section 250 of CrPC are applicable *mutatis mutandis* under this new section. Therefore, now, Special Court can discharge or acquit the accused and may award compensation to the informant or complainant if it is of the opinion that there is no reasonable ground for making accusation against the accused. Prior to taking such action, a show cause notice is to be issued to the informant as to why such compensation should not be awarded and accordingly, hearing is to be conducted and reasons must be recorded. The amount of compensation must not exceed the amount which a Special Court is empowered to award. In default of payment of such compensation, the informant shall undergo simple imprisonment not exceeding thirty days. Such person shouldn't be exempted from any civil or criminal liability.[66]

Application of Fines

The Court shall include the whole or any part of payment of cost of proceedings or payment of any reward to the informant.[67] This provision corresponds to s. 626 of 1956 Act. The only difference between the old and the new provisions is that, the old provision of 1956 Act included courts as well as Tribunal (NCLT) into its ambit as the provision was placed under general provisions related to offences under the Act, whereas the new provision is brought under the chapter exclusively dealing with the Special Courts and includes only these courts in its ambit.

Mediation and Conciliation Panel

The new Companies Act, 2013 has introduced the concept of Mediation and Conciliation Panel as an alternative dispute mechanism. This is a process in which parties discuss and settle over an issue in presence of a mediator or conciliator. It's a time-bound and confidential

65. Section 625(2)-(8) of The Companies Act, 1956 (Act 1 of 1956), s. 625(2)-(8).
66. The Companies Act, 2013 (18 of 2013), s. 445 read with The Criminal Procedure Code, 1973 (2 of 1974), s. 250.
67. The Companies Act, 2013 (18 of 2013), s. 446.

process wherein the information shared by all the parties must be kept confidential. The mediator helps the parties to determine the manner of the settlement of the disputes whereas the conciliator himself suggests the manner of settlement to the parties. All this process is voluntarily done by the parties.[68] Mediation and conciliation concept was incorporated by the Parliament to settle the cases between the parties in a faster way saving time as well as money. This concept has been encouraged to be included in all kinds of cases so that there is faster delivery of justice.[69] Consequently, this concept has also been included and enforced in the new Companies Act under s. 442 discussed below: The Central Government is mandated to maintain number of experts, called the Mediation and Conciliation Panel, qualified for mediation between the parties during the pendency of any proceedings before the Central Government (which includes proceedings before a Special Court), before the Tribunal (NCLT) or Appellate Tribunal (NCLAT). Application for referring the matter to the Panel can be made by either of the parties to the Central Government or NCLT or NCLAT, wherever their proceedings are pending, in such a form along with fees as may be prescribed. On such application, the Central Government or NCLT or NCLAT may appoint one or more experts from the Panel for such case. The fees, procedure and terms and conditions of the Panel shall be as may be prescribed. The Central Government or NCLT or NCLAT may, *suo moto* also refer any matter pending before them to such number of experts from the Panel. The Panel should dispose of the matter referred to it within three months from the date of reference and forward its recommendations to the Central Government or NCLT or NCLAT as the case may be. If any of the parties is not satisfied by the recommendation of the Panel, then it may file objection before the Central Government or NCLT or NCLAT as the case may be.

Conclusion

It is observed that the Special Courts would help in good governance and stricter implementation of Company Law in India. These Courts would compel the Companies to comply with the provisions of this Act

---

68. Chitra Narayan, "Lets sort it out across the table", *Business Line*, *The Hindu*, Dec. 2, 2013, available at: http://www.thehindubusinessline.com/opinion/lets-sort-it-out-across-the-table/article5414876.ece (Last visited on 18th April, 2015).
69. Justice M. Jagannadha Rao, "Would Conciliation & Mediation succeed in our Courts?", available at: http://lawcommissionofindia.nic. in/adr_conf/mediation % 20succed%20Rao%202.pdf (Last visited on 18th April, 2015).

and they would risk themselves if they ignore or avoid the requirements of this Act.[70] But on the other hand, it can be debatable on the question that is the judicial system moving in a correct direction by establishing such Courts wherein vacancies would be created in the general Courts as a Session Judge becomes a Special Judge in a Special Court? Will this not be an additional burden in the system as other criminal cases would pile up in the general Courts because of the vacancies created?[71] The corporate offences in India are increasing rapidly. Every now and then we come across big business houses involved in scams. It is mostly seen that these business houses are money minded, they go to any extend to earn more money even if the manner is illegal. As a result they avoid complying with the provisions of Company Laws as they do not take these laws seriously and continue to commit serious corporate crimes. These offences significantly affect the growth and development of the country. Its impact on the nation's economy can be in the form of inflation, uneven distribution of resources, corruption, creation of black money, etc. If these corporate crimes keep on increasing, then India would lose its reputation globally and investments would get affected from within and outside India. Thus, these corporate crimes are ought to be controlled and regulated as seriously as possible and the creation of Special Courts would ensure not only speedy justice but also the company offender's fear from the laws, take the law seriously and strictly comply with them.

70. Delep Goswami, "Special Court for Speedy Trial of Company Offences", XLIII ICSI 1182-86 (2013).

71. Special Courts: Blurring of Boundaries or an Unnecessary Evil? Available at: http://archanabala.com/2013/05/07/special-courts-blurring-of-boundaries-or-an-unnecessary-evil/ (Last Visited on 26th April, 2015).

CHAPTER V

Cross Border Merger & Amalgamation

9

Corporate Governance of Mergers and Amalgamations in India: Position under the Companies Act, 2013

DR. APARAJITA BHATT

Introduction

One of the main objectives of introducing the concept of corporate governance in India is to make the business or corporate transactions transparent as well as adduce strict accountability to someone in case of any wrong committed to any stakeholder in the corporate sector. An important dimension of it is to check corrupt or mal practices in Merger & Amalgamation transactions. Merger transactions which are important form of corporate restructuring exercise undertaken by companies throughout the world are exposed to many direct or indirect lucrative benefits to one of the parties, which is detrimental to the interests of the shareholders, creditors, minority shareholders or even public interest at large. Thus, the principles of corporate governance which govern merger transactions under the Companies Act, 2013 aim to establish a transparent and fair merger process and merger can be approved only if the companies comply with the procedure as laid down in the Act.

Defining Corporate Governance

The Cadbury Committee Report (1992) on the Financial Aspects of Corporate Governance defines corporate governance as 'the system by which companies are directed and controlled'.[1] This definition was adopted and approved even by the Hampel Committee on corporate governance as well as the Higgs Review of the role and effectiveness of non-executive director.[2] The 1999 OECD definition of Corporate Governance discusses that corporate governance is a system by which business corporations are directed and controlled. The companies and their businesses have to be controlled in such a way that all the transactions made by the companies are fair, just and corruption-free. The theory of corporate governance involves the ways and means by which the shareholders and other stakeholders can be ensured minimum protection. Remarkably, the concept of contractual corporate governance includes the ways and means by which individual companies can deviate from their national corporate governance standards which can result in increasing or reducing the level of protection they offer to their shareholders/stakeholders.

Corporate Governance in M&As in India

The corporate governance principles established in the Companies Act, 2013 go a long way in setting up the principles of accountability, probity, fairness and transparency. Corporate governance means good governance which should be reflected in the manner of doing and controlling business. Corporate Governance makes the directors of a company directly accountable to the company's stakeholders in the event of any mal-practice. It requires the directors and the board of management to work in the best interest of the company and its shareholders, imbibing ethical and value-based management within its day-to-day governance.

Corporate Governance Reforms in M&A

Corporate governance and M&A which is a form of corporate restructuring share an interesting relationship. In fact, it would be apt to state that good corporate governance is a concomitant of a good and successful corporate restructuring activity. If companies practice good corporate governance norms in its day-to-day business transaction, including the M&A deals, it strengthens the corporate health of the country. Similarly, good governance structure acts as a good defence against direct takeover by any company in this highly competitive market. Another dimension to it is that corporate governance standards

1. www.ecgi.org/codes/country_pages/codes.uk.htm.
2. www.dti.gov.uk/cld/non_exec_review).

if applied in M&A transactions are likely to provide better value of the deal to the stakeholders of the company.[3] Most importantly, good corporate governance practices act as corruption check while entering into any M&A transaction. There are many parameters to ascertain the application of corporate governance principles while making a deal of merger or amalgamation. The Companies Act, 2013 has tried to evolve various measures to ensure that the deal or scheme sanctioned under the Act goes through thorough test of verification, surveillance and multi-party check. One such parameter is the role of board of directors in the process of merger deal. The board of directors perform the most important and preliminary duty of reviewing the merits and demerits of the scheme. It is the duty of the board to assess and analyse the effects of the proposed merger on all the stakeholders. The action and decision of the directors have been brought under strict accountability norms under the Act. While making an M&A transaction, the board of directors is no more supposed to act merely as a rubber stamp but is required to think and decide in the interest of all and be responsible for its mal-actions. The board is entrusted with major decision-making responsibility before making a merger deal such as:

(i) Whether or not the merger deal is in the overall interest of the company.

(ii) The board of directors is responsible to monitor the entire deal. The monitoring functions include a proper and careful due diligence conducted on the transferee company, carefully identifying the red flags, double check the involvement of the other company into any illegal business or transaction as well any civil or criminal liability.

(iii) Ensuring fair valuation to the shareholders.

(iv) Giving equal opportunity to the shareholders and other stakeholders to participate in the process of merger approval, raise objections or make any representations.

(v) Giving opportunity to sectoral regulators to make any representation.

(vi) To follow the required accounting and valuation standards honestly believing in the fairness of the procedure adopted and figures arrived at.

To rule out possibilities of mal-practices or corrupt M&A

3. Umakanth Varottil, Corporate Governance in M&A transactions, available at https://papers.ssrn.com/sol3/Data_Integrity_Notice.cfm?abid=2042307.

transactions, it is important that the board should work independently. An independent board of director is the most important requisite in the corporate governance framework especially, independent directors assume great responsibility in M&A transaction between the related parties.

Shareholders' Participation—A Key Corruption Check Mechanism

Shareholders can play a pivotal role in making a sound, corruption free M&A deal if the corporate governance principles are properly followed. The Companies Act, 2013 provides them an equal opportunity to participate in the merger approval meeting by giving them a right to vote, either in person, by proxy or even by postal ballot. This democratic right has been ensured to every single shareholder, no matter he is in minority. The company is bound to send notice of the meeting for the purpose of discussing the prospects of merger scheme to every shareholder so that he can exercise his democratic right to approve or reject the proposal of the merger scheme. But on the flip side of it, the situation of the minority or retail shareholder is not very sound due to the minimum right of participation given to him on his minimum shareholding. But, the institutional shareholders play a significant role in influencing a deal. Such shareholders by their active participation can keep a check on the company's and its director's mal-intentions hidden behind any M&A deal.

Disclosure Norms

The corporate governance norms lay down two kinds of disclosures; quantitative disclosure and qualitative disclosure. The Companies Act, 2013 necessitates both kinds of disclosures to be made by the companies before hitting an M&A deal. The notices sent to the shareholders under section 230 reflects the democratic set-up and are required to be accompanied by a statement disclosing the following details:

- Details of the merger scheme,
- a copy of the valuation report, if any,
- explaining their effect of the scheme on creditors, key managerial personnel, promoters and non-promoter members, and the debenture-holders, and
- the effect of the compromise or arrangement on any material interests of the directors of the company or the debenture trustees.

Thus, these disclosure norms under the 2013 Act would be

instrumental in checking the presence of any corrupt or wrong transaction once it comes within the knowledge of various stakeholders. Many other significant steps have been proposed and taken under the Companies Act, 2013 towards establishing strong governance principles such as the companies are now required to place their notices and related documents on the website of the company. It would facilitate spreading awareness among the general public and the creditors as well as the sectoral regulators about the company's proposal to merge with another company. A merger or amalgamation involves stakes of various parties and thus, the Act attempts to rule out the possibility of transacting such a significant deal in a hidden manner. The Act also mandates that the documents should be notified to the Securities and Exchange Board and the stock exchange where the securities of the companies are listed, in case the company is a listed company. The most important mode of informing the general public is through newspaper publication which should be done in a prescribed manner.

Right to Raise Objection

Democracy gives and appreciates the right of expression. Similarly, corporate democracy which supports corporate governance gives the right to make representation or even right to raise objection if any visible wrong is being committed in the business transactions. The Companies Act, 2013 considering this democratic right which should be given to the stakeholders, allows such shareholders and creditors to raise an objection who hold not less than ten per cent of the shareholding or five percent of the outstanding debt respectively, as per the latest audited financial statement. It simply means that if such shareholders who hold at least ten percent of shares or such creditors who hold minimum five percent of outstanding debt have a strong feeling that the merger deal is tainted with corruption or individual or classes' interest are adversely affected by the proposed merger, they can raise their objections before a Tribunal. The Tribunal shall consider all raise sound objections before approving the scheme. It is to be noted here that under the Companies Act, 1956, the right to raise objection was given to any interested party no matter how miniscule was the percentage of his shares or stakes in the company. Another significant step taken towards strengthening transparency and integrity in the M&A transactions is that the companies shall now be required to send the notice of merger along with all relevant documents to all the regulatory authorities including the Central Government, the income-tax authorities, the Reserve Bank of India, the Securities and Exchange Board, the Registrar, the respective stock exchanges, the Official Liquidator, the Competition Commission of India and such other sectoral regulators or authorities which are likely to be affected by the compromise or arrangement.[4] Not only this, the Act also gives a right to make representations to different regulators within thirty days of the receipt of the notice. The main objective behind this provision is to process the entire deal in a transparent manner. The simple rule is that more the number of people know, it is more easy to keep a check on the mal intentions of the directors of the company. When a company proposes to merge with another company, everyone including the general public as well as the regulatory authorities must be informed about the company's intention. To merge or amalgamate with another company is a power conferred by the Companies Act on the companies and thus, the authorities must ensure that the companies should not use this power for wrongful gain or with wrong motive. If the regulatory authorities fail to make representation within the stipulated time period, it shall be presumed that they have no representations to make on the proposals.

Accounting Treatment

Another anti corruption mechanism provided under the 2013 Act is that while approving or rejecting the scheme, the Tribunal relies on the certificate of the company's auditor. This certificate pertains to the status that the accounting treatment adopted by the company is in conformity with the prescribed accounting standards. No company can merge with another company unless the scheme has received the approval of the Tribunal. Once the scheme is approved by the Tribunal, it becomes equally binding on all the stakeholders. Various judicial precedents have enunciated the basic principles to be applied before a merger proposal can be sanctioned by the Tribunal. The Tribunal before finally approving or rejecting the scheme has to be satisfied on the following grounds:

(a) Whether statutory provisions have been complied with;
(b) Whether the class of shareholders was fairly represented; and
(c) Whether the arrangement is such as a man of business would reasonably approve.

Power of Tribunal to Enforce Compromise or Arrangement

Not only the Tribunal has the power to sanction or reject a scheme

4. Section 230 of the Companies Act, 2013.

but it also has the power to enforce or implement the scheme. The Tribunal shall sanction the scheme only when it is just, fair, reasonable, in public interest and not against the interest of the minority shareholders. But this is not enough, because there might be many obstacles in the enforcement of this order of the Tribunal which cannot be removed without the Tribunal's supervision.[5] In the case of *Subhishka Trading Services Ltd., In re,*[6] it was held that even after an order sanctioning a scheme is passed, Court is empowered to order modification of scheme if it thinks necessary for proper working of scheme and can even go to the extent of ordering winding-up of the company if it is satisfied that a compromise or arrangement already sanctioned cannot be worked out satisfactorily without such modification. The main objective behind conferring this power of enforcement over the Tribunal is to ensure the effective working of the scheme in the same form and manner in which it has been sanctioned. The power of the Tribunal is similar to the High Court and therefore it may make the following orders:

- Approve the scheme;
- Modify the scheme;
- Reject the scheme; and
- Order winding up of the companies where it is necessary to do so for proper enforcement.

Mergers and Amalgamations of Companies

The merger and amalgamation the companies have been facilitated under section 232 of the 2013 Act. The Act prescribes a detailed procedure when two or more than two companies merge or amalgamate. It states the following:

> "Where an application is made to the Tribunal for the sanctioning of a compromise or an arrangement and it is shown to the Tribunal—
>
> (a) that the compromise or arrangement has been proposed for the purposes of reconstruction of the company or companies involving merger or the amalgamation; and
>
> (b) that under the scheme, the whole or any part of the undertaking, property or liabilities of the transferor company is required to be transferred to the transferee company.

The Tribunal, on receiving such an application, has the right to

5. Section 231 of the Companies Act, 2013.
6. (2011) 108 SCL 13 (Mad-Mag).

order a meeting of the creditors or members or their classes separately, as the case may be, to be called, held and conducted in such manner as the Tribunal may direct. If the Tribunal is satisfied that all the statutory requirements have been complied with, it may, by order, sanction the compromise or arrangement or by a subsequent order, make provision for the following matters, namely:—

(a) the transfer to the transferee company of the whole or any part of the undertaking, property or liabilities of the transferor company from a date to be determined by the parties unless the Tribunal, for reasons to be recorded by it in writing, decides otherwise;

(b) the allotment or appropriation by the transferee company of any shares, debentures, policies or other like instruments in the company which, under the compromise or arrangement, are to be allotted or appropriated by that company to or for any person. As a result of compromise or arrangement, a transferee company shall not hold any shares in its own name or in the name of any trust whether on its behalf or on behalf of any of its subsidiary or associate companies and any such shares shall be cancelled or extinguished;

(c) the continuation by or against the transferee company of any legal proceedings pending by or against any transferor company on the date of transfer;

(d) dissolution, without winding-up, of any transferor company;

(e) the provision to be made for any persons who, within such time and in such manner as the Tribunal directs, dissent from the compromise or arrangement;

(f) where share capital is held by any non-resident shareholder under the foreign direct investment norms or guidelines specified by the Central Government or in accordance with any law for the time being in force, the allotment of shares of the transferee company to such shareholder shall be in the manner specified in the order;

(g) the transfer of the employees of the transferor company to the transferee company;

(h) where the transferor company is a listed company and the transferee company is an unlisted company, the transferee company shall remain an unlisted company until it becomes a listed company;

(i) where the transferor company is dissolved, the fee, if any, paid by the transferor company on its authorized capital shall be set-off against any fees payable by the transferee company on its authorized capital subsequent to the amalgamation; and

(j) such incidental, consequential and supplemental matters as are deemed necessary to secure that the merger or amalgamation is fully and effectively carried out."[7]

Towards setting up strong governance in the corporate set-up, the Act specifically carves out the liability in respect of such offences which have been committed by officers in default prior to merger or amalgamation, would continue after such merger also.[8] However, it is to be noted that the provisions of 2013 Act have not been notified by the Central Government in the official gazette. But the provisions of the Act undoubtedly have a strong hold on the intentions as well as the activities of the big corporate houses before, during and after making a business transaction.

Corruption Check in M&A Transactions

There are many corruption related risks involved in contemplating any M&A transaction. The risk depends on various factors such as the buyer, the kind of transaction, the kind of companies, the material effect of the scheme of the management of both the companies, etc. The following are the main corruption-related issues involved in the M&A transaction:

(i) acquisition of a company which is already charged with corruption allegations or is tainted with corrupt practices;

(ii) the consideration or part of the consideration for merger or acquisition or the revenue involved in the scheme is backed by any corrupt source;

(iii) the acquirer or the transferee company bears the direct risk of tarnishing its reputation; and

(iv) the involvement of management in resolving the above mentioned issues can be both expensive as well as time-consuming.

It requires a proper due diligence exercise on the part of the acquirer or transferee company to find out about the number of red flags in order to identify whether or not the transferor company is tainted with corruption. Factors such as the industry or the sector to which the company belongs to, its geographical location, the details of company's

7. Section 232 of the Companies Act, 2013.
8. Section 240 of the Companies Act, 2013.

external consultants, intermediaries or agents, and its interaction with government officials and any already existing civil or criminal liability against the company are the probable red flags which may be identified before finalising the deal. There is greater risk involved when the deal is of the nature of cross-border or joint venture. There may be many hidden facts and liabilities which are revealed post deal and therefore, utmost care should be taken before entering a forced marriage deal with the other company.

Corruption Risks in Cross-Border M&A

Cross-border M&A is an important mode of corporate growth and expansion. It provides both geographical as well as product expansion benefits to companies with the added advantage of reduced labour and operational costs in the new market domain. Thus developing countries tend to encourage such corporate matrimonial knots by providing good investment options to the foreign companies via the merger route. However, there are inherent risks of corruption in cross-border M&A deals. Regulators across the countries are constantly endeavouring to enact strict anti-corruption provisions so that such transactions can be settled according to the corporate governance principles of their respective jurisdictions. In this regard, the steps taken by US and UK governments are appreciable as their anti-corruption policies are most effectively and strictly implemented. The Companies Act, 2013 provides a better platform to facilitate cross-border mergers and amalgamations. Unlike its predecessor, the new Act encourages cross-border mergers from both sides. It simply means that now, both an Indian company as well as a foreign company can merge with each other. But there are high risks of corrupt practices being involved in such a case as there are lesser possibilities of carrying out effective due diligence over the foreign company. Therefore, cross-border mergers are allowed only subject to the approval of the Reserve Bank of India and with selected jurisdictions.[9] A foreign company for the purpose of this section means any company or body corporate incorporated outside India whether having a place of business in India or not.

Position in United States of America

The Foreign Corrupt Practices Act, 1977 directly prohibits any non-U.S. company from committing an act in furtherance of a bribe scheme within U.S. territory. Acts as minor as sending an email to a U.S. bank

9. Section 234 of the Companies Act, 2013.

requesting a fund transfer can constitute an act "in furtherance" of a bribery scheme. Of equal importance, the U.S. government frequently prosecutes individuals, including officials of non-U.S. companies, who face imprisonment if convicted. The stringent Act prohibits bribery of foreign public officials. It embodies the corporate governance principles by requiring issuers to maintain accurate books and records. The Act also lays down provisions to devise and maintain systems of internal accounting control in order to bring out transparency in the accounting procedure. The statute is not only stringent but also aggressive in nature as it has its reach extended over the foreign officials as well as foreign nationals. Effective enforceability of any anti-corruption statute is a big challenge but the FCPA being enforced by the Securities and Exchange Commission (SEC) and Department of Justice (DoJ) has been quite successfully implemented on both civil as well as the criminal matters involving companies, U.S. citizens, nationals and residents, and foreign nationals.[10] The FCPA requires the companies to undertake proper and thorough due diligence process before making any M&A transaction. It is one of the factors in determining whether any enforcement action was ultimately taken if a violation has discovered. The US provisions also state that as a result of acquisition, the acquiring company acquires potential liabilities associated with various regulations, contracts and statutes and that successor liability is a recognized component of corporate, civil and criminal law.[11] There is always a possibility to identify the 'red flags' if proper due diligence is carried out and the corruption risks can be greatly minimised. Otherwise, the successor or the acquiring company will have to directly bear the risk if it fails to identify the obvious 'red flags'.

Conclusion

Corporate governance which denotes good governance is indicative of a healthy economic situation of country. Business transactions such as M&As are most likely to be affected by the evils of the corporate world. Corporate corruption has a strong nexus with corporate governance in the sense that a good corporate governance structure minimises the risk of corruption. Corporate governance principles are based on socially

10. Cross-Border Mergers & Acquisitions: Anti-Corruption Issues, Posted by Noam Noked, co-editor, HLS Forum on Corporate Governance and Financial Regulation, on Thursday, April 11, 2013, last accessed 7th April 2014.
11. http://www.justice.gov/criminal/fraud/fcpa/guide.pdf, last accessed 7th April 2015.

acceptable norms which are valued-based. It imbibes and directs the companies, directors and stakeholders to work in the overall interest of the company and not towards following individual selfish pursuits. Such behaviour acts as an anti-thesis for corrupt actions. Corporate corruption, which has become a global phenomenon needs to be checked through stringent and effective legislative policy. Both developed and developing countries are trying to achieve a corporate culture which is corruption-free. Countries like UK and USA have taken commendable actions in restricting and checking the corruption in the corporate sector. India still needs to do a lot towards checking corporate corruption and establishing a good corporate governance structure which prioritises the interests of the companies and nation first and individuals later.

10

Cross-Border Merger & Amalgamation: An Analysis under the Companies Act, 2013

RUKMA ROY

Introduction

As a business gets bigger, the growth will be organic or inorganic. Organic growth, also called internal growth, occurs when the company grows from its own business activity using funds from one year to expand the company the following year. While ploughing back profits into a business is a cheap source of finance, it is also a slow way to expand and many firms want to grow faster. A company can do so by inorganic growth. Inorganic growth, or external growth, occurs when the company grows by merger or acquisition of another business. An entrepreneur may grow its business either by internal expansion or by external expansion. Thus, in the case of internal expansion, a firm grows gradually over time in the normal course of the business, through acquisition of new assets, replacement of the technologically obsolete equipments and the establishment of new lines of products. But in external expansion, a firm acquires a running business and grows overnight through corporate combinations. These combinations are in the form of mergers, acquisitions, amalgamations and takeovers and have now become important features of corporate restructuring. They have been playing an important role in the external growth of a number of leading companies world over. They have become popular because of the enhanced competition, trade without barriers, free flow of capital across countries and globalisation of businesses. In the wake of economic reforms, Indian industries have also started restructuring their operations around their core business activities through acquisition and takeovers because of their increasing exposure to competition both domestically and internationally. Mergers and acquisitions are strategic decisions taken for maximisation of a company's growth by enhancing its production and marketing operations. They are being used in a wide array of fields such as information technology, telecommunications and business process outsourcing as well as in traditional businesses in order to gain strength, expand the customer base, cut competition or enter into a new market or product segment. Merger and Acquisition (M&A) has always been a sought for transaction in India, as more and more M&A deal is being carried out each and every day in the Indian market. As per Grant Thorton, there have been a total of 480 deals amounting to $27.4 billion during 2013 involving Indian companies.[1] A merger is a combination of two or more businesses into one business. Laws in India use the term 'amalgamation' for merger. Amalgamation is defined as the merger of one or more companies with another or the merger of two or more companies to form a new company, in such a way that all assets and liabilities of the amalgamating companies become assets and liabilities of the amalgamated company and shareholders not less than nine-tenths in value of the shares in the amalgamating company or companies become shareholders of the amalgamated company.[2]

Legal Framework of Cross-Border Mergers before the 2013 Act

Under the Companies Act, 1956, only foreign companies could merge or amalgamate with Indian companies by the procedures laid out in Sections 391 to 394. The reverse scenario was not covered. "Transferee Company"[3] was defined only as a company formed or registered under it or earlier company laws in India. However, "Transferor Company" included any corporate, whether it was a company under the Act or not. Therefore, it was inferred until now that a foreign company could only be a transferor and not transferee, effectively blocking outbound mergers of Indian companies with foreign entities. Thus, the Companies Act, 1956 under Section 394(4)(b)

1. Yogesh Malhan, "*Mergers and Acquisitions*", available at http://www.lexology.com/, last accessed on April 14th, 2014.
2. Section 2 (1B) of the Income Tax Act, 1961.
3. Section 394(4)(b) of the Companies Act, 1956.

restricted cross-border mergers to the Indian transferee companies. This legislative policy was unusually restrictive and ostensibly existed to protect Indian companies. It should be noted, that such restrictive and unnecessarily protectionist condition does not exist in many advanced jurisdictions like, the U.K. and the U.S. No adverse effects have been demonstrated on the U.S. and U.K. companies due to permissive regime in their jurisdictions.

Scenario After the 2013 Act

The Companies Act, 2013 promises to marry corporate law with globalised business needs.[4] Besides several talked-about concepts such as Corporate Social Responsibility, auditors' rotation and one-person company, it brings about a clearer legal framework for cross-border mergers. A forward looking law on mergers and amalgamations needed to recognize that an Indian company ought to be permitted to merge with a foreign company. Both contract-based mergers between an Indian company and a foreign company and court-based mergers between such entities where the foreign company is the transferee, needed to be recognized in Indian Law.[5] The merger provisions are contained in Chapter XV, containing Sections 230 to 240, which deals with 'Compromises, Arrangements and Amalgamations.' Section 234 specifically deals with the cross-border mergers. The 2013 Act proposes to allow both, inbound and outbound cross-border mergers, between Indian companies and foreign ones. It provides for the merger of an Indian company into a foreign one, whether its place of business is in India or in certified jurisdictions (to be notified by the Central Government from time to time)[6], subject to the NCLT's and RBI's approval. However, the practical utility will depend on yet-to-be-enacted Reserve Bank of India regulations on this topic and necessary changes to India's foreign direct investment policy.[7] The Government will also frame rules for cross-border mergers in consultation with the Reserve Bank of India. Also, RBI approval is a must. Interestingly, the

4. Shashishekhar, "Green Signal for Outbound Mergers", *The Hindu*, October 27th 2013.
5. Ministry of Corporate Affairs, Report of the Expert Committee on Company Law, Mergers and Acquisitions.
6. Operational provisions awaited.
7. Rishi Shroff, Key Implications of the Companies Act, 2013 on Board Room Decision-making, India Forbes, July 10, 2014.

new law appears to be silent on cross-border splits or demergers.[8] In this period of challenged macro-economic situation, Merger and Acquisition is viewed as an important tool in improving the financial health of corporate sector. One of the key features of the new act was to promote and regulate the merger and acquisition activity in the country. It intended to bring in reformatory and contemporary provisions, so as to make M&A environment more congenial.

Need for Cross-Border Merger

Businesses no longer limited by borders, cross-border merger and amalgamation transactions present significant opportunities for economic gain and increased shareholder or investor value. Various factors influence the spurt in recent cross-border mergers and acquisitions, including the ever-increasing need of companies to tap new markets and set-up global operations in these, achieve cost and secure natural resources. Cross-border M&A is also supported by technological advancements, low cost financing arrangements and robust market conditions, which have made deal-makers confident and think more creatively about their global growth strategies. The flow of transactions could be inbound (non-residents investing in India) or outbound (Indian businesses making investments abroad). The 2013 Act will provide an opportunity of growth and expansion to Indian companies by permitting amalgamation with foreign company or *vice versa*. This will provide opportunity to form corporate strategies on a global scale and also makes it possible for an Indian company to restructure its shareholdings and transfer its ownership to an international holding structure, and thereby increase its access to foreign markets.[9] Cross-border mergers could have ground-breaking significance in plotting India on the global M&A landscape, since corporate deals have fallen through or failed to meet their desired objectives in the past due to the lack of such provisions in the 1956 Act. Enabling of cross-border mergers is expected to help Indian companies in more ways than one, including the following:

1. Restructuring their shareholdings, wherein they can migrate ownership to an international holding structure.

---

8. Grant Thornton India LLP, Green Signal for Outbound Mergers, 29th October 2013.
9. Pawas Jain, Financeonline. In, Mergers Acquisitions: A New Beginning under Companies Act, 2013, 13th December 2014

2. Facilitating listing of entities, which may have Indian assets in overseas jurisdictions.
3. Providing exit routes to current investors in overseas jurisdictions.[10]

An Insight on Provisions of the Companies Act, 2013

More Comprehensive Reporting: Sub-section (2) of Section 230 at the onset makes the reporting to the tribunal for purpose of calling a members or creditors meeting more comprehensive than prescribed by Rule 67 of the Companies Court Rules, 1959, by filing an affidavit in Form No. 34, as required on an application made under Section 391(1) of the Companies Act, 1956. Most notable changes are the disclosure regarding the Corporate Debt Restructuring (CDR) Scheme to the tribunal; and filing of a share and property valuation report before the tribunal. Easier procedure of objecting to the scheme: As per the existing Companies Act, 1956, an essential requirement for approval of a restructuring scheme is to convene a creditors or members (shareholders) meeting. The new act intends to make things easier by allowing objection to the scheme to be made by only those persons holding not less than 10% of the shareholding or having outstanding debt amounting to not less than 5% of the total outstanding debt as per the latest audited financial statement. *Simplified procedure in certain cases:* One salient provision of the 2013 Act is Section 233, which prescribes for bypassing the tribunal in case of merger or amalgamation of two or more small companies or between a holding company and its wholly-owned subsidiary, apart from other prescribed companies. Section 233 involves the Registrar (RoC) and Official Liquidators (OLs) in such mergers and amalgamations. This simplification of the process should expedite such mergers apart from reducing the transaction costs. Layers of investment companies: All along companies have traditionally created multiple investment subsidiaries at home or at overseas, particularly in tax efficient jurisdictions for routing investments into another company. Large Indian corporates have several subsidiaries to act as investment arms or the subsidiaries of the holding companies which are in turn used to start new ventures, acquire business, etc. To curb/check such layering of investments for funding new ventures or acquisitions, the Bill prohibits a company from making investment through more than two layers of investment companies, i.e. a company whose principle business

10. Ernst and Young Publication, Mergers and Acquisitions in the new era of Companies Act, 2013, February 2014.

is to acquire shares, debentures or other securities. However, this restriction will not apply in case of cross-border mergers. Prescribed time limit to cut short delays: Considering the special needs of smaller companies or holding companies and subsidiaries companies, simpler provisions have been made regarding M&A. To cut short the bureaucratic delays, where the approval of statutory authorities are involved, a prescribed period of thirty days has been specified and in case of failure to make representation between the specified period, it shall be presumed that those authorities have no representations to make.

Cross-Border Mergers: Progressive or Regressive

The unnecessarily strict mindset regarding the merger and amalgamation set-up, should have been long sacrificed in this era of economic liberalisation, where the Indian government is slowly and cautiously moving towards an open door policy for inbound foreign investment, with progressive relaxation on capital account transactions.[11] In such an environment, the restriction on cross-border mergers imposed by Section 394(4)(b)[12] has very correctly been replaced by a much broader and relaxed section 294 of the new act that allows Indian companies to enter into cross-border mergers and amalgamations. These new provisions can be greatly beneficial to Indian companies which have a global presence by providing them structuring options which did not exist under the 1956 Act. Thus, the introduction of Section 234 in the 2013 Act is a welcome step. However, a regressive restriction of allowing such cross-border mergers only with the foreign companies incorporated in the Central Government notified jurisdictions nullifies the progressiveness which was apparent in Section 234. Notably, the Companies Act, 1956 provisions did not restrict cross-border mergers on basis of the nationality of the transferor foreign company. Will this restriction in the 2013 Act actually make it even more regressive than the 1956 Act? This question can only be addressed after the relevant notification is issued, which will enable examination of its scope and contents; and its impact on cross-border M&As can be seen with the passage of time.

---

11. Ajay Kumar Sharma, *India Law Journal*, Cross-border Mergers Provisions under the Companies Act, 2013: Analysis and Implications.
12. Companies Act, 1956.

Key Contents of Section 234 of the Companies Act, 2013

The Central Government framing Rules in consultation with the Reserve Bank: Proviso to sub-section (1) of Section 234 provides, 'that the Central Government may make rules, in consultation with the Reserve Bank of India, in connection with mergers and amalgamations provided under this section.' The consistency and clarity, both within and with other existing laws, of such rules will be important to note. The Companies (Cross-Border Mergers) Regulations, 2007 (U.K.) may be instructional in this regard, as it exhibits considerable foresight in dealing with even offshoot issues like, protection of employees.[13] Consultation from stakeholder and experts should be taken before formulating such rules to ensure majority acceptance and smooth running of the merger and amalgamation framework.

Role of the Reserve Bank in the approval: *Onerous condition:* Sub-section (2) of Section 234 requires a prior Reserve Bank approval in the cross-border mergers. This is unusual and should be left to the wisdom of the authorities managing Foreign Exchange Management Act, 1999 and its Regulations, prescribing the exchange control laws in India. The saving grace is that sub-section (2) is 'subject to any other law for time being in force'. Thus, FEMA Regulations[14] should override the prior approval requirements.

Depository Receipts as payment of consideration to the shareholders of the merging company: One radical feature of sub-section (2) of Section 234 is allowing Depository Receipts (DRs) as payment of consideration to the shareholders of the merging company. Thus, there can be a case of issuance of Indian Depository Receipts (IDRs) by the foreign company as payment of consideration to the shareholders of the Indian merging company. The Indian shareholders who can now receive IDRs or foreign securities in lieu of Indian shares, can as a result, become members of the foreign company or holders of security with a trading right in India (especially in listed companies). The payment in cash or depository receipts would facilitate exit to the shareholders of the merging entity who do not want to be a part of the merged entity.[15]

---

13. Ajay Kumar Sharma, *India Law Journal*, Cross-border Mergers Provisions under the Companies Act, 2013: Analysis and Implications.
14. Regulation 7, FEMA (Transfer or Issue of Security by a Person Resident outside India) Regulations, 2000.
15. PSA Legal Counsellors, Merger Regime Under The Companies Act, 2013, January 2014.

These changes reflect the legislature's intent to facilitate cross-border business. IDRs have been an unpopular and problematic security, which seems to have fallen into disfavour after the Standard Chartered Bank's IDR issue. The RBI and SEBI have created unnecessary restrictions, and have been skeptical in critical areas like redemption, which has only been slowly yet not fully relaxed, to the inconvenience of the foreign companies issuing such IDRs through depositories. The Central Government's interference through the Companies (Issue of Indian Depository Receipts) Rules, 2004 cannot be neglected since it made the whole IDR Regime extremely complex and unattractive. If the IDRs are to be made as attractive and acceptable as securities like American Depository Receipts (ADRs) and Global Depository Receipts (GDRs), then simplification and unification of the IDR legal regime needs to be done with an open mind by the concerned regulatory authorities. Otherwise, such provisions enabling the issuance of IDRs carry little or no meaning.

Tax Considerations of Cross-Border Mergers

The Income Tax Act presently grants tax exemptions on mergers if the transferee is an Indian company and does not recognize a situation where the transferee will be a foreign company, as contemplated under the 2013 Act. The Income Tax Act contains provisions that mergers of companies where the transferee is an Indian company will not be subject to tax if certain conditions, namely, all assets and liabilities of the transferor become the assets and liabilities of the transferee, and at least three-fourth (in value) of the shareholders of the transferor become shareholders of the transferee, are fulfilled. If the two conditions are fulfilled, then the merger is a qualified one for the purpose of the Act and there will be no tax implications in the hands of the transferor and its shareholders.[16] However, corresponding amendments are required in existing laws including the Income Tax Act, Exchange Control Regulations (relating to ownership of real estate in India, sectoral caps, definitions of overseas holdings, etc.), security-related laws (change in rules regarding dual listings), etc[17]. Currently, tax laws do not provide any tax-neutral provisions to enable such cross-border mergers. The debate on whether cross-border mergers should be taxable or not is an interesting one, since in some mergers, companies may be moving some

16. *Ibid.*
17. Ernst and Young Publication, Mergers and Acquisitions in the new era of Companies Act, 2013, February 2014.

value outside India. If they are operating companies, they will need to move out their Indian operations before the mergers, to avoid operational and tax-related complications. Furthermore, the impact of payment of cash/depository receipts or any other modes on the tax neutrality of the amalgamations will need deep analyses. A key aspect to look for will be notification of the "specified jurisdictions" for cross-border mergers and the amendment of Exchange Control Regulations. This may restrict the scope of outbound mergers as well as inbound ones, which are currently allowed from any jurisdiction that allow cross-border mergers under their domestic laws. Moreover, the requirement of approval from the RBI is expected to play a major role in such cross-border mergers. Some key points related to tax considerations of cross-border mergers are as follows:

1. Taxability of assets transferred by Indian company to Foreign Co-Exemption under Section 47(vi) of the Income Tax Act, 1961, available only if the merged company is Indian company—Availing of exemption difficult.
2. Taxability of shares transferred by Indian shareholder in lieu of GDR/cash of Foreign Co-Exemption under Section 47(vii) of the Income Tax Act, available only if the merged company is Indian company—Availing of exemption difficult.
3. Post-merger, the Indian business would be considered as branch/permanent establishment of the Foreign Company.
4. Tax rate applicable to profits of foreign Company would be 43.26% as against 33.99% for domestic companies.
5. Income of the branch to be determined in accordance with the principles of Article 7 of the relevant DTAA, i.e. profits attributable to the Branch.
6. Relatively easy to repatriate profits from the branch to the parent.[18]

Regulatory Framework of Cross-Border Mergers

1. Substantive compliance requirements for Indian companies under Companies Act, would not be applicable.
2. Post-merger the Branch would be considered as a foreign company and provisions of Sections 592 to 602 of Companies Act would be applicable.

---

18. Nangia & Co. Chartered Accountants, Analyzing Impact of the Companies Act, 2013 on Mergers & Acquisitions, February 2013.

3. Compliance with RBI regulations, as applicable to Branch applicable.

Legal Issues or Impacts of Cross-Border Mergers

1. One more exit route will be available for foreign companies which have wholly owned subsidiary/Joint Venture/investments in India.
2. There may be anomalies for companies from non-common wealth countries which do not have similar Law.
3. The FEMA regulation and FDI/ODI policies will be amended to accommodate the new provisions.
4. There is possibility of bringing in additional norms to control outflow of resources.[19]

Conclusion

It would be fair to say that the 2013 Act seeks to streamline and make M&A more smooth and transparent. The new provisions should make it easier for corporations proposing mergers as it spears to have a good system of checks & balances to prevent abuse of these provisions. The merits of some provisions related to merger and amalgamation in the new Act are noticeable at the onset. For example, as discussed, Section 230(2)[20] provides for a more comprehensive reporting relatively than the one under the 1956 Act regime. The simplification of procedure of mergers, in certain cases, under Section 233 is also commendable. As the new law also ushers in short-form mergers (that is, bypassing Court or Tribunal approval) between small companies or wholly-owned subsidiaries and their parents, reorganizing international holding structures may now become simpler. However, many of the enactments are criticisable. Notice requirement to the Competition Commission of India, under Section 230(5)[21] should not be provided for due to the current competition law sufficiently addressing that issue. Involvement of too many regulators in the proceedings before the tribunal may unnecessarily complicate and delay the process of a cross-border merger. In fact, it is surprising to find the inclusion of CCI in this provision considering the government's efforts on the other hand to simplify the regulatory process by initiating measures like the

19. C.S. Ranjeet Pandey, Companies Act, 2013, Restructuring & Revival, 13th September, 2013.
20. The Companies Act, 2013.
21. *Ibid.*

constitution of the financial sector legislative reforms commission (FSLRC) under the chairmanship of Justice Srikrishna.[22] Furthermore, the restriction contained in Section 234 restricting cross-border mergers (both ways) of Indian companies with companies of only notified countries is not only regressive but speaks of the narrow outlook and protectionist mindset of the government. This restriction in practice may turn out to be more regressive than the corresponding one under the 1956 Act having only one-way prohibition. Thus, if the parliament and government seriously seek to liberalize cross-border mergers, then such jurisdiction notification criterion should certainly be done away with. If issues like tax avoidance are a problem in cross-border deals, the solution should be sought under international tax laws regime not through the Companies Act. The mention in Section 234(2) about seeking RBI approval in cross-border mergers, subject to any existing law, is also excessive in view of the FEMA and the gamut of regulations under it, which are meant to act as the foreign exchange control laws. In order for the liberalization process to be effective it is critical to ensure that the list of countries covers all jurisdictions relevant for Indian business. Although the Companies Act has received Presidential assent, the provisions governing amalgamations have not been notified yet. That is likely to happen only when the Government is ready with the corresponding rules. So, even though the new law is good news for cross-border corporate marriages, the prospective brides and grooms still have a long wait ahead. Thus, in a nutshell, the new companies act aims to align the law with current commercial realities and has been drafted, keeping in mind the need of the hour, the necessity to boost the Indian economy, bring transparency in corporate restructuring. However, other allied laws and regulations such as Foreign Exchange Management Act, Income Tax Act, 1961 and the proposed rules to be notified by the Central Government should fall in line with the provisions of the new Bill else, it would make the implementation inefficient and yield inconsistency which in the current economic environment would be an unwelcome experimentation.

22. Ajay Kumar Sharma, *India Law Journal*, Cross-border Mergers Provisions under the Companies Act, 2013: Analysis and Implications.

11

Mergers & Amalgamation: A Comparative Analysis under Companies Act, 2013 and Competition Act, 2002

DR. ANEESH V. PILLAI

Introduction

The enactment of new Companies law in 2013 can be considered as a milestone in the development of company law in India and is likely to have far-reaching consequences on all companies operating in India. This is because the new Act has introduced various new provisions and changes from the old Companies Act, 1956. One of the areas where the new Act has made significant change is the regulation of mergers among companies. Mergers are methods by which distinct businesses may combine[1]. There are many reasons for entering into a merger or amalgamation by business firms. For example, increasing capabilities; gaining a competitive advantage or larger market share; diversifying products or services, etc. As competition increased in the economy, to avoid competition and to face challenges from international and multinational companies, Indian companies are going for mergers or acquisitions, sometimes they may go for even cross-border mergers. In

1. Dr. M. Venkatasubba Reddy, B. Swetha & T. Srinivasarao, "Mergers and Acquisitions in Corporate Sector", *International Journal of Scientific Research*, Vol. 4(1), 2012, 97.

India, the mergers and amalgamations between companies are also dealt under Competition Act, 2002. Thus, there is generally an apprehension that, it is possible to have a conflict with Company law and Competition law when both regulating the same merger.

Mergers & Amalgamations: Concept and Meaning

Merger means any situation in which the ownership of two or more enterprises is joined together.[2] The term merger is not defined neither under Companies Act, 2013 not under Competition Act, 2002. The Companies Act as well as Competition Act considers both merger and amalgamations are identical and prescribes same set of procedures for its regulation though conceptually both are different. The Oxford Dictionary defines merger as a means 'combining of two companies into one.'[3] Thus, a merger is a fusion between two or more enterprises, whereby the identity of one or more is lost and the result is a single enterprise. In merger the assets and liabilities of the companies get vested in another company; the company that is merged loses its identity and its shareholders become shareholders of the other company.[4] The Income Tax Act, 1961 defines, "amalgamation as the merger of one or more companies with another or the merger of two or more companies to form a new company, in such a way that all assets and liabilities of the amalgamating companies become assets and liabilities of the amalgamated company and shareholders not less than nine-tenths in value of the shares in the amalgamating company or companies become shareholders of the amalgamated company."[5] A merger can be of various types depending upon the requirements of the merging entities. The first category of mergers is 'Horizontal Mergers' in which a merger takes place between entities engaged in competing businesses which are at the same level of market structure. The goal of a horizontal merger is to create a new, larger organization with more market share. The second major type of merger is 'Vertical Mergers' in which there is a

---

2. Manas Kumar Chaudhuri, "Mergers & Acquisitions under the Indian Competition Law: A Critical Legal View", available at http://www.jftc.go.jp/eacpf/01/india_mergers0706.pdf, visited on 20.4.2015.
3. Indian Institute of Banking and Finance, *Principles and Practices of Banking*, MacMillan, Mumbai (2nd Edn., 2008), p. 83.
4. Poulami Chatterjee, "Horizontal Merger Guidelines For Competition Commission of India (CCI)", available at http://cci.gov.in/images/ media/ResearchReports/HorrizontalMergerGuidelinesPoulamichatterjee09022007_20080 411100916.pdf, visited on 17.5.2013.
5. See, The Income Tax Act, 1961, Section 2(1A).

combination of two firms that may not compete with each other, but exist in the same supply chain. For example, an automobile company joining with a spare parts supplier is a type of vertical merger. Another major form of merger is 'Congeneric Mergers'. These mergers are between entities engaged in the same general industry and somewhat inter-related, but having no common customer supplier relationship. For example, a soap manufacturer merges with a face cream manufacturer. The fourth category of mergers is 'Conglomerate Mergers' which involves a combination of two unrelated entities. For example, a cloth manufacturing company merges with a toothpaste manufacturing company. Each of the type of these mergers has various effects on the competition in the market. According to Companies Act, 2013, a merger can occur either by absorption or by formation. A merger, where under the scheme the undertaking, property and liabilities of one or more companies, including the company in respect of which the compromise or arrangement is proposed, are to be transferred to another existing company, it is a merger by absorption. On the other hand, in a merger where the undertaking, property and liabilities of two or more companies, including the company in respect of which the compromise or arrangement is proposed, are to be transferred to a new company, whether or not a public company is a merger by formation.[6]

Mergers under the Companies Act, 2013

Generally, two or more companies can merge or amalgamate only when the amalgamation is permitted under their Memorandum of Association. Also, the acquiring company should have the permission in its object clause to cårry on the business of the acquired company. In the absence of these provisions in the Memorandum of Association, it is necessary to seek the permission of the shareholders, board of directors and the National Company Law Tribunal, before affecting the merger.[7] The Chapter XV of the new Companies Act deals with mergers and amalgamations primarily; however, other provisions are also attracted at different stages of the process. The Sections 230-237 of the Act contains major provisions for mergers. These sections would have to be read with the Companies (Court) Rules, 1959 which forms a complete procedural

6. Section 232, Expl. (i).
7. A.P. Dash, *Mergers and Acquisitions*, IK International Publishing House Ltd., New Delhi, 2010, p. 84.

code for implementing mergers.[8] An analysis of the new Companies Act shows that, it regulates different types of mergers in India. They can be categorized as follows:

1. General Mergers

The first and most important categories of mergers which are regulated under Companies Act, 2013 are the ordinary or general merger between two companies. A merger may be made through common agreements between the transferor and the transferee but mere agreement does not provide a legal cover to the transaction unless it carries the sanction of National Company Law Tribunal for which the procedure laid down under Section 230 of the Act should be followed for giving effect to mergers through the statutory instrument of the Tribunal's sanction.

In every company, the board of directors is empowered to approve any scheme of merger with another company.[9] Once the merger partner has been identified and the scheme of merger is approved by the board of directors, both the transferor and transferee should submit the scheme to the tribunal for its sanction. If under the scheme, the whole or any part of the undertaking, property or liabilities of any company is required to be transferred to another company or is proposed to be divided among and transferred to two or more companies, the Tribunal may on such application, order a meeting of the creditors or class of creditors or the members or class of members.[10] In pursuance of Tribunals order, where a meeting is proposed to be called, a notice of such meeting shall be sent to all the creditors or class of creditors and to all the members or class of members and the debenture-holders of the company, individually at the address registered with the company. The notice should be accompanied by a statement disclosing the details of the merger, a copy of the valuation report, if any, and explaining their effect on creditors, key managerial personnel, promoters and non-promoter members, and the debenture-holders and the effect of the merger any material interests of the directors of the company or the debenture trustees, and such other matters.[11] The notice which is being sent should be placed on the website of the company, if any, and in case

---

8. Ashish S. Joshi, "Mergers and Acquisitions in India: A Primer", *The Michigan Business Law Journal*, Summer 2008, 43.
9. Section 179 (i).
10. Section 232(1).
11. Section 230(3).

of a listed company, these documents shall be sent to the Securities and Exchange Board and stock exchange where the securities of the companies are listed, for placing on their website and shall also be published in newspapers. Such a notice for the meeting can also issue by way of an advertisement. The copies of merger scheme should be made available to the concerned persons free of charge from the registered office of the company. The merging companies are also bound to circulate the following for the meeting so ordered by the Tribunal, namely: (*a*) the draft of the proposed terms of the scheme drawn up and adopted by the directors of the merging company; (*b*) confirmation that a copy of the draft scheme has been filed with the Registrar; (*c*) a report adopted by the directors of the merging companies explaining effect of compromise on each class of shareholders, key managerial personnel, promotors and non-promoter shareholders laying out in particular the share exchange ratio, specifying any special valuation difficulties; (*d*) the report of the expert with regard to valuation, if any; (*e*) a supplementary accounting statement if the last annual accounts of any of the merging company relate to a financial year ending more than six months before the first meeting of the company summoned for the purposes of approving the scheme. Every notice sent in pursuance of Tribunal's order should indicate that, the persons to whom the notice is sent may vote in the meeting either themselves or through proxies or by postal ballot to the adoption of the merger scheme within one month from the date of receipt of such notice. However, it is to be noted that, any objection to a merger scheme can be raised only by persons holding not less than ten percent of the shareholding or having outstanding debt amounting to not less than five percent of the total outstanding debt as per the latest audited financial statement. A notice along with all the documents in such form as may be prescribed shall also be sent to the Central Government, the income-tax authorities, the Reserve Bank of India, the Securities and Exchange Board, the Registrar, the respective stock exchanges, the Official Liquidator, the Competition Commission of India, if necessary, and such other sectoral regulators or authorities which are likely to be affected by the merger. These sectoral regulators are supposed to make their representation to the Tribunal within a period of thirty days from the date of receipt of such notice, failing which, it shall be presumed that they have no representations to make on the merger scheme. In the meeting so held in pursuance of Tribunal's order, majority of persons representing three-fourths in value of the creditors, or class of creditors or members or class of members, as the case may be, voting in person or by proxy or by postal ballot, agree to such merger, the Tribunal will sanction the scheme by an order[12]. Once the scheme is sanctioned by Tribunal, it shall be binding on the company; all creditors or class of creditors or members or class of members or in case of a company being wound up, on the liquidator and the contributories of the company. It is to be noted that, o merger scheme shall be sanctioned by the Tribunal unless a certificate by the company's auditor has been filed with the Tribunal that the accounting treatment proposed in the scheme compromise or arrangement is in conformity with the accounting standards. In the order of sanctioning or by a subsequent order, the tribunal can make provisions for the following matters: (*a*) the transfer to the transferee company of the whole or any part of the undertaking, property or liabilities of the transferor company from a date to be determined by the parties unless the Tribunal, for reasons to be recorded by it in writing, decides otherwise; (*b*) the allotment or appropriation by the transferee company of any shares, debentures, policies or other like instruments in the company which, under the compromise or arrangement, are to be allotted or appropriated by that company to or for any person. However, a transferee company shall not, as a result of the compromise or arrangement, hold any shares in its own name or in the name of any trust whether on its behalf or on behalf of any of its subsidiary or associate companies and any such shares shall be cancelled or extinguished; (*c*) the continuation by or against the transferee company of any legal proceedings pending by or against any transferor company on the date of transfer; (*d*) dissolution, without winding-up, of any transferor company; (*e*) the provision to be made for any persons who, within such time and in such manner as the Tribunal directs, dissent from the compromise or arrangement; (*f*) where share capital is held by any non-resident shareholder under the foreign direct investment norms or guidelines specified by the Central Government or in accordance with any law for the time being in force, the allotment of shares of the transferee company to such shareholder shall be in the manner specified in the order; (*g*) the transfer of the employees of the transferor company to the transferee company; (*h*) where the transferor company is a listed company and the transferee company is an unlisted company: (A) the transferee company shall remain an unlisted company until it becomes a listed company; (*B*) if shareholders of the transferor company decide to opt out of the transferee company, provision shall be made for payment of the value of shares held by them and other benefits in accordance

12. Section 230(6).

with a pre-determined price formula or after a valuation is made, and the arrangements under this provision may be made by the Tribunal. (*i*) where the transferor company is dissolved, the fee, if any, paid by the transferor company on its authorised capital shall be set-off against any fees payable by the transferee company on its authorised capital subsequent to the amalgamation; and (*j*) such incidental, consequential and supplemental matters as are deemed necessary to secure that the merger or amalgamation is fully and effectively carried out[13].

2. Amalgamation by Sick Company

The second category of merger or amalgamation under the Companies Act, 2013 is the amalgamation between sick companies. A company which fail to pay or secure a debt, which is fifty percent or more of its total outstanding debt, within thirty days of demand notice it may be declared as sick company[14]. The procedure for amalgamation by a sick company with another starts with a scheme prepared by the company administrator for revival and rehabilitation of the sick company through the amalgamation of (*i*) the sick company with any other company; or (*ii*) any other company with the sick company.[15] The scheme prepared by the company administrator for amalgamation should be placed before the creditors of the sick company in a meeting convened for their approval by the company administrator within the period of sixty days from his appointment, which may be extended by the Tribunal up to a period not exceeding one hundred twenty days. He shall convene separate meetings of secured and unsecured creditors of the sick company and if the scheme is approved by the unsecured creditors representing one-fourth in value of the amount owed by the company to such creditors and the secured creditors, representing three-fourths in value of the amount outstanding against financial assistance disbursed by such creditors to the sick company, the company administrator shall submit the scheme before the Tribunal for sanctioning the scheme. The scheme should also be laid before the general meeting of both the companies for approval by their respective shareholders and no such scheme shall be proceeded with unless it has been approved, with or without modification, by a special resolution passed by the shareholders of that company. On submission of the

13. Section 232 (3).
14. Sick Companies (the Companies Act, 2013), available at https://aishmghrana.me/2014/02/04/sick-companies-companies-act-2013/, visited on 20.4.2015.
15. Section 261.

scheme, it shall be examined by the Tribunal and a copy of the scheme with modification, if any, made by the Tribunal shall be sent, in draft, to the sick company and the company administrator and to any other company concerned. The Tribunal can publish the draft scheme in brief in such daily newspapers as the Tribunal may consider necessary. Any stakeholder can submit their suggestions and objections, if any, within such period as the Tribunal may specify. Further, the Tribunal may make such modifications, if any, in the draft scheme as it may consider necessary in the light of the suggestions and objections received from the sick company and the company administrator and also from the transferee company and any other company concerned in the amalgamation and from any shareholder or any creditors or employees of such companies. The tribunal has to complete all these procedures within sixty days of receipt of application from company administrator, after satisfying that the scheme had been validly approved in accordance with the provisions of this Act pass an order sanctioning such scheme.

3. Compulsory Amalgamation on Public Interest

The third category of amalgamation discussed under the Companies Act, 2013 is the compulsory amalgamation by Central government in the interest of public. There are two situations in which Central Government can order for compulsory amalgamation. They are:

(i) Amalgamation by Ordinary Companies: The Central Government if satisfied that it is essential in the public interest that two or more companies should amalgamate, by order notified in the Official Gazette, provide for the amalgamation of those companies into a single company with such constitution, with such property, powers, rights, interests, authorities and privileges, and with such liabilities, duties and obligations, as may be specified in the order. The Central government can incorporate such modifications in the draft order in the light of suggestions and objections which may be received by it from any such company within such period as the Central Government may fix on that behalf.[16] Every member or creditor, including a debenture holder, of each of the transferor companies before the amalgamation shall have, as nearly as may be, the same interest in or rights against the transferee company as he had in the company of which he was originally a member or creditor. In case the interest or rights of such member or

16. Section 237.

creditor in or against the transferee company are less than his interest in or rights against the original company, he shall be entitled to compensation to that extent. If any person is aggrieved by the assessment of compensation can approach the Tribunal.

(ii) Amalgamation by Special Kind of Companies: The Companies Act confers the power to issue license to allow a person or association of persons to be registered as a limited company without the addition to its name of the word "Limited", or as the case may be, the words "Private Limited"[17]. This is in cases where a limited company establishes for the purpose of promotion of commerce, art, science, sports, education, research, social welfare, religion, charity, protection of environment or any such other object; intends to apply its profits, if any, or other income in promoting its objects; and intends to prohibit the payment of any dividend to its members. However, the license can be revoked by the Central Government, if the company contravenes any of the requirements of Section 8 or any of the conditions subject to which a licence is issued or the affairs of the company are conducted fraudulently or in a manner violative of the objects of the company or prejudicial to public interest, and without prejudice to any other action against the company. On revocation of licence the Central Government can if it deems fit in the public interest order for amalgamation of such company with another registered company having similar objects. The Central Government by order, provide for such amalgamation to form a single company with such constitution, properties, powers, rights, interest, authorities and privileges and with such liabilities, duties and obligations as may be specified in the order.[18]

4. Fast Track Mergers

Fast Track merger is a merger between two or more small companies or between a holding company and its wholly-owned subsidiary company or such other class or classes of companies as may be prescribed. The Act states that fast track mergers can be entered by the eligible companies subject to the following procedures:

17. Section 8.
18. Section 8(8).

(i) The transferor company or companies and the transferee company, has to submit a notice of the proposed scheme inviting objections or suggestions, if any, from the Registrar and Official Liquidators where registered office of the respective companies are situated or persons affected by the scheme within thirty days of such notice.

(ii) The objections and suggestions, if any received are considered by the companies in their respective general meetings and the scheme is approved by the respective members or class of members at a general meeting holding at least ninety per cent of the total number of shares. This meeting has to be convened by giving a notice of twenty-one days along with the scheme to its creditors.

(iii) Each of the companies involved in the merger files a declaration of solvency, in the prescribed form, with the Registrar of the place where the registered office of the company is situated.

(iv) The transferee company shall file a copy of the scheme so approved in the manner as may be prescribed, with the Central Government, Registrar and the Official Liquidator where the registered office of the company is situated.

(v) On the receipt of the scheme, if the Registrar or the Official Liquidator has no objections or suggestions to the scheme, the Central Government shall register the same and issue a confirmation thereof to the companies.

(vi) If the Registrar or Official Liquidator has any objections or suggestions, he may communicate the same in writing to the Central Government within a period of thirty days. In case if he does not communicate his objection within the said period, it shall be presumed that he has no objection to the scheme.

(vii) If the Central Government after receiving the objections or suggestions or for any reason is of the opinion that such a scheme is not in public interest or in the interest of the creditors, it may file an application before the Tribunal within a period of sixty days of the receipt of the scheme stating its objections and requesting that the Tribunal may consider the scheme under section 232.

(viii) On receipt of an application from the Central Government or from any person, if the Tribunal, for reasons to be recorded in writing, is of the opinion that the scheme should be considered as per the procedure laid down in section 232, the Tribunal may direct accordingly or it may confirm the scheme by passing such order as it deems fit. In case, if the Central Government does not have any objection to the scheme or it does not file any application under this section before the Tribunal, it shall be deemed that it has no objection to the scheme.

(ix) A copy of the order confirming the scheme shall be communicated to the Registrar having jurisdiction over the transferee company and the persons concerned and the Registrar shall register the scheme and issue a confirmation thereof to the companies and such confirmation shall be communicated to the Registrars where transferor Company or companies were situated.

(x) The registration of the scheme shall have the following effects, namely: (*a*) transfer of property or liabilities of the transferor company to the transferee company so that the property becomes the property of the transferee company and the liabilities become the liabilities of the transferee company; (*b*) the charges, if any, on the property of the transferor company shall be applicable and enforceable as if the charges were on the property of the transferee company; (*c*) legal proceedings by or against the transferor company pending before any court of law shall be continued by or against the transferee company; and (*d*) where the scheme provides for purchase of shares held by the dissenting shareholders or settlement of debt due to dissenting creditors, such amount, to the extent it is unpaid, shall become the liability of the transferee company.[19]

5. Cross-Border Mergers

The last category of mergers mentioned under the Companies Act is the Cross-Border Merger. An Indian company is entitled to merge or amalgamate with a foreign company, if such company is in the jurisdiction of a country which is notified by the Central Government. The 1956 Act permits cross-border mergers only where the transferor is a foreign company. In contrast, the 2013 Act permits in-principle mergers between an Indian and a foreign company located in a jurisdiction notified by the central government in periodic consultation with RBI. Such a merger would be subject to RBI approval and Scheme

19. Section 233.

may provide payment in cash or depository receipts or both.[20] The detailed procedure for such an amalgamation may be provided by the Central Government through rules made in consultation with the Reserve Bank of India.[21]

Regulation of Merger under Competition Act, 2002

The Competition Act, 2002 is enacted with a primary objective to promote free and fair competition in the market and thereby ensure the interest of consumers. It contains various provisions to deal with practices which affects the competition in the market such as anti-competitive agreements; abuse of dominant position by dominant firms and regulation of business combinations. The mergers are regulated by the Competition Act, 2002 under the provisions of the Act dealing with combinations. The various provisions relating to regulations of mergers and combinations under the Act have come into force from June 1st, 2011.[22] So also a regulation titled, 'the Competition Commission of India (Procedure in Regard to the Transaction of Business Relating to Combinations) Regulations, 2011', was issued by the Competition Commission of India in the year 2011 with a view to provide a broader framework for merger regulation in India. This regulation was subsequently amended in 2012. At present the Competition Act, 2002 regulates mergers under the sections 5, 6, 20, 29, 30 and 31 of the Act and the allied regulations. The regulation of merger under the Act takes place in different stages, which are as follows:

The starting point of regulation of mergers in India is a notification by merging parties. It is mandatory for firms which propose to enter into a merger to give a notice to the Commission within 30 days of approval of such proposal relating to merger by the board of directors of the firms.[23] It is to be noted that, all mergers are not required to give a notice to the Commission. Only those mergers which come within the threshold limit of assets prescribed under Section 5 (c) of the Act are required to submit a notice. So also there are various categories of mergers which are exempted from the purview of Competition Act,

20. The Section 234; Ajay Kumar Sharma, "Cross-border Mergers Provisions under the Companies Act, 2013: Analysis and Implications", available at http://www.indialawjournal.com/volume7/issue-1/article2.html, visited on 20.4.2015.
21. Section 234.
22. Porter Elliott, *Merger Control: Jurisdictional Comparisons*, Thomson Reuters, (2011), p. 309.
23. The Indian Competition Act, 2002, S. 6(2).

2002 and they are also not required to submit a notice to the Commission.

Applicable Threshold Limit: The Section 5 of the Act prescribes separate thresholds for individuals, group and target level which are as follows:

Individual: Either the value of the combined assets of the enterprises is more than 1,500 crores in India or the combined value of turnover of the enterprise is more than 4,500 crores in India. In case either or both of the enterprises have assets/turnover outside India also, then the combined assets of the enterprises are more than US$ 750 millions, including at least 750 crores in India, or turnover is more than US$ 2250 millions, including at least 2,250 crores in India.[24]

Group: The group to which the enterprise remaining after the merger or the enterprise created as a result of the merger would belong after the merger, have or would have either asset of more than 6000 crores in India or turnover more than 18,000 crores in India. Where the group has presence in India as well as outside India then the group has assets more than US$ 3 billion including at least 750 crores in India or turnover more than US$ 9 billion including at least 2250 crores in India.[25]

Target: The target enterprise (including its subsidiaries, units, or divisions) which is being acquired has assets in more than 250 crores in India or a turnover of more than 750 crores in India.[26]

Exemptions: Under the Competition Act, merger arrangements entered into by public financial institutions, foreign institutional investors, banks or venture capital funds, pursuant to a covenant in a loan agreement or an investment agreement are exempted from submitting notice to CCI.[27] However, in such cases, the acquirer will need to notify

---

24. Section 5(c).
25. Section 5(c).
26. This is because the Government of India, through the Ministry of Corporate Affairs, issued a notification dated 4 March 2011, whereby a combination would not require prior notification to, and approval from, the CCI if the target enterprise (including its divisions, units and subsidiaries) has either assets of the value not exceeding 250 crore in India or turnover not exceeding 750 crore in India for a period of five years. This notification was issued by Central Government by exercising the powers conferred by clause (a) of section 54 of the Competition Act, 2002, in the interest of public.
27. Section 6(4).

the CCI of the acquisition within seven calendar days after completion of merger.[28] So also a list of about 11 transactions mentioned in Schedule I of the Combinations Regulations, 2011 are exempted from the requirement of pre notification. This is because such transactions are ordinarily not likely to cause an AAEC, in the relevant market in India. Recently the Central Government exempts banking company from pre notification requirement by a notification issued under Sec. 45 of the Banking Regulation Act, 1949 for five years from 2013.[29]

Thus every proposed merger if it comes within the threshold of asset value and is not exempted either by the Act or its Regulations or by any Government Notifications is bound to submit a notice to the CCI. On receipt of such notice the CCI has to review the proposed merger with in 210 days and to declare its view. In case of any failure on the part of CCI to do so within 210 days, the merger is deemed to be approved by the CCI.[30] After receipt of notice of proposed merger the Commission has a duty to evaluate about its anti-competitive effect on competition in the relevant market[31]. It is to be noted that, the Commission may, upon its own knowledge or any information relating to merger conduct an inquiry about its Appreciable adverse effect on competition in India. However, the Commission shall not initiate any inquiry after the expiry of one year from the date on which such merger has taken effect.[32] The Competition Act, 2002 under Section 20(4) provides various factors to be taken into account by the Commission while evaluating whether a merger would have the effect of or is likely to have an AAEC in the relevant market. Thus in order to apply these various factors it is essential for the Commission to first determine the relevant market in which the proposed merger would take place. 'Relevant Market' refers to the line of commerce in which competition has been restrained and to the geographic area involved, defined to include all reasonably substitutable products or services, and all nearby competitors, to which consumers could turn in the near term if the restraint or abuse raised prices by a not insignificant amount. A relevant market has therefore two fundamental dimensions, product and geographic. The product market describes the good or service. The geographic market describes

28. Section 6(5).
29. See, S.O. 93(E), Date of Notification 8th day of January, 2013, available at http://cci.gov.in/images/media/notifications/S.O.%2093%20(E)_08012013.pdf, visited on 10.7.2013.
30. Section 31(11).
31. Section 20(2).
32. Section 20(1), Proviso.

the locations of the producers or sellers of the product or service.[33] After such evaluation if the Commission is of the opinion that any merger does not, or is not likely to, have an appreciable adverse effect on competition, it shall, by order, approve such proposed merger[34]. If the Commission is of the opinion that the merger has, or is likely to have, an appreciable adverse effect on competition, it shall direct that the merger shall not take effect[35]. So also if the Commission is of the opinion that the merger has, or is likely to have, an appreciable adverse effect on competition but such adverse effect can be eliminated by suitable modification to such merger, the Commission may propose appropriate modification to the merger, to the parties to such combination. If the parties, who accept the modification proposed by the Commission, carry out such modification within the specified period, the Commission shall, by an order, approve the combination. If the Commission is of the *prima facie* opinion that a merger which has already taken place is likely to cause or has caused an appreciable adverse effect on competition within the relevant market in India, it shall issue a notice to show cause to the parties to merger calling upon them to respond within thirty days of the receipt of such notice[36]. Thus, Commission can conduct inquiry into the mergers which has already taken place but within a period of one year of such merger.[37] The Commission after forming a *prima facie* opinion about the AAEC of a merger which has already taken place can issue a show cause notice to the parties. On receipt of the response of the parties to the merger, the Commission may call for a report from the Director General. After analyzing the response of the parties to the merger, if Commission forms a *prima facie* opinion that the merger has, or is likely to have, an appreciable adverse effect on competition, the Commission can direct the parties to publish the details of such merger. The Commission can give such a direction within seven days of receipt of response from the parties or receipt of report from the Director General. The manner and method of publication is decided by the Commission and the parties have to publish details of merger within 10 working days of such a direction. The purpose of this publication is to bring into the knowledge

33. Dr. S. Chakravarthy, Relevant Market in Competition Case Analyses, available at http://www.circ.in/pdf/Relevant_Market-In-Competition-Case-Analyses.pdf, visited on 10.7.2013.
34. Section 31(1).
35. Section 31(1).
36. Section 29.
37. Section 20 (1), Proviso.

of public and other affected parties of such merger. The Commission can receive any written objections from any person or member of the public affected or likely to be affected by the said merger within fifteen working days from the date of publication of details of the merger. If the Commission wants it can ask for additional information's from the parties. After analyzing all this information the Commission will give its Order regarding such merger. The Competition Act, 2002 provides that the Commission can issue an order either permitting[38] or rejecting the proposed merger[39] or it can give directions for its structural modification.[40] In cases where the merger has already taken place the Commission can direct the parties for any structural modification[41] or the Commission can impose any penalty or initiate prosecution as it deems fit[42]. Thus, it can be seen that the Competition Act, 2002 also provides structural and behavioral remedies for regulation of mergers. The parties or any other persons not satisfied with the orders of CCI can approach the Competition Appellate Tribunal with an appeal within a period of 60 days of receipt of the order/direction/decision of the Commission.[43] Section 32 of the Act allows the CCI extra-territorial jurisdiction to examine a combination between parties outside India and pass orders against it provided that it has an 'appreciable adverse effect' on competition in India. This power is extremely wide and allows the Competition Commission to extend its jurisdiction beyond the Indian shores and declare any qualifying foreign merger or acquisition as void[44].

Merger: Companies Act, 2013 *vis-a-vis* Competition Act, 2002

The regulatory framework dealing with mergers in India is primarily governed by the Companies Act, 2013. However, it does not deal with the effects of merger on competition. To this end, the Indian Parliament enacted the Competition Act, 2002. Though both Company Law and Competition Law regulate the mergers between companies, their purpose is entirely different. The object for providing detailed provisions for the regulation of different categories of mergers under the

---

38. Section 31(1).
39. Section 31(2).
40. Sections. 31(3)-31(7).
41. *Ibid.*
42. Section 31(10).
43. Section 53B.
44. "Competition Laws in India, Analysis and Comparison India, US & EU", available at http://www.indiajuris.com/uploads/publications/pdf/o 139297 5574e comlaw.pdf, visited on 20.4.2015.

Companies Act is the protection of rights and interests of various classes of people associated with the Transferor Company and Transferee Company. However, the purpose of regulation of mergers under competition law is to prevent adverse effect on competition due to such mergers and thereby to ensure there is no distortion of competition in the market. Generally there is an apprehension that, since two separate agencies, i.e. Tribunal and Commission regulates a merger; there is a possibility of diverse opinion regarding the sanction of the proposed merger. It is to be noted here that, both these legislations operating in different filed and regulating mergers with different objective. A proposed merger if it comes into effect may have different consequences. Therefore, it is necessary to obtain sanctions from different agencies established by the Government for regulating merger for different purposes. Hence, even if there is a conflicting view by Tribunal and Commission, it should not be considered as a tussle between these agencies, rather it is the fault of the proposed merger scheme. Another apprehension is about the fast track mergers. It is generally considered the provision for fast track merger may come in direct conflict with the regulation of mergers under the Competition Act. It is to be noted that small company means a company, other than a public company, (*i*) paid-up share capital of which does not exceed fifty lakh rupees or such higher amount as may be prescribed which shall not be more than five crore rupees; or (*ii*) turnover of which as per its last profit and loss account does not exceed two crore rupees or such higher amount as may be prescribed which shall not be more than twenty crore rupees. It can be seen that, the fast track merger involving small companies will not come under the Competition law because such companies are not within the threshold limit prescribed by the Competition Act, 2002. Under the Competition law holding company and its wholly-owned subsidiary company is considered as a single economic unit.[45] A merger or amalgamation between such companies will not be an issue under completion law. Thus, the fast track merger does not create any hardship to the operation of competition law. Another significant concern is about the provision for notice to the sectoral regulators under the Companies Act. According to Section 230(5) a notice along with all the details regarding the proposed merger should be submitted to the Competition Commission. If Commission has any objection regarding

45. See for more, John Temple Lang, "How Can the Problem of the Liability of A Parent Company for Price Fixing by a Wholly-Owned Subsidiary Be Resolved?", *Fordham International Law Journal*, Vol. 37:1481, 2014.

the proposed merger it has to make representation before the Tribunal with in 30 days of receipt of the notice otherwise it will be presumed to have accepted by Commission. It is to be noted that the as per the Competition Act, the Competition Commission has to dispose a notice regarding proposed merger only within 210 days of its receipt. Therefore, the 30 days time limit may encroach the powers of the Commission to deal with a proposed merger. However, it is to be noted that there is a duty on the part of Commission to form a *prima facie* opinion about the anti-competitive effect of the proposed merger within 30 days. Thus since the Commission will form a *prima facie* opinion within 30 days, the time limit fixed under Companies Act will not be an encroachment to the powers of Commission. This is because if there is no *prima facie* opinion about the anti-competitive effect, the Commission will approve such merger. In case if the Commission forms a *prima facie* opinion about its anti-competitive effect, they can make a representation to the Tribunal.

Conclusion

The enactment of Companies Act, 2013 is considered as a welcome step as it intends to equip the corporate law in India to meet the challenges posed by the development in international trade and commerce. The Act provides comprehensive provisions for the regulation of mergers and amalgamation between companies. It introduces the concept of fast track mergers as well as it allows the cross-border mergers. Every merger or amalgamation will have bring prospect to the merging parties in one way or other. At the same time this type of business combinations may pose threat to the competitors of the merging companies or it may restrict the competition in the market where such companies are operating. Hence, it is necessary to scrutinize the anti-competitive effect of such mergers and amalgamations. This duty is entrusted to the Competition Commission of India as per the provisions of Competition Act. The effective implementation of both legislations are highly necessary for protecting the interest and rights of various stakeholders involved in a company and to ensure effective and fair competition in the market. Therefore, it can be concluded that, the regulation of merger and amalgamation by Companies, Act, 2013 and Competition Act, 2002 is not contradictory but complementary to each other.

12

Competition Laws and Cross-Border Mergers & Amalgamations

DR. SOUVIK CHATTERJI

Introduction

Cross-Border Mergers had gained momentum in India over the last 15 years. the Indian legal system regulates and governs various aspects of a cross-border Mergers and Acquisitions transaction by a set of laws, most importantly the Companies Act, 1956; the Foreign Investment Policy of the government of India along with press notes and clarificatory circulars issued by the Department of Investment Policy and Promotion; Foreign Exchange Management Act, 1999 (FEMA) and regulations made there under, including circulars and notifications issued by the RBI from time to time (hereinafter together referred to as the FEMA laws); the Securities and Exchange Board of India Act, 1992 and regulations made thereunder (hereinafter together referred to as SEBI laws); the Income Tax Act, 1961 and the Competition Act, 2002, as amended by the Competition (Amendment) Act, 2007.

Framework under Competition Law and Companies Law

The Competition Act, 2002, as amended by the Competition (Amendment) Act, 2007 had defined all types of mergers, acquisitions and amalgamations as combinations under section 5 of the Act. The treatments of combinations are same under the Competition Act for mergers, amalgamations, acquisitions, etc. Sub-section (5) of Section

230 of the Companies Act provides for sending sub-section (3) notice and other prescribed documents to the sectoral regulators and other authorities who are likely to be affected by the compromise or arrangement, to enable these regulators and authorities to make any representations on the proposals within the prescribed 30 days period. Competition Commission of India (CCI), which is arguably the Indian super-regulator, is expressly to be provided with the said notice and documents, *if necessary*. The dual requirement of allowing CCI to make representations before the tribunal and under the Competition Act to seek mandatory sanction is unnecessary, and cumbersome for the companies concerned. Further an anomalous situation may be created, if the CCI does not object or make any representation before the tribunal and later on declines to grant sanction, as required under Section 31(1) of the Competition Act. Instead, representations by CCI should be omitted in the sub section (5) of Section 230, as it will have authority to block the merger when the 'combination' proposal comes for its approval. Mergers and acquisitions are regulated under various laws in India. The objective of the laws is to make these deals transparent and protect the interest of all shareholders. Firstly, they are regulated through the provisions of the Companies Act, 1956. The Act lays down the legal procedures for mergers or acquisitions:

(a) **Permission for merger:** Two or more companies can amalgamate only when the amalgamation is permitted under their memorandum of association. Also, the acquiring company should have the permission in its object clause to carry on the business of the acquired company. In the absence of these provisions in the memorandum of association, it is necessary to seek the permission of the shareholders, board of directors and the Company Law Board before affecting the merger.

(b) **Information to the stock exchange:** The acquiring and the acquired companies should inform the stock exchanges (where they are listed) about the merger.

(c) **Approval of board of directors:** The board of directors of the individual companies should approve the draft proposal for amalgamation and authorise the managements of the companies to further pursue the proposal.

(d) **Application in the High Court:** An application for approving the draft amalgamation proposal duly approved by the board of directors of the individual companies should be made to the High Court.

(e) **Shareholders and creators meetings:** The individual companies should hold separate meetings of their shareholders and creditors for approving the amalgamation scheme. At least, 75 per cent of shareholders and creditors in separate meeting, voting in person or by proxy, must accord their approval to the scheme.

(f) **Sanction by the High Court:** After the approval of the shareholders and creditors, on the petitions of the companies, the High Court will pass an order, sanctioning the amalgamation scheme after it is satisfied that the scheme is fair and reasonable. The date of the court's hearing will be published in two newspapers, and also, the regional director of the Company Law Board will be intimated.

(g) **Filing of the Court order:** After the Court order, its certified true copies will be filed with the Registrar of Companies.

(h) **Transfer of assets and liabilities:** The assets and liabilities of the acquired company will be transferred to the acquiring company in accordance with the approved scheme, with effect from the specified date.

(i) **Payment by cash or securities:** As per the proposal, the acquiring company will exchange shares and debentures and/or cash for the shares and debentures of the acquired company. These securities will be listed on the stock exchange.

The other law which regulates mergers and acquisitions include The Competition Act, 2002, as amended by The Competition (Amendment) Act, 2007. The Act regulates the various forms of business combinations through Competition Commission of India. Under the Act, no person or enterprise shall enter into a combination, in the form of an acquisition, merger or amalgamation, which causes or is likely to cause an appreciable adverse effect on competition in the relevant market and such a combination shall be void. Enterprises intending to enter into a combination may give notice to the Commission, but this notification is voluntary. But, all combinations do not call for scrutiny unless the resulting combination exceeds the threshold limits in terms of assets or turnover as specified by the Competition Commission of India.[1] The Commission while regulating a 'combination' shall consider the following factors:

---

1. The Thresholds are mentioned in section 5 of the Competition Act, 2002, as amended by the Competition (Amendment) Act, 2007.

- Actual and potential competition through imports;
- Extent of entry barriers into the market;
- Level of combination in the market;
- Degree of countervailing power in the market;
- Possibility of the combination to significantly and substantially increase prices or profits;
- Extent of effective competition likely to sustain in a market;
- Availability of substitutes before and after the combination;
- Market share of the parties to the combination individually and as a combination;
- Possibility of the combination to remove the vigorous and effective competitor or competition in the market;
- Nature and extent of vertical integration in the market;
- Nature and extent of innovation; and
- Whether the benefits of the combinations outweigh the adverse impact of the combination.

Thus, the Competition Act does not seek to eliminate combinations and only aims to eliminate their harmful effects.

Mandatory Merger Notification Regime in India

The Competition Act, 2002, in India could not be implemented in 2002, due to writ petitions being filed in Supreme Court and after requisite amendments being made the Act came into force which was titled Competition Act, 2002, as amended by the Competition (Amendment) Act, 2007. Amongst a number of provisions which faced criticism, probably the provisions relating to mergers and acquisitions which are called combinations under the new Act faced the maximum criticism. Stakeholders, lawyers, economists questioned the fact whether making merger notification compulsory will promote the new companies which want to do business in India in different sectors. Mr. M.M. Sharma, a former Registrar of CCI and Head (Competition Law and Policy) at law firm Vaish Associates said that India is perhaps the only nation in recent times that had brought into force its Competition Act in bits and pieces, by notifying one section after the other. China notified its anti-monopoly legislation in August 2008 in one go, said Mr. Sharma. Among the key sections in the amended Competition Act of India the major provisions included Section 3 (on cartels and anti-competitive pacts regarding production, storage, distribution, and supply), Section 4 (abuse of dominant position by companies), Sections 5 and 6 (pertaining to M&A regulations). The Government notified Sections 3 and 4 in May. But it notified Sections 5 and 6 later. As a result, several mergers and acquisitions which otherwise would have come up before the CCI have gone through unquestioned. "Besides, the two-year period to wind up CCI's predecessor, the Monopolies and Restrictive Trade Practices Commission, was too long and has led to forum-shopping," Mr. Sharma said in an interview. Then Corporate Affairs Minister, Mr. Salman Khurshid, recently said the issues surrounding Sections 5 and 6 of the Act are before then Prime Minister, Dr. Manmohan Singh, even as the Government was considering last minute suggestions from stakeholders. As far as the justification for making notification of combinations (Mergers and Acquisitions) in India mandatory, the CCI had thought that with development of infrastructure in different sectors like electricity, telecom, roadways, airways, etc., a lot of combinations are destined to take place between Indian and foreign companies. In that perspective, the CCI can regulate combinations that cross the threshold limit created by the Competition Act, 2002, as amended by the Competition (Amendment) Act, 2007;[2] only if the notification is made mandatory. If it was voluntary, many companies could have escaped the review of the CCI in spite of crossing the threshold limit. At the same time the CCI does not want any of these big companies to gain that amount of market share from where they can control the market and abuse their dominance. Neither the CCI want the giant companies in entering into combinations and get involved in predatory pricing and driving out the rest of the companies from the market. The Competition Act, 2002, as amended by the Competition (Amendment) Act, 2007, had been enacted after examining the competition laws of most of the other countries of the world, like US, UK, Canada, etc. Most of the countries had mandatory notification and India is no exception to it.

The CCI's (Amendment Regulations) of 2011 and (Amendment Regulations) of 2013

The CCI had brought in Amendment Regulations in 2011 and 2013 to amend the thresholds and process relating to combination review under the Competition Act.[3] According to that regulation the value of

2. Section 5 of the Competition Act, 2002, as amended by the Competition (Amendment) Act, 2007.
3. It is called The Competition Commission of India (Procedure in regard to the transaction of business relating to combinations) Amendment Regulations, 2011 and Competition Commission of India (Procedure in regard to the transaction of business relating to combinations) Amendment Regulations, 2013.

assets include the brand value, goodwill, value of intellectual property, but not the depreciation. Highlighting the amendments made to Schedule 1 of the Combination Regulations, 2013 which describes categories of transactions not likely to have appreciable adverse effect on competition in India, the CII Press Release said the change exempting intra-group Mergers and Acquisitions of two or more enterprises where more than 50 per cent shares or voting rights of the other enterprises are held by enterprise(s) within the same group is vital.[4]

Conclusion

It can be said that Indian Competition regime is at its infancy. After the enactment of the Act hardly ten years had not elapsed. In that scenario, any provision under the new law can be analyzed on the basis of experiences from foreign countries. There are not many cases in India that can be studied to back up the efficacy of mandatory regime. The dual requirement of allowing CCI to make representations before the tribunal and under the Competition Act to seek mandatory sanction is unnecessary and cumbersome for the companies concerned in the context of cross-border mergers and amalgamations. Further an anomalous situation may be created, if the CCI does not object or make any representation before the tribunal and later on declines to grant sanction, as required under Section 31(1) of the Competition Act. Instead, representations by CCI should be omitted in the sub-section (5) of Section 230, as it will have authority to block the merger when the 'combination' proposal comes for its approval. It can be predicted that mandatory regime can bring many controversial combinations within the scanner of CCI and the combinations can be ratified after minor changes that are to be made according to the directives of CCI.

---

4. CII Welcomes Amendments to Combination Regulations, 9th April, 2013, available at http://www.indiainfoline.com/Markets/News/CII-welcomes-amendments-to-Combination-Regulations/5655558832

CHAPTER VI

Corporate Social Responsibility

13

Section 135 of the Companies Act, 2013: An Impetus for Promotion of CSR in India

SUBHANKAR DAS

Introduction

Corporate Social Responsibility or CSR as it is popularly known is an important concept in relation to societal welfare schemes adopted by various companies in different countries across the globe. As a discipline pertaining to community welfare, there have been different definitions and conceptions of CSR which have evolved over the due course of time. As enunciated under the Companies Act, 2013, Sec. 135 provides that companies having a net worth of Rs. 500 crores, or having a turnover of Rs. 1000 crore or net profits worth Rs. 5 crore are supposed to invest 2 per cent of their average net profits under CSR activities, formulate an independent CSR board for formulation of CSR activities and provide a detailed layout as to the CSR policies and objectives undertaken by it in the current financial year.[1] In case proper spending is not done on CSR activities in a particular financial year, it is the duty of the CSR committee, set-up by the concerned company, to give details as to why such necessary spending could not be formulated and where the company lagged behind in doing the same. The Government of India had introduced the Companies Bill, 2012 with the objective of making

1. The Companies Act, 2013 (Act 18 of 2013).

CSR spending mandatory among companies in India with the aim of giving an upliftment to CSR activities in India.[2] This bill was later enacted in 2013 and its provisions became enforceable upon all kinds of companies in India after the 1st of April 2014. Though the intention of the Government is aimed at boosting up CSR activities in India by making CSR a duty rather than a privilege for major companies in the markets, yet it cannot be the sole reason of completely regarding it as one which is a proper mechanism for CSR upliftment in the country. In order to develop a comprehensible understanding about the effectiveness of the legal provisions under the Companies Act, 2013, making CSR a statutory or mandatory duty rather than a matter of privilege,[3] there is a need to make a clear-cut analysis as to the provisions enlisted under Section 135 and by virtue of a careful understanding of the provisions, find out the intention or rationale behind adopting the said provision and then conclude as to the extent of its effectiveness in promotion of CSR activities in India.[4]

The Intention Behind Section 135

The Companies Act, 2013 has laid down the pre-requisites or the criteria for Companies who are under an obligation to make necessary contributions to CSR activities under the said Act. But, for the purpose of developing a critical understanding about the applicability of Section 135 as a mandatory provision for Corporate Social Responsibility in India, it is essential to first clearly understand the intention behind enacting the Companies Act and introducing necessary guidelines under the Act for promoting CSR in India.[5] As per the report delivered by the Planning Commission of India in pursuance to collection of data during the 2011 Census, it was found that India had around 21.9 per cent people living below poverty line, i.e. around 269.3 million people are still living below poverty line.[6] Besides that, India is home to 400

---

2. Editorial, "New Companies Bill Mandates CSR Spending", *The Hindu*, Dec. 19, 2012.
3. Monica Vincent, "CSR Can Play a Positive Role", *The New Indian Express*, April 6, 2014.
4. Archit Gupta, "Mandatory CSR in the Companies Bill, 2011: Are We There, Yet?" 8 NSLR 37(2013).
5. Caroline Van Zile, "India's Mandatory Corporate Social Responsibility Proposal: Creative Capitalism Meets Creative Regulation in the Global Market", 13 APLPJ 269 (2012).
6. Press Note on Poverty Estimates, 2011-12, Government of India, July 2013, available at : http://planningcommission.nic.in/news/pre_pov2307.pdf (Visited on April 3, 2015).

million, i.e. around one-third of the world's total poor population resides in India.[7] Besides that, according to a survey conducted by the World Bank, it was found that around 32.7 per cent of the Indian population lived below $1.25 a day, i.e. the minimum standard requirement set by World Bank for fulfilment of basic requirements of individuals.[8] Taking into due consideration the gravity of the situation prevalent to poverty in India, the Government of India felt the need for a regulatory framework or mechanism wherein companies earning a major share of India's income could be made to contribute towards societal welfare schemes for eradication of poverty and unemployment.[9] According to a report published by UNESCO, India contains around 287 million of total illiterates of the world which is a staggering 37 per cent of the world's total illiterate population and besides that it has the highest percentage of the illiterate adults in India.[10] Further, the World Bank in its report has stated that India had an infant mortality rate of 43 births per 1000 in 2013 which is among the highest in the world. The Government of India has aimed at the fulfilment of following Millennium Development Goals formulated by the United Nations for eradication of poverty and promotion of welfare can be briefly elaborated as follows:[11]

1. Eradication of extreme poverty and hunger.
2. Achievement of universal primary education.
3. Promotion of Gender Equality and women empowerment.
4. Reduction of Child Mortality Rates.
5. Improvement in Maternal Health.
6. Combating important diseases such as HIV/AIDS, malaria and other important diseases.
7. Ensuring the environment sustainability.

Taking into account the fact that a major section of India's population still languishes in poverty even after more than 67 years of

---

7. Dean Nelson, "India has one-third of world's poorest, says World Bank", *The Telegraph*, April 18, 2014.
8. The World Bank, available at: http://data.worldbank.org/country/india (Visited on April 2, 2015).
9. Arpita Ghosh, "Mandatory Corporate Social Responsibility in India", 1 CLA 114 (2013).
10. Editorial, "India's illiterate population largest in the world says UNESCO report", *The Hindu*, Jan. 30, 2014.
11. United Nations Millennium Development Goals 2015, available at: http://www.un.org/millenniumgoals/ (Visited on April 3, 2015).

Independence, prompted the Government of India to formulate a mechanism by virtue of which entrepreneurs and major corporate by the application of their minds and ideas could be made to help in formulating effective policies and guidelines in order to ensure that the country goes a long way in its endeavor of poverty eradication and promotion of health care and population.[12] Talking about CSR as such, the government has tried to put in the best of its efforts for the purpose of promoting societal welfare through corporate involvement and that actually forms the core essence of Section 135 of the Companies Act, 2013.[13] Though CSR in India traces its roots back to the times of the British Raj, yet there was no legal framework for the purpose of conducting CSR in India. Many companies in India in the absence of proper legal framework or a regulatory mechanism, except few companies, there were a plethora of companies that were escaping the compulsion of investing in CSR activities as a part of their duty towards society rather than a privilege that could be exercised by them.[14] Thus, with the objective of making CSR contribution legally binding upon companies fulfilling the desired criteria, Section 135 was enlisted as one of the important provisions under the Companies Act, 2013 for promoting CSR in India.[15] Sachin Pilot, then Minister of Corporate Affairs had stated that, because of the Companies Act, 2013, companies fulfilling the satisfactory criteria would be investing around rupees 15,000 to 20,000 crore for the purpose of CSR activities.[16] He further stated this provision was one which was first of its kind and had the capability of leading to an increase in the CSR spending by the Companies having an income of 500 crores or with turnover of 1000 crores or more and would help the Government in involving leading corporate of the country in the societal welfare schemes with the help of Section 135 of the Companies Act, 2013.[17] Thus, with regards to the

12. Akshay, Divanshu Gupta, Dhruv Kaushal and Chitrangada Sharma, "Corporate Social Responsibility in Companies Bill, 2012: A critical dissection", 51 CLA 113(2013).
13. Anshul Agarwal, "The New Spectrum of Corporate Social Responsibility in Emerging Economies", 1 IJEMR 4 (2014).
14. Prachi Arora, "Incorporate Corporate Social Responsibility Strategy into Business", 1 SIJ 2 (2013).
15. Aditi Rani, "Decoding of Provisions relating to Corporate Social Responsibility in Sec 135 of the Companies Act", 43 CLA 122 (2014).
16. Editorial, "Companies to spend Rs. 15-20k crore a year on CSR", *The Economic Times*, Sept. 10, 2013.
17. Editorial, "CSR rules to be finalized by January first week: Sachin Pilot", *The Economic Times*, Dec. 29, 2013.

intention behind the abovementioned act, it can be clearly enunciated that the purpose behind it is for providing a legal framework or provision by virtue of which CSR spending can be done by involving the major companies of India and making it a duty for them to spend a percentage of their profits for promotion of societal welfare schemes as per the Millennium Development Goals laid down by the United nations for eradication of poverty, hunger and illiteracy by virtue of involvement of the corporate players in India. Though this said provision in the particular Act, clearly specifies or enunciates before us the intention of the Government behind the passing of the said Act, yet by merely accepting it as a device for the effective promotion of CSR can in no way said to be correct.

Critical Analysis of the Provision of Section 135

No act or statute passed till date has been immune from errors, ambiguities or lacunas, be it India or in any other country and Section 135 is no exception in this regard. Section 135 has ambiguous provisions in it along with the prospective of making CSR more viable or making CSR more regularized in India. It is a provision which is more like a double-edged sword.[18] It contains both the good and the bad, i.e. neither it is a full proof mechanism or layout for CSR in India nor it can it be completely said to be bad as at presently it functions as the only regulatory device for CSR activities and promotion of CSR in India.[19] For the purpose of ascertainment of the effectiveness of provisions pertaining to Corporate Social Responsibility under Section 135 of the Companies Act, 2013, there is a need to develop a critical understanding of the said provisions enlisted under the abovementioned Act. The biggest problem under the Act is the fact that, though CSR has been given utmost importance the problem lies in the defining what constitutes CSR. By a thorough observation of the provisions enlisted under Section 135, it can be said that this provision lacks the basic definition as to what essentially constitutes "CSR" or what actually is CSR? Can the existence of CSR be possible without the provision of a proper definition as to what it essentially talks about?[20] The said Act,

18. Rama Mohan R. Turaga and George Kandathil, "Defining the Corporate Social Responsibility of Business: Whose Business is it?" 7 EPW 49 (2014).
19. Shachi Rai and Sangeet Bansal, "An Analysis of Corporate Social Responsibility Expenditure in India", 50 EPW 49 (2014).
20. Academike, "Section 135 and the Concept of Revolutionary Legislation: The fine line in between", available at: http://www.lawctopus.com/ academike/

fails to answer this fundamental question as to what exactly constitutes CSR. In the absence of a proper definition as to what the concerned provision actually talks about or constitutes of, the Act on the face of it is deemed to be irrelevant. However, this is just the beginning; the author would be further delving into the so-called ambiguous provisions of the Act to provide an idea as to why the concerned Section 135 is not a conclusive method of promoting CSR in India. Moving ahead, if we take a closer look at the provisions of the said Act, Companies having net profits of 5 crores and 500 crores of valuation or a turnover of 1000 crores per year are legally bound to invest 2 per cent of annual profits for purpose of CSR activities in every financial year. Now, the question that crops up in the present context is, why would a company earning say 450 crores per year or having a turnover of 950 crores or having a net profit of 4.5 crores would not be eligible to invest 2 per cent of its net profits for the purpose of CSR activities? Though the law and policy-makers have clearly laid down the requisite earnings that are essential to make a company legally bound under the Act, to invest in CSR activities, but, the question that has been unresolved is as to why only a company earning profit of 5 crores, valued at 500 crores or having turnover of 1000 crores will be eligible for investing in CSR activities.[21] This Act in no way enunciates clearly as to why companies having a net profit of Rs. 5 crores or 500 crores of net worth and a turnover of 1000 crores are only eligible to take part in CSR activities. The Act fails to explain as to why companies earning less are ineligible to take part in CSR activities. If it is presumed that, if companies having an income or turnover lesser than that of the above mentioned amounts would be unable to invest in CSR in a proper manner and by doing so will neglect their own company's basic requirements and would be more of a burden on them, then why is to so that companies fulfilling the criteria mentioned under the Act would be able to spend on CSR activities in an effective and efficient manner?[22] In relation to the second question, there can be no conclusive answer as to the correctness of this particular

section-135-the-concept-of-revolutionary-legislation-the-fine-line-in-between/ (Visited on March 27, 2015).

21. Sanjay Kumar Sharma, "A 360 degree analysis of Corporate Social Responsibility (CSR) Mandate of the New Companies Act, 2013", 3 GJMBS 7 (2013).

22. *Lawyers Club India*, "Critical Analysis on Corporate Social Responsibility", available at: http://www.lawyersclubindia.com/articles/Critical-Analysis-on-Corporate-Social-Responsibility--5918.asp#.VSoiI_mUe4E (Visited on April 7, 2015).

provision. If the law is based on the general presumption that only companies fulfilling the criteria can effectively contribute to the CSR activities, then only the provision can be said to be of any substance. But, this particular provision leaves two things unanswered: Firstly, whether imposing CSR on companies having lesser earnings is not justified? Secondly, why is it that, only companies with the said earnings can effectively contribute to CSR without feeling any pressure or burden upon them? Thus, the author would like to comment that whether this particular aspect of Section 135 is good or bad, cannot be answered affirmatively, rather this can only be answered once a thorough scrutiny of the said provision is made by law and policy-makers in India. Moreover, Section 135 is a mandatory provision pertaining to Corporate Social Responsibility under the Companies Act, 2013. The question is, whether such a mandatory provision is justified?[23] And whether a company that is not interested in investing in CSR activities be made bound to make investment in such activities?[24] The abovementioned provision of the Companies Act makes CSR mandatory for the companies fulfilling the requisite criteria. The fundamental question raised is whether this is voluntary or involuntary? The biggest problem in this Act is relation to the question as to whether companies should be legally obliged to spend 2 per cent of net profits in the form of CSR activities.[25] The arguments in relation to this can be two-fold. Firstly, unless there is a mandatory provision, there is a possibility of certain companies avoiding CSR spending due to absence of a legal obligation. We are well aware of the fact, that companies have the ability of devising certain methods for tax avoidance and other purposes, and unless there is a strict liability imposed upon them, it is difficult to increase spending on CSR activities.[26] This apparently is the intention of the Government, that is to provide a framework for conducting CSR in a regulated manner, but then this is only one part of the story, there is a need to

23. *Business Today*, "The New CSR rules: Confusion or clarity", available at: http://businesstoday.intoday.in/story/new-csr-rules-ministry-of-corporate-affairs-company-law/1/204363.html (Visited on April 9, 2015).
24. Editorial, "Companies Bill passed with mandate on CSR spending", *The Indian Express*, Feb. 22, 2013.
25. Sarayu Satish, "Corporate Social Responsibility under Companies Act, 2013: Voluntary or Mandatory?" PL November 64 (2014).
26. Mondaq, "India: Corporate Social Responsibility: Mandating Companies To Contribute Towards Society", available at: http://www.mondaq.com/india/x/305620/Corporate+Commercial+Law/Corporate+Social+Responsibility+Mandating+Companies+To+Contribute+Towards+Society.

look at the negative aspect of the Act, i.e. the mandatory CSR provision. The negative aspect of mandatory CSR is the fact this is more of a burden on the companies, rather than an encouragement of earning goodwill through investment in CSR, i.e. societal welfare schemes. The whole point is as to why does the concerned government want to forcibly bring out CSR investments from the companies fulfilling the eligibility criteria under Section 135? Suppose the company suffers a loss, and for some reason or the other unable to make investment in CSR activities, how are they supposed to justify their inability of non-compliance with the CSR policies?[27] The said Act does not give a proper definition in regard to the abovementioned questions. In the opinion of the author, the abovementioned act fails to answer such questions in the affirmative, i.e. it fails to provide a justification for the purpose of CSR making mandatory as a provision under the Companies Act, 2013. Moving further in this section, there is another point to be considered. As mentioned above, Schedule VII of the Act has laid down the defined goals which are parts of the Millennium Development Goals of the United Nations and which our country seeks to achieve through CSR under Section 135 of the Companies Act. There are two problems in relation to having a defined set of goals to be fulfilled. At the first instance, by limiting CSR to the said Millennium Development Goals plans, there is a possibility or there is a risk of limiting the scope of CSR to an extent such that it makes difficult to make investments in other aspects or issues of societal welfare pertaining to India. Secondly, if there is an increase in the scope or the ambit of the societal welfare schemes, there is a risk of always increasing or widening the ambit too much which makes it tough for determining the activities which are to be part of CSR and which are not to be taken into consideration while making investments in CSR.[28] At one point of time, it can be said that by limiting activities coming under CSR we are grossly neglecting other important issues pertaining to societal welfare that need due consideration. At the same time, by increasing the ambit to a wider level there is always a risk of making things too complicated in relation to

27. India Corp Law, "Draft Rules under Companies Act, 2013", available at: http://indiacorplaw.blogspot.in/2013/09/draft-rules-under-companies-act-csr.html (Visited on April 3, 2015).
28. CA Club India, "Corporate Social Responsibility Under Companies Act, 2013: Sec 135", available at: http://www.caclubindia.com/articles/section-135-of-companies-act-2013-csr-19349.asp#.VSqqLPmUe4E (Visited on April 9, 2015).

investments pertaining to CSR activities in India.[29] This is one important aspect of the said provision which fails to explain the logic behind limitation of CSR activities. Furthermore, it is not completely wrong or completely correct to do so, i.e. this is a provision which is not a full proof method of promoting CSR, rather this is one which is confusing in nature and that cannot be construed to be satisfactory by any means.[30] This is an important issue that needs to be addressed in relation to Section 135. The reason being as to the fact whether there should be a limitation on activities, the promotion of which forms the basic purpose or objective behind Section 135. This is one area which remains unanswered and is an unresolved part of the said provision under the Companies Act, 2013 and requires strict scrutiny. Besides the abovementioned points, there is another provision under the Act, which states that the companies are supposed to give preference to the local areas or the geographical area of its operations for the purpose of CSR activities.[31] At one point of time, it is a good example of how there can be a building of a strong network chain between the area concerned and the company, but then, this particular aspect again has its share of lacunas, i.e. it does not talk about increasing the ambit of CSR or the areas in which CSR activities are to be undertaken by the concerned companies.[32] This again leaves a big question mark as to the applicability or effectiveness of the concerned provision. At one point of time there is an attempt made to increase the volume of CSR activities in India, but at the other point the companies are to give preference to local or their own concerned geographical areas of operation.[33] Besides that, companies aren't bound to increase their areas of operation or there is

29. Aksana Neah Ch, Marak and O.P. Singh, "Environmental Protection and Sustainability through Corporate Social Responsibility in India: An Analysis under the Companies Act, 2013 of India", 3 RJAEM 12 (2014).
30. Chhavi Mathur, "Sec. 135, Companies Act, 2013: A Game Changer for Corporate Social Responsibility", 1 IJBMR 1 (2014).
31. KPMG, "New Companies Act, 2013—Insight Series, Volume IV, Corporate Social Responsibility", available at: https://www.kpmg.com/Global/en/IssuesAndInsights/ArticlesPublications/taxnewsflash/Documents/india-sept20-2013no4companies.pdf (Visited on April 7, 2015).
32. Lakshmi Kumaran and Sridharan Attorneys, "Understanding Corporate Social Responsibility (CSR)", available at: http://www.lakshmisri.com/News-and-Publications/Publications/Articles/Corporate/understanding-corporate-social-responsibility (Visited on April 5, 2015).
33. Indian Institute of Corporate Affairs, "Corporate IICA Newsletter Odyssey, 2013", available at: http://iica.in/images/IICA_NL_121113_LR.pdf (Visited on April 3, 2015).

no substantive explanation as to how the areas of operation are to be justifiably increased in a reasonable manner.[34] This is again an important question that remains unanswered and serves to be yet another example as to how Section 135 is an ineffective provision for promotion of CSR in India. Besides the abovementioned criticisms, there is another major unspecified provision in this Act which relates to tax deduction for participation in CSR activities, i.e. the provision pertaining to the payment of additional taxes. There is a provision that talks about a company's eligibility of receiving deduction on taxability or benefits on taxation for investments in CSR activities under the said Act. The provisions under this Act state that there can be a tax deduction if the said company donates the 2 per cent net profits to the Prime Minister's relief fund as part of its investment and contribution to Corporate Social Responsibility activities in India.[35] However, for CSR investments in the other activities concerned, i.e. the activities that are part of the Millennium Development Goals, fulfilment of which is the basic aim or objective behind beside the formulation of Section 135 of the Companies Act, 2013. Besides that 2 per cent net profits is the profit before actual tax, which is a kind of double taxation that has been imposed upon the companies by virtue of this provision.[36] Further, if there is any amount of money left after CSR spending, there is no clarity as to whether this amount is to be a part of the taxes paid by the company or whether it is to be utilized by the company in any other form according to its own will or whether the leftover amount is to be invested in CSR only?[37] This particular provision again brings forth before us an important question or an important aspect as to the taxes to be paid on the company. Though it is important that companies pay the requisite amount of taxes from the earnings they make, however, imposition of an additional tax burden is unjustified on them. Though CSR is largely mandatory by virtue of the said Act, yet if a particular provision is responsible for imposition of an additional tax burden on

---

34. Arjya B. Majumdar, "India's Journey With Corporate Social Responsibility—What Next", available at: http://papers.ssrn.com/sol3/papers.cfm? abstract_id=2545804&download=yes (Visited on April 7, 2015).
35. Afra Afsharipur and Shruti Rana, "The Emergence of New Corporate Social Responsibility Regimes in China and India", 14 U.C. DBLJ 175 (2013).
36. Lubna Kably, "CSR spends to get cost varying tax benefits", *The Times of India*, Aug. 13, 2013.
37. Moving the Law, "CSR under Companies Act, 2013: From Choice, to Necessity, to Compulsion", available at: http://mowingthelaw. blogspot.in/ 2015/03/csr-under-companies-act-2013-from.html (Visited on April 2, 2015).

the Companies, which in a way vitiates the spirit or the essence of having the provision i.e. for encouraging companies to invest under CSR.[38] Even if it is more of a legal duty more than a voluntary form of contributions, yet in no way it should burden the companies so that they are made to think twice before adjusting their expenses in a manner so that they can sustain themselves along with making the requisite contributions to CSR activities in India.[39] There is no justification behind taxation benefits in relation to contribution to the Prime Minister's Relief Fund and imposition of an additional tax burden in the name of contribution to the CSR activities in India. Thus, if a proper involvement is to be sought out from various companies in relation to making investments for the purpose of promotion of CSR activities or societal welfare schemes, the policies pertaining to it are to be devised in such a manner, that it does not impose an additional burden on the concerned companies in the name of making CSR a legal obligation rather than a matter of privilege for most companies in India. Whatever is the case, any act or provision that is responsible for imposition of an additional tax burden on the concerned companies has to be scrutinized in a responsible and thorough manner before actually imposing it upon companies operating in India and making it their duty to invest in CSR schemes in the country.[40] Above all, Section 135 of the Act lays down that a company failing to invest the requisite amount for the purpose of CSR activities is to submit a report of its failure to do so by means of the independent committee formed by it for the purpose of carrying out CSR activities. The Act fails to lay down as to whether a penalty is to be imposed upon companies for non-compliance with CSR regulations or can companies get away with the non-compliance by only submitting a report in that regard? [41] It is well known that if there is an

38. Law Mantra, "Legislative Force Backing Corporate Social Responsibility in India—The Way to Go?, available at: http://lawmantra.co.in/legislative-force-backing-corporate-social-responsibility-in-india-the-way-to-go/ (Visited on April 9, 2015).
39. Legal Services India, "CSR under The Companies Act, 2013", available at: http://www.legalservicesindia.com/article/article/csr-under-the-companies-act-2013-1704-1.html (Visited on April 7, 2015).
40. BCAS Online, "Corporate Social Responsibility—Companies Act, 2013", available at: https://www.bcasonline.org/articles/artin.asp?1133 (Visited on April 9, 2015).
41. Nishith Desai Associates, "New Rules for CSR announced", available at: http://www.nishithdesai.com/information/research-and-articles/nda-hotline /nda-hotline-single-view/article/new-rules-for-corporate-social-responsibility-

Act which prescribes a particular duty upon a particular entity or individual then it should be stringent enough to be able to properly prosecute, penalize or strictly seek justification in a legalized and effective manner for those who act in contravention to the duties imposed upon them by virtue of the concerned provisions under a defined Act in force in a country. If a closer look is taken at the concerned Act, this Act talks about imposing a duty upon the companies to provide a report as to their inability to make spending in relation to CSR activities. But, what if the companies submit a false report? If proper ethics aren't practiced by people who constitutes the CSR committee? This Act prescribes no proper mechanism or device wherein there can be a penalty imposed upon a company for failure in compliance with the mandate of CSR spending. In addition to that, there is also no proper mechanism or manner by virtue of which there can be a punishment that can be imposed for holding liable companies submitting false reports or claims to supplement their inabilities of complying with the CSR provisions, i.e. failure to make investments in CSR activities during a particular financial year.[42] Thus, it can be concluded that the provision of Sec. 135 of the Companies Act, 2013 is in no way sufficient enough for promoting CSR in India and what has been done and what is needed to be done further for the purpose of rectifying the ambiguities surrounding Section 135 of the Act pertaining to Corporate Social Responsibility in India.

The Way Ahead

Though the provision under Section 135 has a certain number of ambiguities in the enlisted provisions, yet there is always a scope for improvement. The Companies Amendment Bill, 2014 is a good example of the efforts that have been made for the resurrecting the errors committed under the Companies Act, 2013 and bring about a sense of reform in relation to the Companies Act itself. However, the bill lacks the capacity or the provisions for bringing CSR reforms in India. There is a need to define as to what essentially is "CSR" for a better understanding of CSR as a provision enlisted under the said Act rather

in-india-its-effectiveness-and-legality.html?no_cache=1&c Hash=c3c9597008f8602ff6430feed1b03360 (Visited on March 29, 2015).

42. Dr. T.P. Ghosh, T.P. Ghosh on *Companies Act, 2013*, 716 (Taxmann Publications, New Delhi, 2nd edn., 2014).

than interpreting it subjectively as per different situations.[43] Moreover, there should be no additional tax burden imposed upon the companies, rather investments in CSR should be a matter of earning recognition rather than burdening companies with taxes.[44] Additionally, there should be a proper channel and mechanism by virtue of which an investment can be made on CSR in a fair and transparent manner. Above all, what is necessary that mere submission of a report should not be sufficient to discharge liability from the companies for failure of compliance with CSR investments, except for exceptional circumstances, penalties should be imposed upon companies failing to comply with the prescribed CSR norms under the said Act.[45]

Conclusion

In comparison to the Companies Act, 1956, the present provision pertaining to CSR is a good attempt at bringing about necessary reforms and imposing duties upon companies to invest in societal welfare schemes in the name of CSR. It is an important device or mechanism for promoting societal welfare which cannot be done away with and for that a regulated legal framework or mechanism is inevitable. However, there is a need to bring about necessary reforms or changes in relation to CSR in India and for that there are necessary changes that are to be brought about under Section 135 of the Companies Act, 2013. Though Section 135 is not a full proof provision for promotion of CSR in India, yet at least it provides a mechanism or a suitable method by virtue of which there can be promotion of CSR in the form of a duty rather than a matter of charity. Thus, Section 135 can be effective in leading to the promotion of CSR in our country provided that necessary reforms are brought about in it and the concerned ambiguities are removed in its provisions for doing the same.

---

43. Forbes India Blog, "The Good Company, CSR Rules Explained", available at: http://forbesindia.com/blog/the-good-company/new-csr-rules-explained/ (Visited on April 9, 2015).
44. Editorial, "The New Companies Act, 2013 to boost transparency", *The Times of India*, Nov. 29, 2013.
45 Deepak Patel, "Cabinet Clears 14 Changes to Companies Act", *Business Standard*, Dec. 3, 2014.

14

Corporate Social Responsibility in the Companies Act, 2013: An Innovative Legislation Lacking Pragmatic Approach

ARPITA SHARMA AND PUJA KUMARI

Introduction

The ultimate *mantra* for the gigantic triumph of a company is to make the meeting of two ends of profitability and stakeholders' interest. Once, the profitability part has been achieved the company must see that it is fulfilling the ethical values simultaneously as well. The meaning of CSR is different for different entities depending upon the task they take up for the welfare of the society but the concept is the same, i.e. Social Responsiveness. When it comes to defining CSR, some have even gone till the extent of saying that the definition and basically there isn't one.[1] After considerable debates in the Parliament, the year 2013 saw a rise of a massive change in the Indian Companies Law. The New Companies Act, 2013, enacted by the assent of the Hon'ble President of India on 29th August 2013, has not only brought in new concepts like One Person Company[2] but also made the companies more accountable to the public bringing in a philanthropic approach for the welfare of the

1. P. Jackson, B. Hawker, Is Corporate Social Responsibility Here to Stay? (200I) http://www.cdforum.com/research/icsrhts.doc accessed 14th December 2013.
2. Section 1(62) of the Companies Act, 2013.

society.[3] CSR, which was just a deliberate involvement by the companies, has now been made a mandate for the giant corporations by the 2013 Act. As people come to expect companies to take up larger social role, the 2013 Act will help companies to build up a societal individuality that is equally essential as brand identity. This will help changing the very nature and characteristic of business and will create a win-win situation.[4] After the passing of the 2013 Act, India comes amongst those selected nations which have mandated CSR for a certain group of companies, like Denmark[5] and Indonesia.[6] If a company devotes itself in some altruistic job, it will help the company to pull-off in a better position in the market thus it will get rewarded by its stakeholders.[7]

Background

The reform process of the company law hit the highest point with the enactment of the 2013 Act which changed the existing scenario of corporate law in India. Latest legislation to regulate CSR came in the form of 2013 Act. Although there were some guidelines regulating CSR prior to this Act but there was no concrete legislation *per se*. A notification with respect to CSR was for the very first time issued by the Ministry of Petroleum and Natural Gas in the form of guidelines directing companies to spend on CSR at least 2% of their net profits.[8]

---

3. ASSOCHAM India & Delliote, 'Companies Act, 2013: New Rules of the Game' (Deloitte, 12th September 2013), http://www.deloitte.com/assets/Dcom-India/Local%20Assets/Documents/Companies%20bill/ASSOCHAM-Companies%20Bill_web.pdf accessed 31st December 2013.
4. J.J. Graafland, S.C.W. Eijffinger, Corporate social responsibility of Dutch companies: Benchmarking and Transparency [2004] 152, No. 3, De Economist, 403.
5. 'Denmark Introduces Mandatory CSR Reporting for Large Companies', *United Nations Global Compact* (New York, 17 December 2008), http://www.unglobalcompact.org/newsandevents/news_archives/2008_12_17.html accessed 2nd November 2014.
6. Noke Kiroyan, 'Corporate social responsibility now the law in Indonesia', *The Jakarta Post* (Jakarta, July 25, 2007), http://www.thejakartapost.com/news/2007/07/25/corporate-social-responsibility-now-law-indonesia.html-0 accessed 2nd November 2014.
7. CA Sanjay Kumar Sharma, 'A 360 degree analysis of Corporate Social Responsibility (CSR) Mandate of the New Companies Act, 2013' [2013], Vol. 3, No. 7, *Global Journal of Management and Business Studies,* 757.
8. Ministry of Petroleum and Natural Gas, Government of India, 'Oil PSUs agree to spend two per cent of profits on Social Responsibilities', *Press Information*

Thereafter notifications were issued by the Ministry of Corporate Affairs[9] in the form of voluntary guidelines. Furthermore, guidelines issued by Central Public Sector Enterprises (CPSEs) in April 2010, mandated the making of 'CSR Budget'.[10] Yet another notification came on April 1, 2013 in the form of 'Guidelines on CSR and Sustainability for Central Public Sector Enterprises'.[11] The CSR law is applicable to both domestic and foreign companies operating in India.[12] As Tom Tyler and Peter Degoey note, re-investing in communities can construct reputational legality, belief, and reciprocity from which companies may in due course benefit.[13] This will help the company to inure long-term benefit, if a company invests its money efficiently.[14] The concept of mandatory CSR will not only meet the economic requirements but also serve towards what is needed most by the nation to eradicate poverty to a great extent.[15]

The Figure 1 showing the CSR provision as incorporated in the 2013 Act.

Bureau (2nd February 2009), http://pib.nic.in/newsite/erelease.aspx?relid=47172 accessed 2nd November 2014.

9. Ministry of Corporate Affairs, 'Corporate Social Responsibility Voluntary Guidelines, 2009', http://www.mca.gov.in/Ministry/latestnews/CSR_Voluntary_Guidelines_24dec2009.pdf accessed 26th October 2014.
10. Ministry of Corporate Affairs, Government of India, 'Corporate Social Responsibility', *Press Information Bureau* (11 August 2011), http://pib.nic.in/newsite/erelease.aspx?relid=74428 accessed 5th October 2014.
11. Department of Public Enterprise, 'Guidelines for CSR and Sustainability for Central Public Sector Enterprises', http://www.dpemou.nic.in/MOUFiles/Revised_ CSR_ Guidelines.pdf accessed 5th October 2014.
12. Rama Lakshmi, 'India mandates increase in charitable giving by corporations; critics fear government control', *The Washington Post* (New Delhi, 13 September 2013), http://www.washingtonpost.com/world/india-mandates-increase-in-charitable-giving-by-corporations-critics-fear-government-control/2013/09/10/e556d53a-157d-11e3-961c-f22d3aaf19ab_story.html accessed 26th October 2014.
13. Tom R. Tyler, Peter Degoey & Heather Smith, 'Understanding Why the Justice of Group Procedures Matters: A Test of the Psychological Dynamics of the Group-Value Model' [1996], *Journal of Personality & Social Psychology*, 913, 913-30.
14. Thomas Donaldson, *Corporations and Mortality* (Prentice Hall College Div. June 1982).
15. Seema G. Sharma, 'Corporate Social Responsibility in India: An Overview', [2009] International Law, 1515.

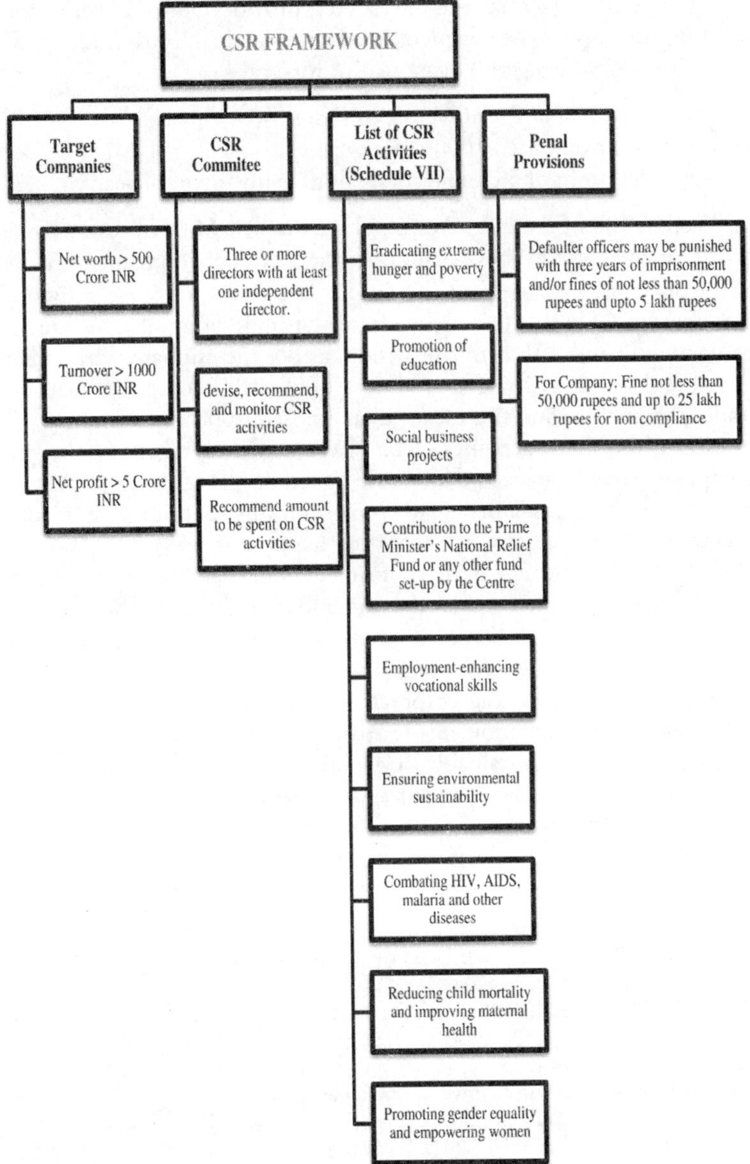

Fig. 1: Overview of CSR Framework in 2013 Act.

The Section 135 of the 2013 Act provides for the companies meeting any of the below mentioned criteria shall constitute a CSR committee comprising of 3 or more directors:

- Networth of Rs. 500 crore or more.
- Turnover of Rs. 1000 crore or more.
- Net profit of 5 crore or more during any financial year.

Section 135 of the 2013 Act stipulates that 2% of three years average profit[16] earned by the above mentioned categories of companies must be spent on CSR.[17] Apart from this it also lays down a list of 'activities' constituting CSR. It aims to inculcate the philosophy of CSR among Indian companies. With this provision, as per the estimates[18] by Indian Institute of Corporate Affairs, almost 6000-7000 companies will fall under the purview and this means that almost 27,000 crore[19] money will be spent on CSR activities. The CSR activities taken up by the companies shall be in accordance with Schedule VII of the 2013 Act. As regards to the mandatory CSR provision, the bottom line is that spending is not necessary but reporting about it is necessary. Also, the CSR Committee which is to be formed under the 2013 Act has to approve a CSR policy[20] and the same has to be published on the company's website.[21] Some difficulties might be encountered in implementing these new provisions in the initial years but it will help in improving society and the corporate would be benefited in terms of enhancement in reputation in the society. CSR is one of the effective methods to achieve sustainable development of any company. So it is needed that it should be accepted as an organizational objective. It is a reality that business and corporate houses can no longer flourish in isolation ignoring its effects on societies and environment and this

16. Akhila Vijayaraghavan, 'On the Course to Mandatory CSR in India' (Just Means, 9th March 2011), http://www.justmeans.com/editorials?action=readeditorial&p=46744 accessed 17th December 2013.
17. 'Cos. to spend Rs. 15-20k crore a year on CSR', *The Economic Times* (New Delhi, 10 September 2013), http://articles.economictimes.indiatimes.com/2013-09-10/news/41937985_1_csr-activities-new-companies-act-corporate-affairs-minister-sachin accessed 26th October 2014.
18. CSR spending may pump in Rs. 27,000 crore a year, *Hindustan Times* (New Delhi, 21 September, 2013), http://www.hindustantimes.com/business-news/csr-spending-may-pump-in-rs-27-000-cr-a-year/article1-1125016.aspx accessed 26th October 2014.
19. *Ibid.*
20. Section 135(3)(a) of the Companies Act, 2013.
21. Section 135(4)(a) of the Companies Act, 2013.

problem to business houses developing externalities has been dully addressed by the 2013 Act by introducing the concept of CSR. The time has come for the companies to contribute to the society from where they make profit and it is no longer possible that the companies may continue to engage in profit-making business and go on ignoring the environment which provides it the requisites resources. They have to be socially accountable and responsible.

Existing Flaws: Acting as Snag

CSR is about amalgamating economic, environmental and social maneuver with companies operations and development. Many consider CSR to be philanthropy, but considering it to be so would amount to limiting its definition. An organization can achieve sustainable development if CSR is integrated with its business functioning. CSR has an influence on almost every area of business operation ranging from hiring to governance and stakeholder benefits sharing.[22] The fact that some companies are now legally required to include CSR committee in their governance structures represents a welcome move towards institutionalizing and legitimizing CSR but this provision of CSR in the 2013 Act is not gratis from predicaments and there are certain points which hunts for sober clarifications. There are certain pitfalls in the existing provisions that will pose challenges in meeting the objectives of the provision. So, it is important that all the grey areas seeking clarifications are made clear and provisions with shortcomings are accordingly amended to formulate a better CSR policy regime that can be properly executed to serve the purpose. Section 135 of the 2013 Act makes a classification of companies and divides the existing companies in India into two categories[23]:

(a) Companies having a net worth of five hundred crore rupees or more, OR a turnover of rupees one thousand crore or more OR a net profit of rupees five crore or more.[24]
(b) Companies not falling under the above category.

Now when the Section is making such a categorization then it becomes imperative to see that it passes the test of Article 14 of the

22. Anirudha Dutta, 'Corporate India & CSR' (Forbesindia.com, 17th August 2013), http://forbesindia.com/blog/beyond-the-numbers/corporate-india-and-csr/ accessed 26th October 2014.
23. Arpit Gupta, 'Mandatory CSR in The Companies Bill, 2011: Are We There, Yet?' 2013, Vol. 8, *NALSAR Student Law Review*, 38.
24. *Ibid.*

Indian constitution[25]. The Apex Court has laid down two important norms to be satisfied for passing the Article 14 validity test,[26] i.e. the classification must be based on an intelligible differentia, i.e. the groups created through the classification must be easily distinguishable from each other and the classification created must have a rational nexus to the object sought to be achieved by the Act. While the former test is easily satisfied by Section 135 but when it comes to latter it fails. The Ministry for Corporate Affairs has already stated that the main aim of this Section is to ensure that 'corporate entities contribute meaningfully' towards the advancement of the nation. Similarly, the Standing Committee[27] on Finance has also raised concern regarding this issue.[28] The legislature has failed to elucidate as to why barely such particular companies have been subjected to such an obligation plus what the basis of such categorization is? What can be perceived from the language of the Section is that only big companies have been subject to such mandate but again what is the definition of "Big Companies" remains unanswered. The question is why should not the companies having net worth of four hundred crores or more but less than five hundred crores be termed as "Big Companies"?[29]

Lack of Effectiveness

The 2013 Act requires the companies that fall within the ambit of Section 135 to spend 2% of its three years average profit on CSR.[30] Furthermore, Section 135(5) states that if the company does not spend 2% of its three year's average profits on CSR initiatives, the BOD are required to furnish a report stating the reasons for such failure under Section 134(3)(o). But this report has to be submitted in the BOD

25. *Ibid.*
26. *In Re*: Special Courts Bill, [1979], AIR 478 SC.
27. The Companies Bill, 2009—Twenty-first Report, Standing Committee on Finance (2009-10), Ministry of Corporate Affairs available at http://www.icsi.edu/webmodules/linksofweeks/ 21_Report_Companies_Bill.pdf.
28. Aneel Karnani, 'Mandatory CSR in India: A Bad Proposal' (Stanford Social Innovation Review Blog, 20 May 2013), http://www.ssireview.org/ blog/entry/mandatory_csr_in_india_a_bad_proposal accessed 26th October 2014.
29. Standing Committee Report (n 28) 38.
30. 'No relaxation: Companies have to spend on CSR initiatives, rotate auditors', *The Economic Times* (New Delhi, 25th November 2013), http://articles.economictimes.indiatimes.com/2013-11-25/news/44449989_1_new-companies-act-national-financial-reporting-authority-auditors accessed 26th October 2014.

meeting,[31] which does not seem to be so prolific, as submitting the report to company's own BOD for non-compliance of such spending is definitely not going to serve the purpose.

Absence of Stringent Penal Provision

Indeed, penalty is levied and if a company contravenes the provisions of this section, the company shall be punishable with fine which shall not be less than fifty thousand rupees but which may extend to twenty-five lakh rupees and every officer of the company who is in default shall be punishable with imprisonment for a term which may extend to three years or with fine which shall not be less than fifty thousand rupees but which may extend to five lakh rupees, or with both.[32] If Section 134(8) is read with Section 135(5) it can be very well made out that the penal provision is only for the non-compliance of submitting the report and not for the failure to spend with respect to CSR. Such penalty is going to be in vain as the companies very well know how to mould things in their favour to escape the liability.[33]

Companies Technically Not Falling under the Category

Another issue is that there may be instances when the companies are not enthusiastic in making such CSR spending because of the reason that the companies are not such colossal profit-making companies but they do fall under the Section 135 category mainly due to triggering net-worth and turnover criteria. Although, there the companies have the option of reporting as to why they will not make CSR spending by giving valid explanation but, what constitutes a "Valid Explanation" has not been defined so the companies might give excuse of not making enough profit so as to contribute to CSR in spite of falling within the category. In that case the purpose of CSR will stand defeated.[34]

List of Activities

Although the Act provides a list of CSR activities but this list is not an exhaustive list. It is unfortunate that the legislature has not provided

---

31. Standing Committee Report (n 28).
32. Section 134(8) of the Companies Act, 2013.
33. Arpit Gupta, 'Mandatory CSR in The Companies Bill, 2011: Are We There, Yet?' 2013, Vol. 8, *NALSAR Student Law Review*, 38.
34. Grant Thornton, 'Implications of Companies Act, 2013 Corporate Social Responsibility', http://gtw3.grantthornton.in/assets/Companies_Act-CSR.pdf accessed 17th December 2013.

more detailed and less ambiguous list as to what all constitutes CSR.[35] Apart from this with corruption spreading its roots in companies the list needs to be more clear as to prevent the companies from carrying on some other profitable activities in the garb of CSR.[36]

Return on Investment

Calculating the return on investment on initiatives undertaken in the name of CSR like benefit to the environment by adoption of cleaner fuels, allocating funds for the scholarship purpose and things like that may have a long time period for return which makes these areas of CSR less attractive.

Voluntary vs. *Mandatory*

CSR which has largely been a voluntary contribution by corporate has now been included in law and made mandatory.[37] But, having binding rules means there will be fraud and temptation to break the rules can be high. Making CSR mandatory will make sure that companies are taking social responsibilities but the problem is that the companies might implement CSR activities just for the sake of implementing and it further might show the way to fraudulent practices in the corporate world to getaway CSR spending.[38] However, the companies those who were voluntarily taking CSR activities even before 2013 Act will continue to take up the same but the corruption in other companies to escape CSR and to refrain from departing from their profits might lure companies to avoid doing CSR voluntarily to be in

---

35. National Foundation for India, 'Comments On Draft CSR Rules Under Section 135 of Companies Act, 2013' http://www.nfi.org.in/sites/default/files/nfi_ files/ Comments%20on%20draft%20CSR%20rules.pdf accessed 26th October 2014.
36. Grant Thornton, 'Implications of Companies Act, 2013, Corporate Social Responsibility', http://gtw3.grantthornton.in/assets/Companies_Act-CSR.pdf accessed 17th December 2013.
37. 'Azim Premji against law on mandatory CSR spending by corporates', *The Economic Times* (24 March 2011), http://articles.economictimes.India times.com/2011-03-24/news/29181451_1_csrspending-corporate-affairs-murli-deora-azim-premji accessed 26th October 2014.
38. IT CEOs back Premji, against mandatory CSR, *The Times of India*, (26 March 2011) http://articles.timesofindia.indiatimes.com/2011-03-26/software-services/29191926_1_csr-azim-premji-corporate-social-responsibility accessed 26th October 2014.

the league of most profitable companies.[39]

Number of Directors in CSR Committee

Section 135 of the New Companies Act requires that CSR committee should consist of a minimum of 3 directors. Now it is important to note that a private company has only 2 directors. So it is a point of clarification that if a private company fits in the category of Section 135 Companies category then will it be required for the private company to increase its board strength to make the number of directors three? Because if it is so it is too stringent provision and private must constitute an exception to it.[40]

No Definition of CSR

Before making rules and regulations for any particular subject it is very important to define the subject so as to develop an understanding of it. The definition is also helpful in drafting suitable policies for the subject. So definition is a must for any subject so that proper rules and regulations can be formulated in the light of the definition. But the 2013 Act surprisingly does not define CSR. The 2013 Act has ignored this point by giving no definition of CSR. Further, Schedule VII of the 2013 provides a list of CSR activities but expect this there is no mention in the Act as to what constitutes CSR. So merely providing a list without any proper definition amounts to narrowing the concept of CSR because it implies that only the activities enlisted in the Schedule VII constitutes CSR and this is the only concept of CSR.[41]

Double Taxation

The 2% of three years average profit is the profit before tax (PBT). So the target companies will have to in a way pay double tax in the way that firstly they will have to part with the 2% of the three years average

39. CA Sanjay Kumar Sharma, 'A 360 degree analysis of Corporate Social Responsibility (CSR), Mandate of the New Companies Act, 2013' [2013], Vol. 3, No. 7, *Global Journal of Management and Business Studies,* 757.
40. *Ibid.*
41. Justine Nolan, 'Corporate Accountability and Triple Bottom Line Reporting: Determining the Material Issues for Disclosure' (UNSW Law Research Paper No. 2007-15); Enhancing Corporate Accountability: Prospects and Challenges Conference Proceedings 1 (March 20, 2007), available at http://papers.ssrn.com/sol3/papers.cfm?abstract_id=975414 accessed 26th October 2014.

profit which is profit before tax and thereafter they will have to pay tax[42] on the remaining profit after deducting that 2% profit. So this CSR is actually imposing double taxation on the companies falling under the purview of the Act.

This concept of CSR is one of the ways of imposing tax and this will result in increasing the already very high corporate tax.[43] Present taxation rate in India for companies are amongst the highest in the world and stands at a level where number of payments are also quite elevated as compared to the global average.[44] This increase in the corporate tax[45] may act as a catalyst to decelerate the interest[46] of the investors to invest in India[47] which might prove to be fatal for the Indian economy.[48] Yet another problem is that some of the activities enlisted in Schedule VII

42. CA Sanjay Kumar Sharma, 'A 360 degree analysis of Corporate Social Responsibility (CSR) Mandate of the New Companies Act, 2013' [2013], Vol. 3, No. 7, *Global Journal of Management and Business Studies,* 757.
43. 'India's corporate tax rates among highest globally: World Bank report', *The Hindu* (New Delhi, 26th November 2013), http://www.thehindu.com/business/Economy/indias-corporate-tax-rates-among-highest-globally-world-bank-report/article5394196.ece accessed 26th October 2014.
44. 'India's corporate tax rates among highest globally: Report', *Business Today* (New Delhi, 26th November 2013), http://businesstoday.intoday.in/story/india-corp-tax-rates-among-highest-globally/1/200885.html accessed 10th October 2014.
45. Abhinav Prakash, 'Critique of Mandatory CSR requirement of the Companies Act' (Academia.edu), http://www.academia.edu/4308942/ Critique_of_Mandatory_CSR_Requirement_of_the_Companies_Act accessed 3rd October 2014.
46. 'Mandatory CSR: India Inc. asks for tax breaks in return', *The Financial Express* (New Delhi, 5th December 2012), http://www.financialexpress.com/news/mandatory-csr-india-inc-asks-for-tax-breaks-in-return/ 1040519 accessed 19th October 2014.
47. 'India Inc. for tax sops on CSR', *Business Standard,* (Mumbai, 20th December 2012), http://www.business-standard.com/article/companies/india-inc-for-tax-sops-on-csr-112122000202_1.html accessed 18th October 2014; 'India Inc. for tax sops on CSR' [2012], Vol. 1, Issue 31, Empower http://freepress journal.in/wp-content/uploads/empower/archive/pdf/21dec2012.pdf accessed 26th October 2014.
48. Abhinav Prakash, 'Critique of Mandatory CSR requirement of the Companies Act' (Academia.edu), http://www.academia.edu/4308942/Critique_of_Mandatory_CSR_Requirement_of_the_Companies_Act accessed 3rd October 2014.

are exempted[49] from tax but the remaining CSR activities have not been exempted. This will generate an attitude in the companies to take up the CSR activities that are tax exempted over the other activities.[50]

Cash Flow Issues

It might happen that the cash and liquidity position of the companies falling the target companies category may be much less than the average profit in the preceding three year's average profit. So in that case it will not be possible for the companies to engage in CSR and spend an amount of 2% of three years average profit, which is a considerable amount of money for companies dealing with cash flow issues or liquidity problem.[51]

Challenges Posed To SMEs

With the enforcement of Section 135, many small and medium enterprises (SME) are expected to qualify. Since, they are engaged in smaller business activities,[52] therefore, the quantum of profits available for CSR with SMEs will not constitute a sizable CSR fund which will not contribute a lot to the improvement of society and it will be of great hardship for SMEs to contribute even this insignificant amount.[53]

Economic Challenges

Total 2% of three years average profit is a significant amount of money. Although spending such amount will not make much difference

---

49. Lubna Kably, 'CSR spends to get cos varying tax benefits', *The Times of India* (Mumbai, 13th August 2013), http://timesofindia.indiatimes.com/ business/ india-business/CSR-spends-to-get-cos-varying-tax-benefits/articleshow/ 21792947.cms accessed 19th October 2014.
50. Lok Sabha Secratariat, 'Corporate Social Responsibility', Reference Note, No. 11 /RN/Ref./2013 (Lok Sabha, 2013), http://164.100.47.134/intranet/ CorporateSociaResponsbility.pdf accessed 18th December 2013.
51. CA Sanjay Kumar Sharma, 'A 360 degree analysis of Corporate Social Responsibility (CSR), Mandate of the New Companies Act, 2013' [2013], Vol. 3, No. 7, *Global Journal of Management and Business Studies,* 757.
52. Malini Goyal, 'SMEs employ close to 40% of India's workforce, but contribute only 17% to GDP', *The Economic Times* (9th June 2013), http://articles. economictimes.indiatimes.com/2013-06-09/news/39834857_1_smes-workforce-small-and-medium-enterprises accessed 26th October 2014.
53. Pradeep Gooptu, 'SMEs to get professional help on corporate social responsibility', *Business Standard* (Kolkata, 5th June 2008), http://www. business-standard.com/article/sme/smes-to-get-professional-help-on-corporate-social-responsibility-108060501090_1.html accessed 7th October 2014.

when the business is going good but during economic slowdown this 2% is really going to bite. Although the defaulter company has the option to explain the reason for non-compliance with such CSR spending by giving valid explanations but what constitutes a valid explanation has no where been explained. Apart from this shareholders have been given no say in the CSR spending by the companies. The 2% PBT to be spent on CSR forms a part of shareholder's wealth. So the question that arises here is that should such funds be diverted to CSR without shareholder's approval?[54] CSR spending creates market ineptitude that might prove to be fatal for the developing economy of India. The Indian economy has been growing at a steady pace post-liberalization and there has been a continuous increase in the GDP at around the rate of eight percent per year.[55] India is one of the fast growing nations in the world.[56] Although there are poverty issues in India but still it can be said that in India we can see the best example of "Trickle down Effect" as not only the upper strata of the society but also the lower strata has benefited from the globalization.[57] According to Greenfield's premise inequality is a market imperfection[58] but the point to be taken note of here is that if a growing economy is disturbed then there are chances that it might get shattered even before it can attain it

54. Tina Edwin, 'New Companies Bill: What India Inc should watch out for', *The Economic Times* (22nd July 2012), http://articles.economictimes.indiatimes.com/2012-07-22/news/32777534_1_csr-activities-new-companies-bill-corporate-social-responsibility accessed 26th October 2014..

55. OECD, 'Economic Survey of India: 2007' (OECD POLICY BRIEF, 2007), http://www.oecd.org/dataoecd/17/52/39452196.pdf accessed 19th December 2013.

56. Sunita Kikeri & John Nellis, 'An Assessment of Privatization', (2004), Vol. 19, No. 1, The World Bank Research Observer, http://econ.tu.ac.th/archan/chaleampong/teaching/ec340/supplement/Ch7_PublicEnterprise/Kikeri-%20and%20Nellis%20(2004)%20An%20Assessment%20of%20Privatization.pdf accessed 19th October 2014.

57. Caroline Van Zile, 'India's Mandatory Corporate Social Responsibility Proposal: Creative Capitalism Meets Creative Regulation in the Global Market' (2012), Vol. 13, No. 2, *Asian-Pacific Law & Policy Journal*, http://papers.ssrn.com/sol3/papers.cfm?abstract_id=2005969 accessed 18th October 2014.

58. Kent Greenfield, 'The Failure Of Corporate Law: Fundamental Flaws and Progressive Possibilities, (Chicago: U of Chicago Press, 2006); Thomas McInerney, Putting Regulation Before Responsibility: Toward Binding Norms of Corporate Social Responsibility, [2007], *Cornell International Law Journal*, 171.

full tune. Similar is the case of India economy. Indian economy is in its growth stage and such burden of CSR spending on the corporate might slow down the pace of development of the economy.

Key to the Predicaments

Since 2 per cent of a company's average profits is a significant chunk of money, it is important to ensure that it is spent wisely. The provision of CSR in 2013 Act mainly suffers from the problem of vagueness. So in order to cure this problem which is paralyzing the Act, it is important to provide certain clarification to make the provisions clear and free from any ambiguity otherwise in future it will pose significant challenges in the execution of the new provisions. In order to ensure that the purpose of this CSR provision in 2013 Act is served, a well planned and structured body is required which will be regulating the CSR activities and related issues of companies. Forming a team of experts and professionals for the purpose of constituting CSR committee is a must. But all these efforts will be in vain if policies and guidelines are not made clear. So making a good law is not the end of the story. In fact a new story starts from here and presents a further challenge to ensure that the law or legislation is properly followed or executed. There are solutions to some of the major problems that the 2013 Act is confronted with:

Explaining "Valid Explanation"

Suppose, a company makes CSR spending and so has to prepare a report giving explanations as to why it is not adhering to such CSR mandate, it is first of all important to explain as to, what constitutes a "Valid Explanation"? Because in absence of such clarity companies might give any random explanations and contest that it should be considered as to be valid due to the reason that there is no definition of validity. So in order to avoid such circumstances curative actions must be taken to make sure that no such confusion occurs.

Stringent Penal Provisions

Although, 2013 Act has a provision of penalty in case of non-compliance of the mandate to make 2% CSR spending and if no spending then submitting report explaining the reasons. But this is not going to be very effective because it gives companies all the possible chances to save itself by taking advantage of the ambiguity in the provisions laid down in the Act. So it is important to make such penalty provision more deterrent and there should be no scope to escape the punishment.

Expanding the Area of CSR

The New Companies law requires the companies to spend two percent of its average net profits made in the preceding three financial years on CSR. The Act also contains a list of government approved CSR activities. But it is not for the government to define as to in which area of CSR the companies should spend. Apart from this the list is not exhaustive and covers very limited area. But if the Government wants the companies to spend on government approved CSR activities then the list should be made more exhaustive giving companies ample number of choices. Also, reference can be taken from circular[59] issued by SEBI concerning the list of CSR activities which listed down a broader area as to what constitutes 'responsible business practices'.[60]

Homogeneous CSR Development

Further, the Act also requires the companies to give preference to the local area where the companies operate but this concept is not a well thought concept as it may lead to the development of areas where companies but the rest of the areas where there are not many companies may remain underdeveloped. It might happen that there might be an area where many companies operate then if every company operating in that area start giving preference to that area then it will not be very useful because many companies focusing on small area and ignoring rest of the areas will not contribute the uniform advancement of society and will give birth to disparity.

Independent CSR Committee

In the 2013 Act it is mentioned that companies to form a "CSR committee" within the board of directors consisting of three or more directors, at least one of which must be an "independent director" (defined in Section 149(6)). But it is recommended that CSR committee must be entirely an independent committee with no person from the board of the committee so as to ensure the efficient and effective working of the committee.

---

59. Business Sustainability Reports, Circular No. CIR/CFD/DIL/8/2012, Securities and Exchange Board of India (SEBI), Aug. 13, 2012 available at http://www.sebi.gov.in/cms/sebi_data/attachdocs/1344915990072.pdf.
60. Arpit Gupta, 'Mandatory CSR in The Companies Bill, 2011: Are We There, Yet?' 2013, Vol. 8, NALSAR *Student Law Review,* 38.

Number of Directors

Furthermore, this provision of CSR committee consisting of 3 directors must be relaxed for private companies because if it is not done then it would mean that private companies will be required to increase their board strength to fulfil the condition laid down in the provision. This completely does not make any sense.[61]

Tax Sops should be given

Legislations should exempt[62] CSR activities from tax as this will not only generate company's interest in CSR but will also benefit the society simultaneously.[63] Imposition of tax on CSR activities is implying that government has got a means to collect revenue and When the Government imposes a tax, it need not identify a specific benefit accruing from the same.[64] This is defeating the rationale behind Section 135 of the 2013 Act.

Consideration of Cash and Liquidity Position

It is important that the CSR provision takes note of the problem of tax and liquidity related issues so as prevent company's interest from getting hampered. Identifying the current liquidity position of the target companies which is required to take up CSR initiatives is a must. So CSR committee must consider this point and if the liquidity position of the company is found to be in adverse situation it must be exempted from CSR spending.[65]

Conclusion

In the year 1953, when H.R. Bowen's "Social Responsibilities of the Business"[66] became an academic topic, this is where the idea of

---

61. Grant Thornton, 'Implications of Companies Act, 2013, Corporate Social Responsibility', http://gtw3.grantthornton.in/assets/Companies_Act-CSR.pdf accessed 17th December 2013.
62. David F. Williams, Tax and Corporate Social Responsibility, (KPMG, September 2007), http://www.kpmg.co.uk/pubs/Tax_and_CSR_Final.pdf accessed 15th December 2013.
63. *Ibid.*
64. *Jindal Stainless Steel Ltd.* vs. *State of Haryana*, AIR 2006 SC 2550.
65. CA Sanjay Kumar Sharma, 'A 360 degree analysis of Corporate Social Responsibility (CSR), Mandate of the New Companies Act, 2013' [2013], Vol. 3, No. 7, *Global Journal of Management and Business Studies*, 757.
66. H.R. Bowen, Social Responsibilities of the Businessman (New York: Harper & Row 1953).

Corporate Social Responsibility (CSR) evolved[67] and here stands the 2013 Act with mandatory CSR provision. The evolution has been appreciable with considerable shifts in attitude and approach. It is anticipated that the 2013 Act will smoothen the progress for more corporate-friendly guidelines, safeguarding the interests of the investors and augmenting the accountability.[68] If a company devotes itself in some altruistic job, it will help the company to pull-off in a better position in the market thus it will get rewarded by its stakeholders.[69] To conclude, the purpose of CSR, we must comprehend that it is only one of a number of diverse liability approaches that can control behavior in and around corporations, with an objective of benefitting the society. As highlighted, stringent provisions are called for in case of non-compliance with the CSR provision, as a just punishment embraces the ethical condemnation of the society. Instead of serving just as a sheer supplement to corporate fines, ground breaking corporate sentences should be the key objectives of CSR of serving the society. One step forward has been taken by Indian Institute of Corporate Affairs (IICA)[70] in this regard. The Institute is planning to initiate a certificate program on Corporate Social Responsibilities activities for working executives.[71] This incorporation of mandatory CSR provision in India is acting as a "Global Watch". India is at the forefront of CSR law with the passing of 2013 Act. As such, India is an experimenting ground for CSR laws of this kind. Indeed, a drift is already evident in CSR law as the European Union is making an allowance for a commandment that would entail CSR reporting and disclosure for certain companies, something the

67. Lok Sabha Secratariat (n 45).
68. 'Companies Bill Likely in Monsoon Session: Ministry', *The Economic Times,* (New Delhi, 11 February 2010), http://articles.economictimes.indiatimes.com/2010-02-11/news/27578096_1_monsoon-session-companies-bill-internal-corporate-processes accessed 17th December 2013.
69. CA Sanjay Kumar Sharma, 'A 360 degree analysis of Corporate Social Responsibility (CSR), Mandate of the New Companies Act, 2013' [2013], Vol. 3, No. 7, *Global Journal of Management and Business Studies,* 757.
70. 'CSR certificate programme on the anvil', *The Economic Times* (New Delhi, 8th September 2013), http://articles.economictimes.indiatimes.com/2013-09-08/news/41873771_1_certificate-programme-corporate-affairs-ministry-csr-committee accessed 18th October 2014.
71. Indian Institute of Corporate Affairs (Ministry of Corporate Affairs), 'Invitation For Expression of Interest (EoI)' (IICA, 25th July 2013), http://www.iica.in/images/EOI_for_UP_and_Bihar_ICP_in_CSR.pdf accessed 26th October 2014.

European Union calls "non-financial information."[72] Also, Legislative measures are also being contemplated in Canada, where the current Bill C-300 would regulate the behavior of Canadian mining companies in developing countries.[73] Companies squabble that setting up minimum standards stops innovation.[74] Considerable debate environs the corporate world that force tends to increase corruption[75] and current CSR law will act like the same force. However, CSR is only in its inception stage and this makes the area available for constant review and up-gradation. Lastly, the authors firmly believe, it is necessary to slot in the proposed recommendations through necessary amendments and serious strides are called for at the earliest in order to put off the corporations from indulging into corporate misconduct and fabrication of corporate profits by the corporate agents.[76]

72. European Commission, 'CSR—Reporting and disclosure' (7th August 2013), http://ec.europa.eu/enterprise/policies/sustainable-business/corporate-social-responsibility/reporting-disclosure/index_en.htm accessed 26th October 2014.
73. John Manley, 'Bill C-300 would impose serious burdens on Canada's mining industry' (Canadian Council of Chief Executives, 27th September 2010), http://www.ceocouncil.ca/publication/bill-c-300-would-impose-serious-burdens-on-canadas-mining-industry accessed 26th October 2014.
74. 'The Arguments against CSR', *Corporate Watch,* http://www.corporatewatch.org/?lid=2688 accessed 26th October 2014.
75. Mushtaq H. Khan, 'Patron-Client Networks and the Economic Effects of Corruption in Asia' [1998], *European Journal of Development Research,* http://eprints.soas.ac.uk/2419/1/Corruption_EJDR.pdf accessed 24th October 2014.
76. Amy Chua, 'World On Fire, How Exporting Free Market Democracy Breeds Ethnic Hatred And Global Instability'? (Anchor Books 2003).

CHAPTER VII

Independent Directors

15

Role and Duties of Directors under the Companies Act, 2013

GUNJAN ARORA

Introduction

Directors play a fundamental role in the management and governance of a company. They oversee the business of the company and all its affairs. Given their key position in the company, they are required to act in the best interest of all the stakeholders of the company. Therefore, the law seeks to regulate their conduct by mandating duties and imposing liabilities on them. The new companies' act of 2013 has brought about major changes and has introduced many new provisions regarding directors and their duties, liabilities, roles and responsibilities. These new provisions seek to enlarge, clarify and re-define director's roles and responsibilities. Companies and directors have to now prepare themselves for these heightened standards that are being imposed by the new act in relation to the conduct of directors of a company.

Definition of Director

"Director" means a director appointed to the Board of a company.[1] A director is either appointed or he is elected. It is not necessary that the director has to be an employee or shareholder of the company. A

1. Section 2(34) of the Companies Act, 2013.

managing director is someone who has been entrusted with substantial powers regarding management of the company. The director gets this power by virtue of Article of Association, Shareholder's resolution or agreement. Whole-time director means a director who is in the whole time employment of the company. Directors would also be covered under the definition of "officer who is in default"[2] under the new act. The term "officer who is in default" covers full time directors, managing directors and also Key Managerial Personnel (KMP). In absence of KMP, other directors as specified by the board would be covered under the definition of 'officer who is in default'. Apart from these categories of directors, if any other director is aware of the act/omission or if such act/omission takes place with his consent, then he would also be covered under the definition of "officer who is in default."

Role of Directors

Directors play different roles and acts as an employee, agent, trustee and officer of the company. The legal position of the directors is as follows:

Directors as Agents: A company is an artificial person. It has been given status of a person under law. To carry on its activities, directors are appointed. They carry out the activities on behalf of the company. Thus, they act as agents of the company. They take decisions for the company.

Directors as employees: Whole time or full time directors are considered as employees of the companies. They are involved in day-to-day affairs of the companies. They are paid remuneration for the same.

Directors as trustees: Directors are considered trustees of money and property of the company. They hold the same on company's behalf. They have a fiduciary duty towards the company and its members.

Directors as officers: Section 2(60) of the new companies act, includes director in the definition of "officer who is in default". Directors are considered as officers of the company and can be held liable for any contravention of the provisions of the companies act.

Duties of Directors under the New Act

The 1956 Companies Act did not mention the duties of the director's explicitly. Courts relied on common law principles while deciding a particular case. The number of cases decided by the courts are

---

2. Section 2(60) of the Companies Act, 2013.

also very few in number and hence there was uncertainty regarding the duties of directors. The new act of 2013 has tried to fix this situation by stating the duties of directors under the act. The duties codified are very similar to that under the U.K. Companies Act of 2006.[3] Codification of duties will provide the directors, greater certainty as to their conduct and also the courts will now be able to judge the breach of duty by a director in an objective manner. The following are the Duties of Directors under the 2013 Act (section 166).[4] All the duties are subject to the other provisions of the companies act. Further, the section also clarifies that a director is under a duty not to assign his office to any person. Any such act would be void. The duties under the act can be classified mainly into two heads, i.e fiduciary duty and duty of reasonable care and diligence. According to the act, a director of a company should:

Act in good faith and promote the objects to the company;

Act for the benefit of the members, employees and shareholders of the company;

Act in the best interest of the company;

Act in the best interest of the community and protection of the environment; and

Do his duties with due and reasonable care. He should also conduct his duties with diligence. He should exercise independent judgment;

---

3. Section 172.
4. Section 166: (1) Subject to the provisions of this Act, a director of a company shall act in accordance with the articles of the company.

(2) A director of a company shall act in good faith in order to promote the objects of the company for the benefit of its members as a whole, and in the best interests of the company, its employees, the shareholders, the community and for the protection of environment.

(3) A director of a company shall exercise his duties with due and reasonable care, skill and diligence and shall exercise independent judgment.

(4) A director of a company shall not involve in a situation in which he may have a direct or indirect interest that conflicts, or possibly may conflict, with the interest of the company.

(5) A director of a company shall not achieve or attempt to achieve any undue gain or advantage either to himself or to his relatives, partners, or associates and if such director is found guilty of making any undue gain, he shall be liable to pay an amount equal to that gain to the company.

(6) A director of a company shall not assign his office and any assignment so made shall be void.

(7) If a director of the company contravenes the provisions of this section such director shall be punishable with fine which shall not be less than one lakh rupees but which may extend to five lakh rupees.

Again according to the Act, a director of a company should not compete with the company. He should not involve himself in a situation, either directly or indirectly, where his interest and interest of the company will conflict and make personal profits. He should to achieve or attempt to achieve any undue gain or advantage either to himself or his partners, associates or relatives.

In case the director achieves any undue gain/advantage or causes someone else related to him to achieve some undue gain, he would be liable to compensate the company. He would be liable to pay an amount which is equal to the gain which was made. The section also provides that in case of any contravention of the duties mentioned above, the director shall be liable to pay fine of minimum one lakh rupees. The director can be asked to pay a fine up to five lakh rupees.

Related Party Transactions: Director of the company also has the duty not to enter into related party transactions which will cause undue loss to the company. It is the duty of the director to disclose such a transaction and obtain consent of the company and its members through the process provided in the law. The Act defines who is a "related person." Transactions include leasing/sale/purchase/disposal of property, rendering of services, supply of goods and also appointing an agent for these activities. Non-cash transactions are also included. It is the duty of the director to give priority to the interest of the company and not cause any undue gain to him or any one related to him.

Critical analysis of Section 166: Codification of the duties is a right step forward. Many aspects have been made clear now. The ambits of the duties have been clarified and the act tries to minimise the uncertainties regarding the duties of the directors.

Ambit of the duties clarified: Interest of the company is generally understood as interest of the shareholders. However, the new act specifically mentions that it is the duty of the director, to act in the best interest of not only the shareholders but also the employees of the companies. Therefore, the act makes it clear that it would not be sufficient for the director to act for the shareholder's interest alone. The director must also take care of the interest of the other stakeholders of the companies. Thus, the Board of Directors should keep in mind not only the interest of the shareholders but all other stakeholders, while making a decision for the company.

Duties of the Directors for Corporate Social Responsibility (CSR): Under the 2013 Act, there is a lot of emphasis on CSR of the companies. It has been made mandatory, though non-compliance does not attract penalty. In furtherance of this, the new act imposes a duty on the director to act in the best interest of the community and protection of environment.

Since the duties attract penalty, it is necessary that directors strictly comply with them. However, there is no further clarification about this particular duty in the act. It is not clear up to what extent the director needs to act for the protection of environment and community, while acting in his official capacity of director. A situation might arise in which the director's duty to protect the environment and community is in conflict with his other duties. No guidance is provided by the act for such situations. Such situations will have to be dealt by the courts as and when the matter comes up before them.

Duties of the Directors and Decision-making

It seems that duties will complicate the decision-making process of the directors. Non-compliance with Section 166 of the new act attracts penalty for the directors. Hence, it is necessary that the directors follow the duties under the act strictly. These duties are not just guidelines to the directors, but have to be necessarily complied with. It is not clear how should the board make a decision if the interest of the shareholders and other stakeholders of the company is in conflict. A normal tendency is to prefer the rights of the shareholders but in doing so the directors might contravene their duty under section 166(2) of the act. Section 166(2) specifically states that interest of non-shareholders such as the employees of the companies have to be taken into consideration by the directors. This dichotomy would have to be dealt by the Board of Directors very carefully. Though, a question also remains that whether the employees of the companies have a justifiable right under this situation. Similar situations of conflict of duties of directors are likely to arise in the future.

Concept of Independent Directors

Independent directors are also sometimes known as outside directors. These directors do not have any interest in the company whether pecuniary or material. They are not allowed to hold stock in the company. These directors are rewarded by sitting fees. These directors are appointed so that they act without any prejudice or bias while taking the decisions of the company. The appointment of an independent director has been made mandatory under the new act of 2013. According to the new act, IDs should represent one-third of the Board of Directors in case of a listed company. All the duties mentioned under section 166 of the Act, as discussed above, are applicable to all the directors of the companies. However, for independent directors other provisions have been incorporated under the act. The act discusses in detail the duties, responsibilities, roles and liabilities of the Independent Directors under Schedule IV and other provisions. According to section 149(8) of the act, the company and the Independent Directors have to abide by Schedule IV of the Act.

Code for Independent Directors under the Schedule IV of the Act

First time company law introduced a detailed code for Independent Directors in Schedule IV of the new statute. The Schedule has eight parts consisting guidelines of professional conduct, role & functions, duties, manner of appointment, re-appointment, resignation or removal, separate meetings and evaluation mechanism about Independent Directors.

Guidelines of professional conduct: An independent director is supposed to act objectively and conduct his duties in a *bona fide* manner and in the interest of the company. He should not be negligent towards his duties, give proper time and attention to his work so that he can make informed decisions. He should not abuse his position or achieve undue advantage. He should not do anything that would lead to loss of his independence. In case he cannot act impartially under any circumstance, he should inform the Board of Directors immediately. It is also his duty to assist the company in following the best corporate governance practice.

Roles and functions of the Independent Directors: An independent director should help in bringing an objective view and independent judgement especially in important board decisions. It is his role to safeguard the interest of all the stakeholders of the companies including minority shareholders. He should also try to balance the conflicting interests of different stakeholders of the companies. He also has to monitor and scrutinise the performance of management of the company and integrity of financial information. Determining appropriate remuneration of executive directors and key managerial personnel is also his duty. His role also includes recommending their removal whenever it is necessary and circumstances so demand. He should also arbitrate a conflicting situation between the management and shareholders.

Duties of the Independent Directors in the Code: The Schedule has given a list of 13 duties of the Independent Directors. Some of the important duties are; Take advice of experts for clarification and amplification of information, where necessary and required; Regularly update and refresh their skills and knowledge; Regularly attend all the meetings of the board and board committees; Be well informed about the company and its affairs; Bring up concerns regarding the running of the company to the Board of Directors and ensure that appropriate action is taken; Not to obstruct the functioning of the board; Ensure that enough deliberations are held for approval of a related party transaction; Report unethical behaviour, suspected fraud or violation of code of ethics; Protect interest of stakeholders of the company; Not to disclose confidential information.

Critical Analysis of Role and Duties of Independent Directors

Independent Directors will serve a very important function in the governance of the companies. Role and duties of them are incorporated in the act with an aim that they will ensure that the company is being governed in an effective and transparent manner. However, the effectiveness of appointment of Independent Directors will be a challenge because of the concentrated shareholding patterns in most of the listed companies. Moreover, manner of appointment of Independent Directors is same as that of appointment of other directors. This means that promoters will have discretion and can influence the process. Though, Nomination and Remuneration committee can take care of such a situation to an extent. Independent Directors have been entrusted with many important duties. Their role is multi-facet. They have been assigned the role of guardians of the members of the companies. They have to take care of their interests. Their role is also to supervise the activities of the companies and report any fraud or mismanagement. They also have to carry out board evaluation. They also are supposed to play the role of arbiter in case of conflict of interest between the shareholders and management or between different stakeholders of the companies. Their role also includes approving of various activities of the companies such as, CSR activities, approving a related party transaction, etc. There are many roles assigned to Independent Directors under the act, however they will be held liable only in certain circumstances. Schedule IV of the act clarifies that liability of Independent Directors will be limited to the following situation:

(a) When the acts/omission occurred because the Independent Directors did not act diligently.

(b) When the acts/omissions occurred with the knowledge of Independent Directors.
(c) When the acts/omissions occurred with the consent or connivance of Independent Directors.[5]

The provisions in the new act clarify to a large extent the roles and duties of Independent Directors. However, most of the provisions are very prescriptive in nature. This will make the role of Independent Directors onerous. But the flipside is that such provisions will increase the monitoring of the companies, which is very important for good corporate governance and is urgently needed in the current business scenario. Some of the other provisions relating to Independent Directors are qualitative in nature and proving compliance with the same would be difficult in certain situations. For example, the act does not provide any guidance as to how the Independent Directors should conduct the board evaluation and what are the parameters for the same. Also, how should the Independent Directors arbitrate the conflict between the interest of different stakeholders and company and the formalities to be observed for the same is not clear under the Act.

Conclusion

Two main changes have been brought about by the new Companies Act of 2013 with respect to the directors. Firstly, duties of the directors are now codified and contravention of the same attracts penalty. Secondly, the concept of independent directors has been introduced by the act. The act has endowed many responsibilities on the directors and has introduced high standards of conduct for them. After analysis of the provisions of the new act, it can be said that Independent Directors will assume a very important position in the governance of the companies. However, many onerous duties and liabilities have been placed on them. Certain mitigating factors have been incorporated under the act itself so that liabilities of Independent Directors are restricted to certain situations only. This has been done so that appropriate persons are not discouraged from serving the board. So many roles and duties of the directors are provided under the act and non-compliance with the same attracts penalty. Given this fact, it would be advisable that the directors do not take up too many directorships as they would now be needed to spend considerable amount of time and effort in carrying out their duties. The provisions of the new Act have increased the involvement and risks for the directors. Therefore, the board should adequately

5. Section 149(12).

remunerate the directors. This will ensure that appropriate and capable people take up the job. The new provisions aim to bring about a change in the corporate governance of the companies and have tried to ensure responsibility and accountability of the directors. However, only strict enforcement of these provisions will ensure their effectiveness.

16

Independent Directors: Evolutionary Changes Elevating Corporate Governance

Varun Tandon and Amit Pande

Introduction

The Companies Act, 1956 did not define the term 'Independent Director' though, it is being required by the Indian Listing Standards to include Independent Director in the board of the listed companies. But neither the Act nor the Listing Agreement precisely defines the roles, duties and liabilities of the Independent Director which places them on the equal footing as of other directors in the Board and therefore, the duties, liabilities, roles and functions they ought to perform could not be incurred. However, the Companies Act, 2013 clarifies such roles, powers, duties and functions that have to be performed by the Independent Directors by laying down certain norms and non-exhaustive list of duties to be performed by them. SEBI for the first time in the year 1999 set-up a committee under the Chairmanship of Shri Kumara Mangalam Birla to report to the matter of Corporate Governance and one of the recommendations that laid the emphasis on Independent Director states that, "Good corporate governance dictates that the board be comprised of individuals with certain personal characteristics and core competencies such as recognition of the importance of the board's tasks, integrity, a sense of accountability, track record of achievements, and the ability to ask tough questions. Besides, having financial literacy, experience, leadership qualities and the ability to think strategically, the directors must show significant degree of commitment to the company and devote adequate time for meeting, preparation and attendance."[1] Also in 2002, the Naresh Chandra Committee and in the year 2003, the Narayana Murthy Committee were set-up by the SEBI for the examination of various aspects relating to Corporate Governance. Both the Committees laid down great emphasis on the roles of Independent Director but the term 'Independent Director' was first introduced in India when SEBI incorporated Clause 49 in the Listing Agreement. The need for strict regulations in the code of conduct of Independent Director was felt after the greatest scam in the history of corporate world of India, i.e. Satyam Computer Scam. After the public announcement of Satyam scandal on January 7, 2009, Mr. Ramalingam Raju confessed that notified SEBI of having falsified the account with Balance Sheet as on 30 September 2008 contained:

1. An inflated (non-existent) cash and bank balances of Rs. 5,040 crore (as against Rs. 5,361 crore reflected in the books) on the balance sheet as on September 30, 2008.
2. An accrued interest of Rs. 376 crore which is non-existent.
3. An understated liability of Rs. 1,230 crore on account of funds.
4. An overstated debtors position of Rs. 490 crore (as against Rs. 2,651 reflected in the books).
5. For the September quarter, Satyam fraudently reported a revenue of Rs. 2,700 crore and an operating margin of Rs. 649 crore (24% of revenues) as against the actual revenues of Rs. 2,112 crore and an actual operating margin of Rs. 61 crore (3% of revenues).[2]

The lack of concern of Independent Directors in the Satyam Company has given a way to such a huge scam that had occurred just below their own nose and survived for years. But just after the investigation began, the scam could not survive a weak and everything got revealed.

Such a huge Scandal has highlighted the need of the strict corporate

1. Securities and Exchange Board of India, Report of the Kumar Mangalam Birla Committee on Corporate Governance (May 1999).
2. Manpreet Kaur, "Corporate Governance in India: Case Study of Satyam", 2, IJR 30(2013).

governance and has also exposed its weaknesses. The Satyam episode has instilled fright in the minds of the Independent Directors in India as the most essential issue of Corporate Governance was brought to enlightenment by this Scandal. This gave a path to the strict regulation of code of Independent Directors in the Companies Act, 2013. As per the Section 149(6), an Independent Director in relation to a company, means a director other than a Managing Director or a Whole-time Director or a Nominee Director,—

(a) Who in the opinion of the Board, is a person of integrity and possesses relevant expertise and experience;

(b) (i) Who is or was not a promoter of the company, or its holding, subsidiary or associate company;

(ii) Who is not related to promoters or directors in the company, its holding, subsidiary or associate company;

(c) Who has or had no pecuniary relationship with the company, its holding, subsidiary or associate company, or their promoters, or directors, during the two immediately preceding financial years or during the current financial year;

(d) None of whose relatives has or had pecuniary relationship or transaction with the company, its holding, subsidiary or associate company, or their promoters, or directors, amounting to two percent or more of its gross turnover or total income or fifty lakh rupees or such higher amount as may be prescribed, whichever is lower, during the two immediately preceding financial years or during the current financial year;

(e) Who, neither himself nor any of his relatives—

(i) holds or has held the position of a key managerial personnel or is or has been employee of the company or its holding, subsidiary or associate company in any of the three financial years immediately preceding the financial year in which he is proposed to be appointed;

(ii) is or has been an employee or proprietor or a partner, in any of the three financial years immediately preceding the financial year in which he is proposed to be appointed, of—

(A) a firm of auditors or company secretaries in practice or cost auditors of the company or its holding, subsidiary or associate company; or

(B) any legal or a consulting firm that has or had any transaction with the company, its holding, subsidiary or associate company amounting to ten percent or more of the gross turnover of such firm;

(iii) holds together with his relatives two per cent or more of the total voting power of the company; or

(iv) is a Chief Executive or director, by whatever name called, of any non-profit organisation that receives twenty-five per cent or more of its receipts from the company, any of its promoters, directors or its holding, subsidiary or associate company or that holds two per cent or more of the total voting power of the company; or

(f) Who possesses such other qualifications as may be prescribed.[3]

Appointment and Board Composition

According to the Code for Independent Directors, "the appointment process of independent directors shall be independent of the company management; while selecting independent directors the Board shall ensure that there is appropriate balance of skills, experience and knowledge in the Board so as to enable the Board to discharge its functions and duties effectively and their appointment to be approved at the shareholder's meeting."[4] Clause 49 of the Listing Agreement states that the composition of the Board should be the optimal combination of Executive Directors (ED) and Non-Executive Directors (NED) and should also satisfy some of the following criteria:

- If Chairman is an Executive Director, at-least half of the Board should be Independent Directors (ID).
- If Chairman is a promoter or related to promoter, at-least half of the Board should be Independent Directors (ID).
- If Chairman is related to anyone occupying management position at the Board level or one level below the Board, at-least half of the Board should be Independent Directors (ID).
- If the Chairman is an Independent Director, at-least one-third of the Board should be Independent Directors (ID).
- If the Board does not have a regular non-executive Chairman, at-least half of the Board should be Independent Directors (ID).[5]

3. See Section 149 of the Companies Act, 2013 (No. 18 of 2013).
4. Schedule IV, Manner of Appointment, The Companies Act, 2013 (No. 18 of 2013).
5. Revised Clause 49, New Corporate Governance Norms for India Listed Companies, available at http://www.ingovern.com/wp-content/uploads/2014/05/

The Independent Directors are to be considered as the 'watchdogs' of the Company and they have a very crucial role to play in managing the affairs of the Company. Since the Companies Act, 2013 has recognised the Independent Directors as vital component in the operation of the Company, therefore, the Companies Act, 2013 has also set-up certain criteria for qualifying to be an Independent Directors. An Independent Director shall possess appropriate skills, experience and knowledge in one or more fields of finance, law, management, sales, marketing, administration, research, corporate governance, technical operations or other disciplines related to the company's business.[6] The Central Government under the Regulation has notified that there would be at-least two Directors as Independent Directors for the following class or classes of companies—

(i) Public Companies having paid up share capital of Rs. 10 crore or more;

(ii) Public Companies having turnover of Rs. 100 crore or more; and

(iii) Public Companies, which have, in aggregate, outstanding loans, debentures and deposits, exceeding Rs. 50 crore.[7]

The Companies Act, 2013 attempts to bring the constitution of the Board of Directors in India at par with other international capital markets by mandating at least one-third of the board to be independent directors in case of public listed companies. The Companies Act, 2013 states that, "every public listed company shall have at least one-third of the total number of directors as Independent Directors"[8] and such number of Independent Directors "may be selected from a data bank containing names, addresses and qualifications of persons who are eligible and willing to act as an Independent Directors, maintained by anybody, institute or association, as may be notified by the Central Government."[9] The Companies Act, 2013 also provides that the Independent Director shall hold office up to five consecutive years once elected. The Act further states that an Independent Director can further

---

Revised-Clause-49-New-Corporate-Governance-Norms-for-India-Listed-Companies.pdf, (Visited on April 24, 2015).

6. Rule 5 of the Companies (Appointment and Qualification of Directors) Rules, 2014.
7. See Rule 4 of The Companies (Appointment And Qualification of Directors) Rules, 2014, Ministry of Corporate Affairs Notification, 19th January, 2014.
8. Section 149(4), The Companies Act, 2013 (No. 18 of 2013).
9. Section 150, The Companies Act, 2013 (No. 18 of 2013).

hold office for the next consecutive five years, which means that the Independent Director can hold office for two consecutive terms at a single go. Provided the re-appointment for the third term shall only be possible after the period of three years from the end of the second tenure or term. This period of three years is known as cooling off period where the Independent Director shall not be appointed or associated with company in any other capacity, either directly or indirectly. The Corporate Ministry Affairs has also clarified that "if a company intends to continue an existing independent director, his appointment would need to be made expressly afresh under the Act before March 31, 2015, and his earlier tenure will not be counted for such fresh appointment under the Act."[10]

Independence

Schedule IV of the Companies Act, 2013 defines the code for Independent Directors from which two-fold definitions can be interpreted, they are as follows:

(a) Independent Directors are those who help in bringing an "Independent Judgment".

(b) Independent Directors are those who do not have any pecuniary relationship with the company either directly or indirectly.[11]

It has been considered that having truly independent directors on the Board of the Private or Public Company is the 'best practice'. A series of appalling corporate governance failures around the nation triggered pervasive changes to the regulations and policies in the Companies Act, 2013, including new requirements for director independence. With the change in scenario of the Corporate Governance since the Satyam Scandal, there has been much emphasis on the independence of the directors and it is clearly evident from the introduction of 'Independent Directors' in the Companies Act, 2013. Independence is a state of mind and cannot be codified through a statute. A lot of promoters bring someone on the board that they have known for long. The chosen individual is either expected to add value or toe the line without constructive challenge. However, if the non-executive director chooses

---

10. See General Circular No. 14/2014, Government of India, Ministry of Corporate Affairs, available at http://www.mca.gov.in/Ministry/pdf/General_Circular_14_2014.pdf, last (Visited on May 02, 2015).
11. See Section 149(8) of the Companies Act, 2013 (No. 18 of 2013).

to engage in constructive challenge within the board room, that is real independence. In the long-run, such constructive dissent is bound to result in more effective decision-making.[12] Therefore, it is being considered that Independence allows the directors to be rational and helps in evaluating the performance of the company without any conflicts and unjustified control of any of the interested parties. A board with a majority of independent directors, can bring expertise and objectivity which:

(i) Assures owners that the company is being run legally, ethically, effectively and in the best interest of its owners;
(ii) And that they have "representatives" who are objective and have no "axe to grind"; and
(iii) Who will look at issues with no vested interest or 'hidden agendas'.[13]

Therefore, the main purpose underlying the introduction of Independent Directors on the Board is to act as a catalyst against any discrepancies by the company's management.

Roles and Duties

Neither the Companies Act, 1956 nor the Equity Listing Agreement described the scope of roles and duties of the Independent Directors in the company. However, Independent directors may be viewed as repositories of vigilance intended to ensure that the promoters and executive directors carry on the activities of the company in conformity with the interests of the shareholders as a whole.[14] To ensure the conformity with the interests of the shareholders of the company, the Companies Act, 2013 has mandate the Independent Directors to hold at-least one meeting in a year without the presence of Non-Independent Directors and the members of management so as to review the performance of the directors and the Board and also of the Chairperson of the company.[15] The minority shareholders are dependent upon the Independent Directors for providing transparency in working of the

---

12. KPMG, ASSOCHAM, Role of Independent Directors: Issues and Challenges.
13. Leslie Dashew, "Importance of Independent Directors", available at http://www.lesliedashew.com/pdf/importance-of-independent-contractors.pdf, last (Visited on May 10, 2015).
14. Shinoj Koshy, Preetha S. and Vandana V., "The responsibilities, rewards and liabilities of independent directors will be transformed by the new Companies Act", 7, IBLJ 28 (2014).
15. See Schedule IV of the Companies Act, 2013 (No.18 of 2013).

company. Therefore, the Companies Act, 2013 has laid down a new dimension that Independent Directors in the public listed company has to balance the conflicting interests of the stakeholders while protecting the rights of the minority shareholders. The Independent Directors also has a significant role to play in the internal affairs of the company since there is greater risk from inside the company than outside. It is being expected that the Promoters and the management of the company has better quality information regarding the internal affairs and the strength and weakness of the company and for that they meticulously try to work for protecting their personal interests. The Companies Act, 2013 cast upon the Independent Directors to act within his authority and assist in safeguarding the legitimate interest of the company, its employees and its shareholders. Since, it is being expected from the Independent Directors to attend all shareholder meetings and 'scrutinize the performance of management in meeting agreed goals and objectives and monitor the reporting of performance'[16] therefore, it is the duty which has been cast upon the Independent Directors to report to the Registrar of Companies (ROC) concerns related to any unethical behaviour or any suspected fraud or violation of company's code of conduct.

The Companies Act, 2013 has also laid down rules regarding external affairs of the company. It is the duty of Independent Directors to keep him/her well equipped with the information about the company and the external environment in which the company operates. It is also the duty of the Independent Directors to not to disclose any credential information which includes technologies, advertisement and sales promotion plan, commercial trade secrets, etc. provided that such disclosure has been approved by the Board or is required by law. There has also been a shift in the role of the Independent Directors after the Satyam Scandal in fraud prevention and detection management. Recently, it has been a trend where Independent Directors are taking up tasks and showing interest in reviewing the fraud risk management structure for mitigating the risk of fraud. Since the list of specific duties to be performed by the Independent Directors has been provided by the Act, it by no means is to be considered as exhaustive and also the liability of the Independent Directors does not end or Independent Directors would not be exempted from the liabilities even if they have performed their duties but they have to comply with all the necessary and effective duties which is required for the efficient business of the company.

---

16. *Ibid.*

Meetings and Committees

For ensuring the better, proper and smooth functioning of the Board of Directors of the Company, the Companies Act, 2013 requires all the Independent Directors to meet at least once in the calendar year. This meeting shall be conducted without the presence of non-Independent Directors of the company and members of the management of the company so as to evaluate and review the performance of the whole of the company without any biasness and discrepancies. The Companies Act, 2013 further provides for the evaluation of the Chairperson of the company by the Independent Directors of the company. Thus, it helps in aiding for the smooth functioning of the management of the company. The Independent Directors shall also 'assess the quality, quantity, timeliness of flow of information between the company management and the Board that is necessary for the Board to effectively and reasonably perform their duties.'[17] The Companies Act, 2013 has also emphasized on the role of Independent Directors on various Public Sector Undertaking Committees so as to ensure good Corporate Governance.

Audit Committee: This committee is required to carry out the duties of the parent company and shall supervise the integrity of the financial statements of the company and is also associated with the internal controls and the risk management systems. According to the Companies Act, 1956, the Audit Committee shall consist of minimum three directors and two-third of the members of the committee would consist of directors other than the managing and whole-time director.[18] Thus, the act of 1956 did not include Independent Directors in the Audit Committee. As per the Companies Act, 2013, 'the Audit Committee shall consist of a minimum of three directors with independent directors forming a majority.'[19] The Equity Listing Agreement, Clause 49 also states that 2/3rd members of the Audit Committee shall be an Independent Director and it also mandates the Chairman of the Audit Committee to be an Independent Director.

Nomination and Remuneration Committee: The Companies Act,

---

17. Grant Thornton, Strengthening Corporate Governance: Amendments to Clause 49 of the Equity Listing Agreement, available at http://gtw3.grantthornton.in/assets/Strengthening_Corporate_Governance.pdf, (Visited on April 25, 2015).
18. See Section 292A of the Companies Act, 1956 (1 of 1956).
19. See Section 177(2) of the Companies Act, 2013 (No. 18 of 2013).

1956 did not provide for the creation of nomination and remuneration committee but the Companies Act, 2013 states that the Board of Directors of every listed company and such other class or classes of companies, as may be prescribed shall constitute the Nomination and Remuneration Committee consisting of three or more non-executive directors out of which not less than one-half shall be Independent Directors.[20]

The major tasks that the committee is being engaged with are as follows:

(i) identification of persons that are qualified to become directors;
(ii) recommendation for the appointment and removal of directors; and
(iii) evaluation of director's performance.

Corporate Social Responsibility Committee: The concept of Corporate Social Responsibility rests on the ideology of give and take.[21] With the change in time, we see that the trend of Corporate Governance is on radar of corporations as were never earlier. India has visited a vast change in the norms of public corporation and with this adverse change, there has also been a change in the cultural norms by including Corporate Social Responsibility so as to contribute back to the communities, societies, environment its resources that have been utilized while carrying out one's business. The Companies Act, 1956 did not mandate for spending on CSR activities and therefore, there was no mandatory requirement for the construction of CSR Committee but the introduction of CSR policy to the Companies Act, 2013 has a wider ambit, therefore, the regulation needs to be monitored and hence there has been an inclusion of Independent Director in the Board of CSR Committee. The Companies Act, 2013 provides that every company having net worth of Rs. 500 crore or more shall constitute a Corporate Social Responsibility Committee of the Board consisting of three or more directors, out of which at least one director shall be an Independent Director.[22]

Stakeholder Committee: The Companies Act, 1956 did not require to constitute Stakeholder Relationship Committee but the Companies

20. See Section 178 of the Companies Act, 2013 (No. 18 of 2013).
21. Mansukhlal Hiralal & Co., "Corporate Social Responsibility: Indian Companies Act, 2013", available at www.mondaq.com (Last Modified 14/01/2015).
22. See Section 135 of the Companies Act, 2013 (No. 18 of 2013).

Acts, 2013 has included the Stakeholders Relationship Committee[23] that has to be constituted by any company that has a combined total of all its shareholders, debenture-holders, deposit-holders and security holders to be more than one thousand members shall constitute a Stakeholders Relationship Committee and the chairperson of that committee is to be the non-executive director of the company and any other member as per the decision of the Board. Since the role of the committee is to consider and resolve the grievances of the security holders of the company, therefore, the inclusion of non-executive director as the Chairperson of the committee has been made so as to provide independence to the justice delivery system without any biasness.

Liabilities

Under the old Act,[24] a contention can be made by the Independent Director for not considering him as an "officer in default" and consequently for non-liability for the actions of the Board. Also in the case of *S.M.S. Pharmaceuticals Ltd. v. Neeta Bhalla*[25], it was laid down by the Supreme Court of India that the liability arises on account of conduct, act or omission on the part of a person and not merely on account of holding an office or a position in a company. Thus, such a provision and judgment was a great relief to the Independent Director of a company who were being prosecuted merely by virtue of their presence on the Board. But with the enforcement of the Companies Act, 2013 such controversy has been put to rest. Since the Act has provided certain roles to be played by the Independent Directors; the Act has also laid down the liability which arises out of the roles. In order to safeguard the Independent Directors out of the unwelcome consequences arising out of Non-Independent Directors, the Companies Act, 2013 has expressly laid down that an Independent Director 'shall only be liable for such acts of omission or commission by a company which had occurred with his knowledge, attributable through Board processes, and with his consent or connivance where he had not acted diligently.'[26]

Remuneration

The Companies Act, 2013 restricts or expressly restrains Independent Directors from receiving remuneration other than sitting

23. See Section 178(5) of the Companies Act, 2013 (No. 18 of 2013).
24. The Companies Act, 1956 (1 of 1956).
25. 2009 (3) CC (NI) 194.
26. See Section 149(12) of the Companies Act, 2013 (No. 18 of 2013).

fees and reimbursement of travel allowances for attending the Board meeting, shareholders' meeting or any other meetings. The Act also laid down that the Independent Directors would not be entitled to any stock options.[27] The restriction from receiving remunerations has been included in the Act in order to maintain Independence by preventing Independent Directors to have a personal financial nexus with the company.

Removal

The Independent Directors can resign or be removed from the company as per the provision of Section 168 and 169 of the Companies Act, 2013. From the date of such resignation or removal, the Independent Director has to be replaced by a new Independent Director within a period of 180 days. On April 1, 2014, when Section 149 was notified by the Ministry of Corporate Affairs, the clock started ticking from then for the Independent Directors and it was really fortunate that it did not have a retrospective effect for them. Therefore, all the Independent Directors serving on the Board could continue serving on the Board for a period of ten years but they have to fulfil the necessary requirement as per the provisions of Section 149 of the Companies Act, 2013. Section 169 of the Companies Act, 2013 lay down that a special notice is to be required for the removal of the Directors. The same requirement of special notice has also been found in the Section 284(2) of the Companies Act, 1956, but there is one major difference and an important one too – Section 115 of the Companies Act, 2013 and Rule 23 of the Companies (Management and Administration) Rules, 2014 when read together indicates that a special notice may be given by members holding at least one percent of the total voting power or shares on which Rs. 5,00,000 has been paid.

Conclusion

Independent Directors on the Board of the company is to keep a check and balance in decision-making and the need for good Corporate Governance in India has been felt over a decade since the government started implementing its policy of economic liberalisation.[28]

It is being presumed that one cannot be independent while at the

27. See Section 197(7) of the Companies Act, 2013 (No. 18 of 2013).
28. P.N. Shah, "Role of Independent Directors in Corporate Governance", available at https://www.bcasonline.org/articles/artin.asp?41, (Visited on April 20, 2015).

same time one is serving the liabilities pertaining to the company. Therefore, Independent Directors are the outsider to the company, they serve, due to which they are being referred as Independent as they do not hold any pecuniary relationships with the company either directly or indirectly. This has also been mandated by the Act. The introduction of the concept Independent Directors in the Companies Act, 2013 must be seen as a positive measure taken by the Government in ensuring good Corporate Governance. The changes brought by the new Act are to ensure greater amount of accountability and transparency along with the independence in the management of the public listed companies thereby, casting greater responsibilities on Independent Directors since the Act lays down that any decision taken in the Board meeting without the presence of Independent Director has to be ratified by at least one of the Independent Director without which the decision would not hold valid. With the increase in measures taken by the Ministry of Corporate Affairs for augmenting corporate governance, there are evidences that are increasing complexities as well. The duties and responsibilities casted upon the Independent Directors are so tedious that the person who may have joined the Board would not be able to continue in that position under the provisions of the new Act. Also finding the adequate number of persons with compliance with the provision of Schedule IV and Clause 49 of the Equity Listing Agreement who will quality to be Independent Directors would also be difficult. Also the Independent Directors are not allowed to take any sort of remuneration other than the sitting fee and that too has a ceiling limit of Rs. 20,000 per meeting which is only possible for huge profit-making public listed companies. Therefore, this will find difficulty in attracting people of much high competence.

Efforts should also be taken to remove some of the discrepancies as in the case of allotment of stock options to the Independent Directors where Section 149[29] of the Act restricts Independent Directors from receiving any kind of stocks from the company while on the other hand Clause 49 of the Listing Agreement allows the public listed companies to allot stock options to the Independent Directors provided it has been approved by the Shareholders. Similarly, the ethical standard of code as specified in the Code for Independent Directors[30] does not mention what would be the basic standard of ethical behaviour and also the

29. See Section 149(9) of the Companies Act, 2013 (No. 18 of 2013).
30. See Schedule VI, Section 149(8) of the Companies Act, 2013 (No. 18 of 2013).

definition of Independent Director as per the provision of Companies Act, 2013 and Listing Agreement differs because 'the 2013 Act provides for quantitative threshold for the evaluation of significance of the relationship and both material and immaterial aspects of pecuniary relationship has been covered by the 2013 Act, thus, this would lead to the disqualification from the 2013 Act, though being considered Independent as per the Listing Agreement.'[31] Thus, elevating corporate governance in true sense needs smooth, efficient and transparent working of the management, promoters and Independent Directors which will help promote the interest of both the minority shareholders and the public listed companies as whole.

31. Grant Thornton, Implications of Companies Act, 2013: An Overview, available at http://gtw3.grantthornton.in/assets/Companies_Act-Governance.pdf (Visited on April 25, 2015).

17

Happy Independents: An Analysis on Concept of Independent Director

Hansa Sinha

Introduction

The board of directors can be said to be the soul of a company and the driving force. It is the board of directors who can give direction to company towards greater heights through its prudent and timely decisions. There is no doubt that the directors are qualified and able, however, often while leading a group of persons can involve some restrictions and these in turn affect the independence of the directors and for ensuring the high standards of corporate governance this independence is indispensable. The Companies Act, 1956 did not define the term "independent director". The previous Act placed an independent director on the same level as any other director for the purposes of decision making and no privileges, duties or functions were specified. It can be said that this has lead to an uncertainty with respect to the roles to be performed by independent directors. The Independent Director has recently gained importance with the introduction of the New Companies Act, 2013; however the concept is not new. In the 1950's this concept first saw the light of day in the USA. At the time it was seen as a solution to the Manager-Share Holder Agency problem. One thing common among some of the important jurisdictions was that this concept was introduced in the aftermath of various scams. Whether it was the Enron, World Com or Tyco in case of USA that resulted in the Sarbanes Oxley Act in the year 2002 or whether it was the Maxwell and Polly Peck scams in the UK. The Indian concept of independent directors had a similar series of events provoking it into existence and more specifically the Satyam Scam in the year 2009. To bring about transparency the concept of independent director has now been introduced. Many committees have deliberated on this concept like, Kumara Mangalam Birla Committee (1999), Naresh Chandra Committee (2002), Narayana Murthy Committee (2003) and recently the J.J. Irani Committee.[1] The new companies Act has laid down a non-exhaustive list of duties to be performed by the independent directors. This places the Indian independent director on the global map next to its UK and USA counterparts where the codified duties and roles of an independent director exist.

Legal framework for Independent Directors

At first this term found expression in various committees' reports. Further, to these proposals, the term "independent director" was introduced for the first time in India when the Securities and Exchange Board of India ("**SEBI**") incorporated clause 49 in the Listing Agreement.[2] Again Section 2(47) of the Companies Act defines "independent director" to mean an independent director as referred to in Section 149 of the Act. An independent director means a director other than a managing director or a whole-time director or a nominee director who does not have any material or pecuniary relationship with the company/directors.[3] Section 149(6) of the Act prescribes the criteria for independent directors, which are as follows:

(a) Who in the opinion of the Board, is a person of integrity and possesses relevant industrial expertise and experience;
(b) Such individual shall not be a promoter or related to promoter of the company or its holding, subsidiary or associate company;

---

1. Divesh Goyal, "Independent Directors" *CA Club India,* dated 17 December 2014 available at http://www.caclubindia.com/articles/independent-directors--22423.asp#.VTfrdyGqqko (Visited on April, 22, 2015).
2. Shinoj Koshy, Preetha S and Vandana V, "New Directions: The responsibilities, rewards and liabilities of independent directors will be transformed by the new Companies Act"; Vol. 7, Issues 6, *Indian Business Law Journal* (Dec 2013/Jan 2014).
3. Companies Act, 2013, Appointment and Qualifications of Directors; The Institute of Company Secretaries of India, Available at: http://www.icsi.edu/portals/0/APPOINTMENT%20AND%20QUALIFICATIONS.pdf.

(c) Such individuals must not have any material or pecuniary relationship during the two immediately preceding financial years or during the current financial year with the company or its promoters/directors/holding/subsidiary/associate company;

(d) The relatives of such person should not have had any pecuniary relationship with the company or its subsidiaries, amounting to 2% or more of its gross turnover or total income or Rs. 50 lacs or such higher amount as may be prescribed, whichever is less, during the two immediately preceding financial years or in the current financial year;

(e) He must not either directly or any of his relatives

  (i) Hold or has held the position of a key managerial personnel or is or has been employee of the company or its holding, subsidiary or associate company in any of the three financial years immediately preceding year in which he is proposed to be appointed.

  (ii) is or has been an employee or proprietor or a partner, in any of the three financial year in which he is proposed to be appointed of:

    (A) a firm of auditors or company secretaries in practice or cost auditors of the company or its holding, subsidiary or associate company; or

    (B) any legal or a consulting firm that has or had any transaction with the company, its holding, subsidiary or associate company amounting to ten per cent or more of the gross turnover of such firm;

  (iii) holds together with his relatives two per cent or more of the total voting power of the company; or

  (iv) is a Chief Executive or director, by whatever name called, of any non-profit organization that receives 25% or more of its receipts from the company, any of its promoters, directors or its holding, subsidiary or associate company or that holds 2% or more of the total voting power of the company, then also he is not eligible for office of independent director; or

  (v) who possesses such other qualifications as prescribed in Rule 5 as an independent director shall possess appropriate skills, experience and knowledge in one or more fields of finance, law management sales marketing administration research, corporate governance, technical operations or other disciplines related to the company's business.[4]

The Companies (Appointment and Qualification of Directors) Rules, 2014 cover the appointment, qualification, etc. of independent directors and for instance Rules pertains to number of independent directors.[5] It provides that the following class or classes of companies shall have at least two directors as independent directors-

(i) the Public Companies having paid up share capital of ten crore rupees or more; or

(ii) the Public Companies having a turnover of one hundred crore rupees or more; or

(iiii) the Public Companies which have in aggregate, outstanding loans, debenture and deposits exceeding fifty crore rupees:

Provided that in case a company covered under this rule is required to appoint a higher number of independent directors shall be applicable to it. Provided further that any intermittent vacancy of an independent director shall be filled up by the Board at the earliest but not later than immediate next Board meeting or three months from the date of vacancy whichever is later. Provided also that where a company ceases to fulfill any of three conditions laid down in sub-rule (1) for three consecutive years, it shall not be required to comply with these provisions until such time as it meets any of such conditions;

Under the Rules the qualifications of independent director have been elaborated as an independent director shall possess appropriate skills, experience and knowledge in one or more fields of finance, law, management, sales, marketing, administration, research, corporate governance, technical operations or other disciplines related to the company's business.[6]

J.J. Irani Committee Recommendations

This Committee introduced the rationale and the concept of independent directors. It provided that given the responsibility of the Board to balance various interests, the presence of independent directors

4. *Ibid.*
5. Rule 4, the Companies (Appointment and Qualifications) of Director Rules, 2014.
6. Rule 5 the Companies (Appointment and Qualifications of Director) Rules, 2014.

on the Board of a company would improve corporate governance. This is particularly important for public companies or companies with a significant public interest. While directors representing specific interests would be confined to the perspective dictated by such interests, independent directors would be able to bring an element of objectivity to Board process in the general interests of the company and thereby to the benefit of minority interests and shareholders. Independence therefore is not to be viewed merely as independence from Promoter Interests but from the point of view of vulnerable stake holders who cannot otherwise get their voice heard. Law should therefore recognize the principle of independent directors and spell out their role, qualifications and liability. However requirement of presence of Independent Directors may vary depending on the size and type of the company. There cannot be a single prescription to suit all companies. Therefore number of Independent Directors may be prescribed through rules for different categories of companies.[7] The Committee recommendations were readily accepted and incorporated in the new Companies Act.

Qualifications and Disqualifications of Independent Director

Any person who is not disqualified to be a director, who has a Director Identification Number (DIN) and gives declaration to the extent that he is not disqualified to be a director, who has given the necessary consent and has been declared eligible for appointment by the Board is qualified to be an independent director. The disqualifications for an independent director can be deduced from the provision of section 149 elucidated before herein. Further, Section 164 provides general guidelines on disqualifications for appointment of director.

Declaration of Independence

Every Independent director needs to provide a declaration of independence. This Statement contains information about the applicant's relevant experience, a declaration against all such issues that may hold him/her disqualified. It is addressed to the Board of Directors and contains all the relevant details of the applicant such as DIN, complete address with phone number, etc. It is important that an

7. Ministry of Company Affairs, Dr. J.J. Irani Committee Report (Expert Committee on Company Law), published on 31st May, 2005 available at http://www.primedirectors.com/pdf/JJ%20Irani%20Report-MCA.pdf.

independent director satisfies all the criteria required by this Declaration.

Code for Independent Directors

To ensure professional conduct by the independent directors reference to Schedule IV is found in Section 149(8). This prescribes certain guidelines which must be adhered to by the independent directors. Adherence to these standards by independent directors and fulfillment of their responsibilities in a professional and faithful manner will promote confidence of the investment community, particularly minority shareholders, regulators and companies in the institution of independent directors. Code of Conduct includes guidelines of professional conduct, role and functions, duties, manner of appointment, re-appointment, resignation or removal, separate meetings, evaluation mechanism.[8]

The Director Remuneration Debate

The important provisions for consideration here are sections 149(9), 197 and 198. On a collective reading we find that an independent director is not entitled to any stock option. But he may receive sitting fees, reimbursement of expenses incurred for attending board or other committee meetings and commission linked to profits. The sitting fees cannot exceed Rs. 1,00,000. Further the profit related commission as may be approved by the share holders by passing of resolution in General Meeting.[9] The reason for denying monthly/yearly remuneration is to preserve his independency. The deprivation from stock option is not being perceived well by many quarters. Some observe that had it been allowed, it would have been an incentive in the absence of good remuneration.[10]

---

8. The Companies Act, 2013, Appointment and Qualifications of Directors; The Institute of Company Secretaries of India, Available at: http://www.icsi.edu/portals/0/APPOINTMENT%20AND%20QUALIFICATIONS.pdf.
9. Divesh Goyal, "*Independent directors are now a crucial part of Indian Company Law*", 9th July, 2014 (Unpublished Article, Goyal Divesh & Associates) available at http://canextstep.com/wp-content/uploads/user_uploads/vikrampurohit288@yahoo.com/Independent_Director_ACS_Divesh_Goyal.pdf
10. G.S. Rao, "*The Companies Act, 2013: Provisions relating to Independent Directors*", 13 September, 2013 (Unpublished Article DGM (Legal) at OCL India Limited); available at http://www.caclubindia.com/articles/the-com

Resignation and Removal

The resignation or removal of an Independent director shall be in the same manner as is provided in sections 168 and 169 of the Act. The notice of resignation can be given in writing to the Company. The Board of receipt of such notice shall file the same with Registrar in Form DIR-12 within 30 days from the date of receipt of such notice. The Company shall then place the fact of such resignation in Director Report laid in the immediately following general meeting by the company. A copy is forwarded by director in DIR-11 within 30 days. As far as removal is concerned a company may by ordinary resolution remove a director, before expiry of his period after giving a reasonable opportunity of being heard.[11] A special notice is required of any resolution, to remove a director under this section, or to appoint somebody in place of a director so removed. A copy of notice should be sent to the concerned director and shall be entitled to be heard on the resolution at the meeting. A vacancy created by the removal of a director under this section may, if he had been appointed by the Company in general meeting or by the Board, be filled by the appointment of another director in his place at the meeting at which he is removed. The director that has been removed from the office, shall not be appointed as a Director by Board of Directors. The vacancy created by the resignation or removal shall be replaces by a new independent director within a period of not more than 180 days. If the company fulfills the requirement of independent directors in its board without filling the vacancy created by such resignation or removal as the case may be then in that case the requirement of replacement by a new independent director will not be necessary.

Tenure of Independent Directors under Law

An independent director holds the office for a term up to five years. This may be extended by another five years pursuant to special resolution by the company but cannot be more than consecutive ten years. After expiration of three years after ten years, such a person can again be appointed as independent director. This is subject to the condition that during those three years when he is not an independent director with the company he should not be appointed or be associated

panies-act-2013-provisions-relating-to-independent-directors-18363.asp#.VTfQFROUdp9

11. PWC Report on Companies Act, 2013 (Key Highlights & Analysis), 30th November, 2013; available at https://www.pwc.in/en_IN/in/assets/pdfs/publications/2013/companies-act-2013-Key-highlights-and-analysis.pdf

with the company in any other capacity. The independent director should be re-appointed based on report of performance evaluation.

Independent Directors of Asset Management and Trustee Companies

The SEBI has dedicated provisions to this extent. It is provided that the two thirds of the board of directors of a trustee company shall be independent persons and shall not be associated with the sponsors or be associated with them in any manner whatsoever.[12] At least 50% of the Board of Directors of an asset management company must be independent directors, i.e. directors, who are not associates of the sponsor or any of its subsidiaries.[13] AMC and Trustee companies are required to send bio data of its directors to SEBI in the specified format.[14] Persons providing any type of professional service to the Mutual Fund, Asset Management Company, Trustee Company and the sponsors shall be considered as associate directors of AMCs or trustee companies, as the case maybe. Also, the persons having any material pecuniary relationship with these entities which in judgment of the trustees may affect the independence of directors shall be treated as associate directors.[15] AMC or Trustee Company must appoint independent director(s) in the place of resigning director(s) within a period of three months from the date of resignation. Where a mutual fund is unable to meet this time limit, it should report to SEBI explaining the reasons for non-compliance.[16]

Role in Corporate Social Responsibility Committee Diminished

Section 135(1) of the Act provides that every company having net worth of rupees five hundred crore or more, or turnover of rupees one thousand crore or more or a net profit of rupees five crore or more during any financial year shall constitute a Corporate Social Responsibility Committee of the Board consisting of three or more directors, out of which at least one director shall be an independent director. The Companies (Corporate Social Responsibility Policy) Rules, 2014 further this objective. The Rules however have done away with the requirement of independent directors for unlisted public company or a private company as they can have its CSR Committee without the independent director. Further the CSR Rules have relaxed the

12. Regulation 16(5) SEBI (Mutual Funds) Regulations, 1996.
13. Reg. 21(1)(d) ibid.
14. SEBI Circular No. MFD/CIR/11/354/2001, dated 20.12.2001.
15. SEBI Circular No.MFD/CIR/13/16799/2002, dated 29th August, 2002.
16. SEBI Circular No.MFD/CIR/17/21105/2002 dated 28th October, 2002.

requirement regarding the presence of three or more directors on the CSR Committee of the Board. In case where a private company has only two directors on the board, the CSR Committee can be constituted with these two directors. The CSR Committee of a foreign company shall comprise of at least two persons wherein one or more persons should be resident in India and the other person nominated by the foreign company.[17]

Independent Directors by Chamber of Indian Micro Small and Medium Enterprises

The sudden change has created a void in the corporate world. Now suddenly there is a greater demand for independent directors suitable for Indian companies. Keeping this in mind a dedicated portal by the name of www.indianindependentdircetors.org has been initiated by Chamber of Indian Micro Small & Medium Enterprises (CIMSME). This is in consonance with Section 150(1) of the Act which provides for Manner of selection of independent directors through data banks maintained by anybody, institute or association, as may be notified by the Central Government. Firstly it aims to create a data bank of independent directors. Secondly, it intends to reach out to the companies that need such independent directors based on newly formed legal provisions of the Companies Act. The Initial Due diligence promised by the portal is a step towards verifying the profiles of the persons to be hosted on the website. Apart from Due Diligence Process, this portal provides for Professional Zone, wherein professionals can register themselves for inclusion of their names in the online database. The Listed Company Zone is specifically for the PSU's, Listed Company and Other Government and Private Companies. It is expected that there will be a huge demand for qualified and capable independent directors and this portal will be handy in such situations.

Conclusion

As opposed to the old Act the new Act prescribes liability of independent directors in relation to some activities of the board. It seems that the concept under the Act has been streamlined to

17. Rahul Rishi, Ankita Srivastava & Dr. Milind Antani, "*New Rules for Corporate Social Responsibility Announced* dated". 12 March, 2014, Social Sector Hotline, available at: http://www.nishithdesai.com/information/research-and-articles/nda-hotline/nda-hotline-single-view/article/new-rules-for-corporate-social-responsibility-in-india-its-effectiveness-andlegality.html?no_cache=1&c Hash = c3c9597008f8602ff6430feed1b03360

incorporate the good principles of the UK jurisdiction, i.e. the UK's Companies Act, 2006 and the Combined Code of Corporate Governance and various practices adopted by UK. These changes are keeping in mind the changing times and needs. It is expected to bring greater transparency and independence and value to the company. With greater power comes greater responsibility. Thus, through clear defining of roles, duties, functions, code of conduct, etc. a greater responsibility and accountability is bestowed upon the independent directors. With the greater responsibilities and power it still remains to be seen how they deal with the limitation of being a minority, i.e. one-third of the board. The conflicts between the new Act and others for instance the Listing Agreement, if any, will have to be smoothen out. The blocking of the stock option to the independent directors raises the doubt that whether good qualified persons can be attracted to perform the job. Moreover, it is the hope for better corporate governance, particularly for public companies or companies with a significant public interest that encourages the concept. The independent director gives objectivity to the board process so that the general interest of the company is served. It brings a fresh perspective to the company operations which is knowledgeable, professional and which dedicates its attention to the minority interests and small shareholders as well.

CHAPTER VIII

Women Directors

18

Women Directors in Boardrooms: Starting of a New Era

DR. ARUNDHATI BHATTACHARYYA

Introduction

The World Economic Forum has predicted that women will not attain equal economic participation levels and opportunities until 2095.[1] This is not very good news for the present generation and there is need to correct the imbalances in the skewed participation levels. India's low parity level among the genders is a fact. The discriminations against Indian women are found both at the private and the public spaces. Their poor status has been reflected in the workplace. According to the International Labour Organization's Global Employment Trends 2013 report, India's labour force participation rate for women has dropped. In 2004-05, it was just over 37 per cent in 2004-05 and in 2009-10 it was 29 per cent. India ranks 11th out of 131 countries from the bottom in female labour force participation.[2] India is quite low in gender diversity in the boardroom. The percentage of women executives in the

1. Lauren Davidson, "Gender Equality will Happen—but not until 2095," *The Telegraph*, Oct. 28, 2014, available at: http://www.telegraph.co.uk/ finance/ economics/11191348/Gender-equality-will-happen-but-not-until-2095.html (Visited on March 29, 2015)
2. "India: Why is women's labour force participation dropping?" available at: http://www.ilo.org/global/about-the-ilo/newsroom/comment-analysis/WCMS_ 204762/lang--en/index.html (Visited on May 20, 2015)

corporate ladder decreases as one scale higher. They are only 4.7 percent of India's corporate directors. India's position is very low compared to Norway, Finland, France and Sweden. These countries have over 30 percent women representation in corporate boards. India is also lower than China and Brazil.[3] Indian companies reflect the Indian society where glass ceiling is a norm. One way of correcting the disparity is by providing representation of women through quota. Several influential business leaders, like, Christine Lagarde, the managing director of the International Monetary Fund, and Sheryl Sandberg, Chief Operating Officer at Facebook, stated that the controversial quota for women in executive roles are unfortunate but necessary.[4] As board members, women gain influence over policy-making. In the United States, members of boards acquire greater status in society and higher level of presence in boards of non-business institutions. These institutions may have greater say in governmental agencies or even in preparation of curriculum regarding research purpose.[5]

Indian Position on Woman Director

Diversity in the composition of the company boards has been a topic of discussion in India. But, it has acquired serious dimension in India after the passing of the Companies Act, 2013. The government has supported the inclusion of quota for women in the boards of companies. It is the starting of a new era in the running of companies in India. Companies need to have at least one woman director. The categories of companies which need to comply with the requirement of having at least of one woman director are as follows [section 149(1) of 2013 Act]:

(i) Every listed company, within one year from the commencement of second proviso to sub-section (1) of section 149.

3. Kiran Mazumdar Shaw, "Women On Boards: Why India Inc Needs The 'Diversity Edge'?" April 6, 2015 available at: http://www.dnaindia.com/analysis/standpoint-women-on-boards-why-india-inc-needs-the-diversity-edge-2075206 (Visited on May 2, 2015).
4. Szu Ping Chan, "Quotas needed for women in executive roles", Jan. 25, 2014, available at: http://www.telegraph.co.uk/finance/financetopics/davos/10597233/Quotas-needed-for-women-in-executive-roles.html (Visited on March 2, 2015).
5. James D. Westphal and Ithai Stern, "Flattery Will Get You Everywhere (Especially If You Are a Male Caucasian): How Ingratiation, Boardroom Behavior, and Demographic Minority Status Affect Additional Board Appointments at U.S. Companies," 50 *AMJ* 267-288 (2007), available at: http://www.jstor.org/stable/20159854 (Visited on May 5, 2015).

(ii) Every other public company that has paid–up share capital of one hundred crore rupees or more, or a turnover of three hundred crore rupees or more within three years from the commencement of second proviso to sub-section (1) of section 149.

The punishment for not following the directives is serious. According to the order of the Securities and Exchange Board of India, the companies that missed the deadline of March 31, 2015 but who appoints a female director before June 30 must pay Rs. 50,000 as fine. An additional daily fine of Rs. 1,000 per day will be added for companies that obey between July 1 and September 30. After October 1, the fine rises to Rs. 1.42 lakh and Rs. 5,000 for every day of disobedience. The Securities and Exchange Board of India (SEBI) had issued an order in February 2014 for proper execution of the provisions of the Act. It was found that one in every six companies appointed relatives of the promoters as directors. 987 companies of the 1,478 listed on the National Stock Exchange did not meet the requirement of one woman director on board. But, companies took fast action to comply the Act and between February 2014 and March 30, 2015, 674 of the 987 companies appointed a woman director. Several critics have stated that it would be wrong to say that competent women are unavailable who are suitable for the post of a director. But, the problem lies in the patriarchal mindset of the men in power who are not ready or comfortable with a woman director on board. The aim of the Act is to provide the platform for women to have their say heard at the higher company levels. The Act does not specifically mention the need for independent women directors. So, several large companies, like Reliance Industries, Videocon Industries, JK Tyre and Industries, Bajaj Corp and TVS Motor Corp have preferred to appoint their relatives on the board. Supporters of choice of relatives as woman director state that the relatives may be equally efficient in her work. So, she should have the opportunity to contribute to the company.[6] The Corporate Affairs Ministry has notified that every listed company and those public firms having paid up share capital of Rs. 100 crore or more should have at least one woman director on their board. It will be also applicable to entities with a minimum turnover of Rs. 300 crore. The rule would also

---

6. Shruti Srivastava and Sandeep Singh, "Deadline near, India Inc scrambles to get women directors on board", available at: http://indianexpress.com/article/india/india- others/deadline-near-india-inc-scrambles-to-get-women-directors-on-board/ (Visited on May 22, 2015).

apply to public companies having minimum paid up share capital of Rs. 10 crore. Those companies whose aggregate "outstanding loans, debentures and deposits" exceed Rs. 50 crore also need to have a woman director.[7] But, the ground situation is really difficult as on March 31, 2015, 313 National Stock Exchange-listed companies did not have a single woman director. Several reasons put forward by several quarters, behind difficulty in recruiting women in boards are small pool of talent, inability to retain women in the workforce due to their focus on family rather than job and plain reluctance to induct women due to the patriarchal mindset developed for years. In order to increase the resource pool for women directors and to allow diversity in the workforce, the middle level management needs to be re-arranged. It is from here that the gender parity becomes skewed with more women dropping out. The attempt to create gender diversity must extend across the workforce. The SEBI order may trigger recruitment of more women in the highest level, but the impact will be fruitful only when the diversity is reflected at every level. The position of women representation in the corporate sector is dismal in India as she occupies one of the lowest ranks among the Asian countries. According to a 2012 report from the consultancy McKinsey, women account for 29 percent of the workforce at the entry level. It falls to 9 percent at the mid-to-senior management level. The situation becomes worse at the level of chief executives where women constitute less than 1 percent. Kiran Mazumdar Shaw has advised companies to recognize talented women professionals and provide opportunity to bring value to the boardroom in the long-run. She has reinforced and reflected the idea of global studies that companies with greater gender diversity do well financially and they have better leadership, accountability, innovation, operational efficiency and motivational work culture. She has also prescribed the view that companies need to invite skilled economists, social scientists, chartered accountants and women with diverse competencies to bring a fresh perspective to corporate decision-making. She has mentioned a recent study of the top 100 Indian companies (BSE 100) by Randstad. It has reinforced her belief that companies with women on their boards perform better. They bring balance of views and opinions that allow for more informed decision-making. She has mentioned that ensuring

7. "New Companies Act: Firms to have at least one woman, two independent directors", March 28, 2014, available at: http://articles.economictimes.indiatimes.com/2014-03-28/news/48662757_1_new-companies-act-share-capital-corporate-affairs-ministry (Visited on March 29, 2015)

gender balance in the board does not mean compromise of the quality of the board. The selection of women directors based on their professional capabilities, will enhance the quality of the boards, leading to much better outcomes. She advised that Indian companies should respect the spirit behind the SEBI directive. Competent women need to be inducted in the board, to support good governance and effective management of the company.[8] At present, it is stated that competent women with experience in boards are few in number. Some of them are on multiple boards. It is necessary to prescribe a criterion of an active work experience as the precondition to be a board member.[9]

World Scenario

Internationally, there is paucity of women on boards. A study by Deborah E. Arfken *et al* on the presence of women on boards in Tennessee found out that women in board rooms were almost non-existent. Total 63 percent of the companies surveyed had no women directors on their boards.[10] Terjesen and Singh in their study concluded that those countries with a long tradition of political representation have less chances of having more women on boards. On the other hand, representation of more women on boards has a better male-female wage ratio and has higher women in the levels of the corporate ladder. The study is based on the data received from 43 countries.[11] A study by Catalyst regarding gender diversity on boards provides a picture of the representation of women on boards around the globe. Norway has been a model for gender diversty. It is the first country in the world to mandate that women account for 40 percent of its board seats. At present, it has 35.5 percent women on boards of its OMX-listed

---

8. Kiran Mazumdar Shaw, "Women On Boards: Why India Inc Needs The 'Diversity Edge'?" April 6, 2015, available at: http://www.dnaindia.com/analysis/standpoint-women-on-boards-why-india-inc-needs-the-diversity-edge-2075206 (Visited on April 8, 2015).
9. Anirvan Ghosh, "Mandatory Rules to appoint more women directors not working in India", March 30, 2015, available at: http://www.huffingtonpost.in/2015/03/30/where-are-the-women_0_n_6966632.html (Visited on March 30, 2015).
10. Deborah E. Arfken, Stephanie L. Bellar and Marilyn M. Helms, "The Ultimate Glass Ceiling Revisited: The Presence of Women on Corporate Boards", 50 *JBE* 177-186 (2004), available at: http://www.jstor.org/stable/25123205 (Visited on May 5, 2015)
11. Siri Terjesen and Val Singh, "Female Presence on Corporate Boards: A Multi-Country Study of Environmental Context", 83 *JBE* 55-63 (2008), available at: http://www.jstor.org/stable/25482353 (Visited on May 5, 2015)

companies. Finland has 29.9 percent women on boards. In France, it is 29.7 percent of board seats. France has ordered its companies to reach the target of 40 percent by January 2017. Sweden (28.8 percent), Belgium (23.4 percent) and United Kingdom (22.8 percent) are in the fourth, fifth and sixth place, respectively, regarding female representation on its boards. Japan is at the bottom of the list with only 3.1 percent female boardroom representation. Italy has 6 percent female representation. Kenya has 15 percent women in the boardrooms which is less than half of its desired 33 percent quota. Similarly, Canada has 20.8 percent representation which is less than half of its 50 percent quota. Both Australia and the United States, have less than a fifth of their board seats filled by women directors.[12] Germany has 18.5 percent female representation on board. It has introduced a quota for women in non-executive boards.[13] The quota is of 30 percent which will be implemented in 2016.[14]

Benefits of More Women in Boardrooms

It is necessary that the companies realize the business sense of more women in workforce, even at the highest level. There are several advantages for companies with more women in boardrooms. They have better information, increased creativity, less of bad decision-making and have varying perspectives. They add legitimacy to the organization and provide alternative solutions to problems. Moreover, women board members can easily feel the pulse of the women customers. This helps in taking smart decisions as purchasing power of women are well understood by women board members. Some of the institutional investors invest in companies with female representation. So when women are there in the boards, there is access to resources from these investors. Proper gender representation provides opportunity to employ from wider variety of potential employees.[15] Research confirms that the

---

12. Lauren Davidson, "Proof that women in boardrooms quotas work", January 13, 2015, available at: http://www.telegraph.co.uk/finance/newsbysector/banksandfinance/11341816/Proof-that-women-in-boardrooms-quotas-work.html (Visited on March 10, 2015).
13. Justin Huggler, "German boardrooms to introduce female quotas", Nov. 26, 2014, available at: http://www.telegraph.co.uk/news/worldnews/europe/germany/11255970/German-boardrooms-to-introduce-female-quotas.html (Visited on March 28, 2015).
14. Caroline Copley, "German parliament approves legal quotas for women on company boards", Mar. 7, 2015, available at: ETReutershttp://www.cnbc.com/id/102485489 (Visited on March 28, 2015).
15. Amy J. Hillman, Christine Shropshire and Albert A. Cannella Jr.,

benefits of diversity are improvement in financial performance, leveraging talent, reflecting the marketplace and building reputation and increasing innovation and group performance. Insecurities in the economy have transformed the corporate governance climate in every country. Diversity in board rooms brings in fresh ideas and ideas to solve problems. Women in the boards usually create better consumer and employee connections. The diversity helps in the growth of the business which is the ultimate aim of every company. More women in board rooms increase the moral imagination. It helps to imagine the possible issues which would need attention, possible challenges that the company may face and the possible solutions that would make the company more competitive and productive.[16] The re-entry of women in middle level or at any rank in the corporate ladder requires company support. It has been seen that some companies go out of their way in order to support employees, including women, who have leadership potentiality. When companies realize the integrity of the women employees towards the company, most of the companies will be happy to provide them with flexible schedules and other support bases to help them. This will help the company to groom the leadership in the pipeline. Companies want to retain their best employees and for that purpose, they are also ready to go to great lengths.[17] Companies are providing support system to help women to strike a balance between work and life. For example, in Accenture maternity leave benefits have been extended to 5 months of paid leave from 12 weeks. Additional maternity benefit option of 1 month is being provided. Option of unpaid leave of absence for further 12 weeks is provided. Maternity returners programme helps ease the transition for new parents back into workforce by providing career guidance and support in finding the ideal re-entry roles. It also assists women employees during maternity to remain in workforce, if they chose. Maternity counselling sessions enables an expecting or new mother to enroll for six telephonic sessions with a trained counsellor. Employee assistance program helps employees cope with personal and

---

"Organizational Predictors of Women on Corporate Boards", 50 *AMJ* 941-952 (2007), available at: http://www.jstor.org/stable/20159898 (Visited on May, 5 2015).

16. Catherine M. Daily and Dan R. Dalton, "Are Director Equity Policies Exclusionary?" 13 *BEQ* 415-432 (2003), available at: http://www.jstor.org/stable/ 3857965 (Visited on May 5, 2015).
17. Robin Ely and Colleen Ammerman, "Discussing Gender Diversity," *Mint*, May 13, 2015, p. 29.

professional issues.[18]

Challenges in the Way

Lack of informal networking among the women in the corporate sector, compared to men, prevents them from advancing.[19] Women in the boards should voice their opinion and should not act as puppets or as proxy to others. All organizations need to detect the real obstacles to representation of women at the senior levels. Harvard Business School initiated a study on the career and life expectations of its alumni. A constant gender gap was found at multiple dimensions of corporate leadership. Factors like lack of role models and influential mentors could be challenges in the path for women leaders.[20] Women after marriage and children find it hard to carry on with the demands of job. Several studies have found that Indian women are hardly helped by their husband in the household chores.[21] So, the whole focus shifts for the women in running the house. Few years of support from the company in terms of flexi-hours, leaves, etc. may help the women employees to adapt themselves to the changing work-life balance after marriage. In return, companies will get loyal and sincere women employees who will stand by the company even during the worst times.

Conclusion

Mandatory inclusion of at least one woman director to the Board of every prescribed class of companies in India can be considered as being a highly elegant and revolutionary initiation by the Government of India. It will have strong ripple impact on empowerment of women in the Indian corporate world. India will advance economically with solid contributions of women in the corporate sector.[22] For that end, India

---

18. Rica Bhattacharyya, "Accenture Extends Maternity Leave to 5 Months", *The Economic Times*, May 5, 2015.
19. Deborah E. Arfken, Stephanie L. Bellar and Marilyn M. Helms, "The Ultimate Glass Ceiling Revisited: The Presence of Women on Corporate Boards", 50 *JBE* 177-186 (2004), available at: http://www.jstor.org/stable/25123205 (Visited on March 27, 2015).
20. Robin Ely and Colleen Ammerman, "Discussing Gender Diversity", *Mint*, May 13, 2015.
21. Amit Bhandari and Amritha Pillay, "Why India Inc struggles with women on its Boards", April 21, 2015, available at: http://www.thenewsminute.com/article/why-india-inc-struggles-women-its-boards (Visited on April 22, 2015).
22. Hemant Goyal and Sandhya Aggarwal, "New Indian Companies Act of 2013 Towards Women Empowerment," May 15, 2014, available at: http://www.mondaq.com/india/x/313748/Corporate+Governance/Woman+Directorship+

needs more women representation on boards. Companies are trying to create a pipeline one level below. The search for women as board members has increased among the Indian companies after the mandatory representation of women on board has been passed by the Indian legislature. Earlier, Multi-National Companies were only interested in stepping up recruitment of women at senior management levels. Now, the Indian companies are doing the same.[23] Such recruitment drive also improves the ethical image of the company.[24] But, many feel that mere tokenism of the presence of women as directors on board will not help. It will take some time for the fruits of diversity in the composition of the boards, on the basis of gender, can be seen. The talent pipeline of the company needs to be strengthened. Value addition to the company is not done when tokenism of women director is happening. A study by Catalyst found out that more females on board improves financial performance of the companies. Between 2005 and 2009, the top quartile of Fortune 500 companies by female boardroom representation, outperformed those in the lowest quartile with a 16 percent higher return on sales and a 26 percent increase in return on invested capital respectively.[25] Women's representation in the company boards are influenced by overall societal, political, economic and cultural condition of the country.[26] India needs to be fair and supportive towards its daughters. A country can only advance with an equal contribution from both the genders. It is high time that Indians realize it; otherwise, the future of India will be a gloomy one.

A+Laudable+Initiative+Of+The(Visited on May 20, 2015).

23. Prachi Verma and Rica Bhattacharyya, "India Inc's New Formula to Rework Gender Math", *Economic Times*, March 31, 2015.
24. Val Singh and Sébastien Point, "(Re)Presentations of Gender and Ethnicity in Diversity Statements on European Company Websites", 68 *JBE* 363-379 (2006), available at: http://www.jstor.org/stable/25123923 (Visited on May 5, 2015).
25. Lauren Davidson, "Proof that women in boardrooms quotas work", January 13, 2015, available at: http://www.telegraph.co.uk/finance/newsbysector/banksandfinance/11341816/Proof-that-women-in-boardrooms-quotas-work.html (Visited on March 26, 2015).
26. Siri Terjesen and Val Singh, "Female Presence on Corporate Boards: A Multi-Country Study of Environmental Context", 83 *JBE* 55-63 (2008), available at: http://www.jstor.org/stable/25482353 (Visited on May 6, 2015).

19

A Revolutionary Move to Women Empowerment: Woman Director on Board

PRIYAM RATNAM

Introduction

The work place is a setting where gender inequalities are easily noticed. Men are always found in a number much greater than that of Women. Initially women participation was not seen in areas such as army, air force but then the situation changed as several efforts are being made in this field to ensure equal status to women by providing women reservation designed only for the betterment, protection and empowerment of the women. The Companies Act, 2013 has taken a revolutionary step in this direction which is appointment of at least one woman director in certain class of companies' board. Board of Directors is an important body responsible for running of the company and members are elected by Shareholders. Hence, it is very important to have women participation in the board. The second proviso to section 149(1) of the act makes it mandatory the every listed company shall appoint at least one woman director within one year from the commencement of the second proviso to Section 149(1) of the Act.[1] According to an estimate, nearly one-third of the top-500 listed companies do not have any female representation on their respective

1. The Companies Act, 2013.

Boards. Securities and Exchange Board of India (SEBI) has taken necessary action against listed firms which fail to appoint at least one woman director on their Boards. SEBI has written to more than 160 such companies to ensure compliance. Still, a large number of companies are yet to comply.[2] The norms were finalized by the regulator after detailed discussions were held between SEBI and concerned stakeholders for over a year and the regulations are stronger for listed companies than those prescribed under the Companies Act for non-listed entities.

Legal Provisions on Composition of Board

The Constitution of India guarantees gender equality and so many social legislations have been made in modern times to fulfill this constitutional objective. But in corporate laws such type of provisions are very rare. There was no clear provision prescribing composition of Board of Directors in the Companies Act, 1956 though Clause 49 of the Listing Agreement has provided for Composition relating to Board of Directors. Where the Board of directors of the company shall have an optimum combination of executive and non-executive directors with not less than fifty percent of the board of directors comprising of non-executive directors and Where the Chairman of the Board is a non-executive director, at least one-third of the Board should comprise of independent directors and in case he is an executive director, at least half of the Board should comprise of independent directors. Provided that where the non-executive Chairman is a promoter of the company or is related to any promoter or person occupying management positions at the Board level or at one level below the Board, at least one-half of the Board of the company shall consist of independent directors.[3] Now Second Proviso to Section 149(1) of the new law provided further that such class or classes of companies as may be prescribed shall have at least one woman director.[4] The Companies (Appointment & Qualification of Director) Rules, 2014 have to be read along with Section 149 of the Companies Act. Earlier, these draft rules gave arbitrary rights in the hands of government for the appointment of women directors. But as the rules got notified and enforced from 1st day of April, 2014, the position became clear, but only to a limited extent which is providing a

2. http://www.business-standard.com/article/pti-stories/sebi-to-take-action-against-cos-with-no-woman-director-govt-115031700585_1.html.
3. Clause 49 of the Listing Agreement.
4. Section 149, Companies Act, 2013.

choice for company in regard to appointment of the women director. These rules provide the class of companies which shall appoint at least one woman director, these are (i) every listed company; (ii) every other public company having (a) paid–up share capital of one hundred crore rupees or more; or (b) turnover of three hundred crore rupees or more as on the last date of latest audited financial statements. Proviso added to the rule is providing that a company, which has been incorporated under the Act and is covered under provisions of second proviso to sub-section (1) of section 149 shall comply with such provisions within a period of six months from the date of its incorporation.[5] According to Section 152(5), the Companies Act, 2013, every person appointed as a director including women director shall not act as a director unless he gives his consent to hold the office as director. So woman director has to give a declaration that she is not disqualified to hold this office. This will ensure independence of woman director. Hence, the position is clear with regard to the companies which are required to comply with this provision but it is not clear with for the companies which have capital below these prescribed limits. However, it will be worthwhile to see that whether companies will be able to meet these requirements.

Penalty for Non-compliance

SEBI on 8th April, 2015 issued a Circular for non-compliance with the requirement of Clause 49(II)(A)(1) of Listing Agreement to all Managing Directors/Executive Directors and all recognized Stock Exchanges. SEBI announced a four-stage penalty structure wherein fines will increase with the passage of time in 2015.

(i) Firms will have to pay only the monetary fine and can escape further regulatory action if they start complying till September 30, 2015.

(ii) The listed companies complying between April 1 and June 30, 2015 will have to pay only Rs. 50,000.

(iii) Those complying between July 1 and September 30, 2015 this year will need to pay Rs 50,000 and an additional Rs 1,000 per day till compliance.

(iv) The listed companies complying on or after October 1, 2015 would have to pay Rs 1.42 Lakh, plus Rs 5,000 per day till the date of compliance.[6]

---

5. Rule 3, Companies (Appointment & Qualification of Director) Rules, 2014.
6. Circular No. CIR/CFD/CMD/1/2015 and subject as "Fine structure for non-compliance with the requirement of Clause 49(II)(A)(1) of Listing Agreement".

Also, for any non-compliance beyond September 30, 2015, SEBI may take any other action, against the non-compliant entities, their promoters and/or directors or issue such directions in accordance with law, as considered appropriate.

A Step towards Women Empowerment

Apart from diversity in age, experience, areas, educational background and expertise of directors, it would be a significant effort if companies start working on gender diversity as well. It has been observed that only 4 % of directors in Indian listed companies are women. Companies generally do not hire women as director for wide variety of reasons. Safety issues, maternity leaves, stereotyping about women are some of the reasons. According to 2014 Catalyst census report (a corporate research organization in America), among Fortune 500 companies those companies with greater representation of women on board have performed better than those having less representation of women. This Catalyst study again demonstrates the very strong correlation between corporate financial performance and gender diversity. The report said that well managed diversity produces better results. And smart companies appreciate that diversifying their boards with women can lead to more independence, innovation, and good governance and maximize their company's performance.[7] The lack of women at the top in business is now referred to as a "brain drain," and a "crisis of talent retention." More and more businesses are realizing the potential of workplace flexibility to harness the talent of women and new moms and keep them in the workforce. Indeed, workplace flexibility has become accepted by leading businesses as a valuable talent management and retention tool, not only to allow their female employees to manage their family lives, but also to enable workers go to school while working, thus developing critical talent in their workforce.[8] The Companies Act, 2015 is a revolutionary start for empowering women in the corporate world. There are several of capable women around who can add value to the boards, by this provision deserving women candidates will get a chance to prove their worth and Indian

7. Companies with More Women Board Directors Experience Higher Financial Performance, According to Latest Catalyst Bottom Line Report. http://www.catalyst.org/media/companies-more-women-board-directors-experience-higher-financial-performance-according-latest
8. The changing role of women and the case for workplace flexibility, by Yvonne Siu, https://corporatevoices.wordpress.com/2010/06/17/the-changing-role-of-women-and-the-case-for-workplace-flexibility/

companies will be able to perform at par with the foreign companies performing extremely well with women directors on board.

Women as Independent Directors

Simultaneously with the provision for Women director, the Companies Act framed provision for independent directors in section 149 of the same Act. However, there is no provision for women as independent director. To comply with the woman director requirement, companies will start appointing promoter's friends or relative for the post irrespective of their qualification. Hence, in future if government notifies a provision which makes appointment of women as independent director necessary then such situation could be avoided.

Will Women Directors make an Impact?

A study by researchers at the University of California, Berkley found that companies with one or more women on their boards are significantly more likely to have improved sustainability practices, which are considered indicators of risk management, opportunity recognition and strong leadership.[9] According to Forbes, women on board help the company to make more profit. With increasing numbers of female customers and employees, companies' boards need to work to understand their clients and their own employees. According to the CED report, "The pull from the top can have powerful economic effects throughout the various strata of a company and overall society." In other words, women at the top allow greater representation and draw for women in the workforce and better outcomes for their companies. As women's college graduation rate meets and surpasses that of men, creating an environment that draws talented women is crucial for success.[10]

Global Perspective on Women Directors

Norway is the first country to pass such a law, mandating that public companies achieve 40 percent representation of women on their boards within five years. Non-compliant companies risked fines or even

---

9. Secret of Successful Companies: Women Board Members, by Chad Brooks, Business News Daily Senior Writer http://www.businessnewsdaily.com/3447-women-boards-companies-success.html
10. The New Case for Women on Corporate Boards: New Perspectives, Increased Profits, http://www.forbes.com/sites/katetaylor/2012/06/26/the-new-case-for-women-on-corporate-boards-new-perspectives-increased-profits/

dissolution. In Germany, All listed companies to fill 30 percent of their supervisory board seats with women. Among the European Union fewer than 40 percent women on the all listed companies Board. In France, 40 percent of executive Board member shall be female on the board by 2016. In Belgium, Minimum 1/3 of board is female directors and Spain has introduced a quota at 40%, to be reached by 2015. However, Developed countries like, USA, UK, Canada, Singapore, Australia and many more do not have gender quota systems. In Malaysia at least 30 percent representation of women are in decision-making positions.[11]

Indian Scenario

More than 50% of India's current population is below the age of 25 and over 65% below the age of 35, this demographic potential offers India and its growing economy an unprecedented edge over BRICS economies. According to India's National Sample Survey, the proportion of working women in urban areas has increased from 11.9% in2001 to 15.4% in 2011. Since, female participation in the workforce rising along with educational levels, India can reap the huge dividend. For this, India needs not only an employment revolution but also educational revolutions that will allow and encourage women play their full part in a modern Indian economy.[12] As Indian companies scramble to meet a deadline to appoint women to their boards, some wealthy business owners have a solution that meets the letter if not the intention of the law: appointing their wives. India's market regulator, the Securities and Exchange Board of India, made it compulsory for all of the country's listed companies to name at least one female director. In the 12 months after the SEBI order was first announced in February 2014, only 580 companies out of thousands had appointed women, according to local reports. More than 80 appointments were family of company owners. India's wealthiest are setting a high profile example of applying the letter of the law. Mukesh Ambani, the second richest Indian who heads the petrochemicals to telecoms conglomerate Reliance Industries Ltd., appointed his wife Nita Ambani to the company's board. Industrialist Gautam Singhania named his wife Nawaz Singhania as a non-executive director of his company, Raymond Group, one of the world's largest textile manufacturing conglomerates. Both women have

11. Women Director-Governance and Empowering: Bridging the Gap, by Hariom Rastogie http://www.academia.edu/8002091/Women_Directors_-_Provision_and_Governance_under_Companies_Act_2013_and_Listing_Agreements
12. *Ibid.*

business experience though not directly applicable to overseeing a conglomerate. Globally, women lag far behind men in making their way to top management positions and corporate boards. But the situation is dire in Asia where among the leading economies China tops the list with women making up 8 percent of corporate board directors. Japan with 2 percent and South Korea with 1 percent are at the bottom of the heap. In India, women are 5 percent of directors. There are about 9,000 listed companies in India. The Bombay Stock Exchange, which is the biggest Indian bourse, has about 4,200 active member companies. The rest are divided between the NSE and a clutch of smaller regional stock markets. Experts say while the intention of appointing women was to bring about diversity in the boardroom, naming kin to the board might not add to healthy debate and decision-making since someone close to a powerful figure in the company would be unwilling to challenge them. Others feel appointing family members should not necessarily be viewed as negative. Tata International appointed investment banker Vedika Bhandarkar as a non-executive independent director. Bajaj Auto named business historian Gita Piramal to its board after SEBI's notification. Tata's IT services arm, Tata Consultancy Services, appointed Aarthi Subramanian as an executive director for a three year term. She was already a senior executive at TCS. Network-18, the Ambani-led media company that owns television channels CNN-IBN and CNBC in India, appointed Nirupama Rao, a former foreign secretary and ambassador to the U.S., as an independent director on the board. Women with years of experience in areas such as finance and banking find themselves serving on the boards of multiple companies. Renu Sud Karnad, the managing director of housing finance company HDFC Ltd. is on the board of more than half a dozen major companies but still many companies are yet to comply with SEBI requirement.[13]

How to Create the Talent Pool

The law is unclear on the level of transparency for board vacancies. This lack of clarity is evident across both organizational as well as at individual level. The law does not clearly stipulate how to drive awareness across interested candidates who are aspiring to be included in the Board. In this context, it is also not very clear as to whether companies need to advertise Board position vacancies or build awareness

13. Indian Companies Scramble to Find Women Directors, http://www.newindianexpress.com/business/news/Indian-Companies-Scramble-to-Find-Women-Directors/2015/03/28/article2733982.ece

in an alternate way. Adding to these concerns is the fact that there is an ongoing challenge in building a leadership pipeline in organizations. In an environment where large numbers of organizations are looking to recruit from the same talent pool, high attrition rates are hindering the process of leadership development. MNCs pose an added threat to the process, since many of these organizations source Indian talent for global leadership positions, thereby depriving Indian recruiters of future leaders. Although companies are more committed today towards improving the talent and leadership potential of female employees, there continue to be many talented women who leave senior positions or experience stalling careers. The steps that can be taken for talent pool creation are:

1. *Awareness:* Developing the talent pool of future women leaders requires greater awareness at management level, along with a robust bottom-up approach for creating supply. Furthermore, there is also a need for greater clarity in the law, and a need for a framework related to roles, responsibilities, and competencies.
2. *Training and development:* Along with an adequate quota allocation at each level to ensure a consistent talent supply all the way to top management levels, a strong training and development program is required to continuously groom the right kind of talent. On hiring suitable Board-ready women, organizations need to establish retention policies for such employees.
3. *Benchmarking:* Benchmarking can be an added incentive for organizations grooming female talent. This can be accomplished through a Diversity Certification, akin to an analyst rating such as ISO/Moody's 500 or CMM certification.
4. *Government mandates and incentives:* There is need for greater government involvement in mandating a robust company-wide policy that includes more women on boards without any kind of discrimination. Other interesting recommendations included tax incentives for organizations building and maintaining gender diversity.
5. *Societal Sensitization:* While there should be initiatives at organizational level, external factors, such as creating awareness through a diversity program, encompassing gender sensitization,

education and mentoring at a countrywide level will empower and give flexibility to the ecosystem.[14]

Conclusion

The Companies Act, 2013 is a laudable initiative for empowerment of women in corporate world. SEBI is also doing proper follow up to achieve the goal. Though such legislation and quota can be effective to bring women to the top positions in the companies, its benefits will be short lived if there are no proper guidelines to implement it and if it is not properly supervised by the Government. The need therefore is to have an enabling mechanism and to create infrastructure to educate and train women (and men) to effectively discharge this responsibility. A certificate course by industry bodies like CII, FICCI, etc. in partnership with educational institutions like ICAI or ICSI to develop an understanding of Board processes, application of financial judgment and overall corporate governance framework, will be a game-changer. This move is an opportunity to dramatically level the playing field, ensuring diversity at the highest levels, and creating effective women role models at the top for the younger generation to emulate. Women should be accepted for their skills and not just because they are women. It's indisputable that only experienced women with the right qualifications should be appointed as a director of the boards. There are lots of talented women out there; the deserving and qualified women should be brought on board.

14. Women on Boards A Policy, Process and Implementation Roadmap, A study by Biz Divas, http://www.bizdivas.in/wp-content/uploads/2014/09/ women_on_boardV3-PRINT.pdf

CHAPTER IX

Fund Raising

20

Evaluation of Raising Finance by Way of Equity and Debt Respectively under the Companies Act, 2013

RISHIKA LEKHADIA

Introduction

Company law recognizes two types of capital; share capital and debt capital.[1] Debt and equity are both legal obligations in the form of a money commitment by one person to another for a specific purpose. It is extremely difficult to demarcate between share and debt capital although it is possible to identify typical patterns of entitlements which are attached to them in certain business situations. The present legal framework in India is affecting the company's decision of selection in various forms of capital.

Fund Raising for Capital

The capital of the company is usually divided into indivisible units of fixed amount. These units are called the shares of the company.[2] Shareholder is the member of the company and invests in the company is lieu of shares of the company. On the other hand, debt is the right to repayment of the amount invested in the company. The debt holder gets

1. Section 32(4) of the Companies Act, 2013.
2. A.K. Majumdar, G.K. Kapoor, Taxmann's *Company Law,* 158 (13th Edn., 2010).

the inherent right to recover his investment by way of institution of the suit for the same. The first capital that the company typically gets is share capital and the proprietors of the business are usually amongst the first people who will provide the funding for their new venture. Our law also requires the minimum amount of capital to be present for the formation of the company. Private Company requires a minimum paid up share capital of rupees one lakh for its incorporation.[3] On the other hand, the public company requires a minimum paid up share capital of rupees five lakh for its incorporation.[4] At the stage of incorporation, if the promoters or the founding shareholders of the company take the loan, then the same will be taken personally by the shareholder and that shareholder will be personally liable for the repayment of that loan. The liability for the loan taken to finance the minimum share capital will not fall on the company. This reasoning is validated by the fact that section 11 of the Companies Act, 2013 states that the company shall not exercise any borrowing power unless the declaration is filed by the Director that the paid-up share capital of the company is not less than the minimum prescribed amount.[5] Once the company has been incorporated, then the investment usually comes from the venture capitalists and the angel investors. At this stage, the company would have exhibited prospects of doing well but it may not have enough assets for taking secured loan from the lenders. Therefore, a large amount of capital inflow will be in the form of equity. There will be proportionately large returns to these shareholders if the company manages a stellar performance, but there may not be any security on the investment. Hence, it is rightly said that the first amounts are usually the riskiest amounts in the business. After the company acquires assets, it can approach the banks and the commercial institutions for raising debt capital in the form of loans. Moreover, the company can also issue debentures to the public at large. This debt is taken by the company either to finance its working capital requirements or to purchase assets or to invest in new venture of the company. There is a fixed return on this form of capital by way of either fixed or floating interest.

Equity and Debt

The definition of 'shares' in Indian law refers to share capital of the

3. Section 2(68) of the Companies Act, 2013.
4. Section 2(71) of the Companies Act, 2013.
5. Section 11 of the Companies Act, 2013.

company and it includes stock within its ambit.[6] The term 'stock' has been defined as 'the aggregate of fully paid up shares of a member merged into one fund of equal value'.[7] Thus, stock is a set of shares put together in a bundle.[8] There are two main forms of share capital as per the Companies Act, 2013, i.e., equity shares and preference shares.[9] Our present law prohibits the issue of shares on discount and any such issuances are considered void.[10] Therefore, the shareholders will be bound to pay the face value of the shares at the time of its issue. The only exception to this rule is the issue of sweat equity shares of the company.[11] Sweat equity shares are given to the employees of the company as an incentive for their contribution. This issuance can only be made after a year of the commencement of business of the company by way of a special resolution.[12] Additionally, listed company needs to comply with the requirements laid down by the Securities and Exchange Board of India (SEBI) in this regard.[13] Preference share gives preferential rights to its holder with respect to payment of dividend. The dividend may be a fixed amount or could be a fixed rate on the profits of the company.[14] It is to be noted that the dividend that is declared by the company and is not paid will constitute the debt of the company. Preference shareholders will also have priority over the equity shareholders with reference to repayment at the time of winding-up of the company.[15] The new Act has expressly prohibited the issue of irredeemable preference shares.[16] The term within which the preference shares are to be repaid by the company is twenty years, barring the infrastructure projects.[17] Therefore, preference shares are issued with a fixed maturity date, i.e. the date when the capital will be repaid by the company to shareholders. One can compare such an issue of preference shares to the raising of an unsecured debt by the company. This is so because, the shareholders are entitled to dividends and their voting rights in the company are limited. These are usually the characteristics of

6. Section 2(84) of the Companies Act, 2013.
7. Majumdar, at 160.
8. *Id.*
9. Section 43 of the Companies Act, 2013.
10. Section 53 of the Companies Act, 2013.
11. Section 54 of the Companies Act, 2013.
12. Section 54(1) of the Companies Act, 2013.
13. Section 54 and Section 40 of the Companies Act, 2013.
14. Section 43, Explanation (ii)(a) of the Companies Act, 2013.
15. Section 43, Explanation (ii)(b) of the Companies Act, 2013.
16. Section 55(1) of the Companies Act, 2013.
17. Section 55(2) of the Companies Act, 2013.

a debt like instrument which yields regular interest and repayment of principle within a fixed period of time and does not normally grant management rights to the debt-holders. Nonetheless, there are key legal differences in raising finance by way of preference share capital and debt capital. Firstly, the issue of preference share capital within the limits of the authorised share capital of the company, does not require any permission from the existing debtors as per the existing loan agreements. Moreover, the companies need to pass a special resolution for certain kinds of borrowings under section 180 of the Act.[18] This compliance is not mandated for the issue of preference shares by the company. Furthermore, the Income Tax Act also treats preference share capital distinct from the debt capital and hence accords different accounting treatments to both these forms of capital. Besides, law mandates that preference shares can only be redeemed out of the profits of the company or out of the proceeds of fresh issue of shares made for the purpose of such redemption.[19] There is no statutory mandate governing the manner of repayment of debt capital by the company. These peculiarities of preference shares influence the close knit private companies to raise equity by way of preference shares in comparison to equity shares for short-term financing because the redeemable nature of the preference shares ensures that any loss or dilution of the rights of the existing shareholders is only temporary. In *Kesoram Industries case*,[20] the courts have defined debt to be a pecuniary claim or an obligation that is subsisting as on the date. Further, debt must be ascertainable although the amount could be paid either in the present or in the future.[21] A debt instrument can be in the form of a note, bond, debentures or a loan. Our legal framework does not restrict borrowing of money *generally*, except in specified circumstances. The company can issue the debentures with an option to convert such debentures into shares at the time of redemption.[22] Such debentures will be considered a debt instrument until the option of conversion has been exercised. Once these debentures are converted into an equity instrument, the same will be treated as shares of the company. These hybrid instruments blur the line between debt-like and equity-like instruments. Another such example is a loan given in perpetuity. In this case, the borrower's right to enforce will be

---

18. Section 180 of the Companies Act, 2013.
19. Section 55(2)(a) of the Companies Act, 2013.
20. *Kesoram Industries and Cotton Mills* vs. *Commissioner of Wealth Tax*, AIR 1966 SC 1370.
21. *Id.*
22. Section 71(1) of the Companies Act, 2013.

severely restricted as the cause of action is unlikely to arise.

Rights of Shareholders and Securities Holders

A share is a chose in action.[23] This means that the shareholders have the all rights in the company except for the right of possession.[24] Therefore, shareholders have various rights in the running of the company but they do not have right to possess specific assets of the company. Shareholders are granted their rights both under the statute of the Companies Act, 2013 as well as under the shareholder's agreement. Section 47 of the Companies Act, 2013 states that every equity shareholder shall have the right to vote on all the resolutions passed by the Company in proportion of their shares.[25] On the other hand, the law has specifically prohibited the debenture holders from exercising any voting rights in the matters of the company.[26] Equity shareholders can be divided into different classes and each class can be given different rights by the company.[27] There are special types or classes of shares that grant exclusive rights to its holders such a 'golden share'. This share is usually given to the founding family of the company when the company goes public or goes under the governmental control and it attaches a special right to the shareholder.[28] For instance, the family of Volkswagan was given the golden share in the company. The preference shareholders are given preference with respect to the distribution of dividends. But preference shareholder's voting rights are limited to resolutions that directly affect the rights attached to the preference shares and with respect to any resolution for winding up of the company.[29] The law further states that in case the preference shareholders are not paid their dividend for two years, then they shall be entitled to vote on all the resolutions passed by the Company.[30] The authorised share capital is the maximum amount of share capital that is prescribed in the Memorandum of Association of the company.[31] The company can alter

23. *Sri Gopal Jalan & Co.* vs. *Calcutta Stock Exchange Association Limited* [1963] 33 Comp. Case. 862 (SC).
24. *Id.*
25. Section 47(1) of the Companies Act, 2013.
26. Section 71(2) of the Companies Act, 2013.
27. Section 48(1) of the Companies Act, 2013.
28. Eilis Ferran, Look Chan Ho, Principles of Corporate Finance Law, 329 (2nd Edn., 2014).
29. Section 47(2) of the Companies Act, 2013.
30. Section 47 of the Companies Act, 2013.
31. Section 2(8) of the Companies Act, 2013.

its memorandum of association in a general meeting and increase the authorised share capital.[32] This means that the shareholders are vested a statutory right to decide whether they want to increase the share capital of the company. Therefore, any further issue by the company without the shareholder's approval for increasing the authorised capital is void. On the other hand, the debtors in general do not have any statutory right to prohibit the company from taking any further debt. They can have a contractual provision seeking their approval before the company decides to undertake further debt obligations. But if the company does not seek the approval from the existing shareholders, then the same will not make the further borrowing by the company void ab initio. It will only constitute an event of default in the existing loan agreements and therefore, the debtors shall have the right to accelerate the payment of the loan or they can ask for damages for the breach of the existing loan agreement. The only statutory provision protecting the interest of debenture holders in this regard states that if the debenture trustee concludes that the assets of the company are insufficient to discharge the principal amount, then the debenture trustee can file a petition to that effect in the tribunal. The tribunal, after hearing can impose restriction on the company from incurring any further liability.[33] Furthermore, the law states that if the company wants to issue any further capital, then the company is bound to first offer the same to the existing shareholders by providing them a reasonable notice to that effect.[34] But the debt holders do not have any such pre-emptive rights granted by the statute. The company is further allowed to issue bonus shares to its members out of its free reserves, or securities premium account or its capital redemption reserve account.[35] But the caveat is that the company is prohibited from any bonus share issues if it has defaulted on any of its debt obligations.[36] Therefore, it can be noted that the law has given extensive rights to the holder of equity but at the same time ensured that the debt holders do not suffer as a result. The shareholders have the right to appoint the directors of the company who will in turn protect their interest in the company. The debenture holders have the right to appoint a debenture trustee to protect their interest.[37] Sometimes, under the loan agreements, the creditor also has the right to appoint a nominee director on the

32. Section 61(1)(a) of the Companies Act, 2013.
33. Section 71(9) of the Companies Act, 2013.
34. Section 62 of the Companies Act, 2013.
35. Section 63(1) of the Companies Act, 2013.
36. Section 63(2) of the Companies Act, 2013.
37. Section 71(6) of the Companies Act, 2013.

Board of Directors of the Company. This nominee director ensures that the rights of the creditor are duly protected.[38] There are several factors that will influence debtor's control over the management of the company such as the amount and duration of the loan, whether the loan is secured or unsecured, nature of the company and its business activity as well as the credit rating of the company. It has been seen that by subjecting the management of the company to the scrutiny of the debt providers, the management of the company is sending out strong and credible signals to the shareholders of their confidence in business based on the information advantage that the debtors will have in comparison to the ordinary shareholders of the company who do not participate in its management.[39] Therefore, it can be concluded that, from the corporate governance perspective, debt should be added to the company's capital structure upto the point where the costs involved in obtaining the controlling mechanisms that are present in debt finance outweigh their benefits to the shareholders.[40] One of the main advantages that the debt holders have is the option of creating a security interest in the assets of the company. A 'secured creditor' of the company is not an absolute term. A creditor is secured or unsecured creditor only in relation to a specific asset of the company. Therefore, the creditor is 'secured' with respect to the specific assets of the company and 'unsecured' over other property rights of the company. This security is primarily created to reduce the default risk and to give priority to the creditor during the liquidation process.[41] Furthermore, it also gives some control to the debtors over the functioning of the company.[42] The company will not be at a liberty to dispose the asset if there is a fixed charge over that asset.[43] The debtor can create either a fixed charge or a floating charge on the assets of the company. A floating charge or a floating security does not relate to a specific asset, but to an identifiable fund of assets.[44] The debtor is free to use these assets in the normal course of business.[45] There are four types of consensual securities that can be created over the assets of the debtor; pledge, contractual lien,

38. Explanation to section 149(7) of the Companies Act, 2013.
39. Ferran, at 492.
40. Ferran, at 492.
41. Louise Gullifer, Goode on Legal Principles of Credit and Security, 1 (5th Edn. 2013).
42. *Id.*
43. *Id.*
44. Gullifer, at 12.
45. *Id.*

mortgage and charge.[46] Pledge is the actual or constructive delivery of possession of the asset to the creditor by way of security.[47] Lien is the right under law to detain the goods until the money owed to the detainee has been paid.[48] Right of lien can also be created by a contract. The main difference between a lien and a pledge is that lien is simply a possessory right while pledge also grants right of sale and appropriation. Mortgage includes transfer of interest in the property.[49] Notwithstanding this interest, there are rights over the mortgaged assets, which are transferred with the assets as well.[50] In all forms of mortgage where the contract is entered between the mortgagor and mortgagee, it is open to exercise the right of possession and sale without the intervention of the court. The main difference between the pledge and mortgage is that possession is granted by definition in a pledge while possession may or may not be granted by definition in a mortgage. A security interest created on the immovable property apart from the mortgage has been defined as a charge.[51] The company creating a charge on its assets or its undertakings is bound to register the same with the Registrar of the Company (RoC) within thirty days of its creation.[52] This provision grants statutory protection to the future creditors of the company who can verify whether the asset has already been encumbered before creating any additional charge over the same. Creation of security interest over an asset has to be distinguished from other contractual provisions relating to the disposal of assets. A common provision in many facility agreements is the creation of a negative pledge. A negative pledge is a promise made by the debtor to the creditor that the former shall not encumber any asset to any other creditor by way of security which will rank ahead of or *pari pasu* with the security given to this creditor.[53] It is to be noted that if the debtor breaches this obligation, then that would constitute a breach of the loan agreement. But the same will not vitiate the charge created on the asset by the other creditors. Another common clause in many loan agreements is the creation of subordination agreement. This is an agreement in which the creditor agrees to subordinate his claim against the debtor or the security taken by him

46. *Id.* at 31.
47. *Id.* at 32.
48. *Id.* at 34.
49. Section 58 of Transfer of Property Act, 1882.
50. *Id.*
51. Section 100 of Transfer of Property Act, 1882.
52. Section 77(1) of the Companies Act, 2013.
53. Gullifer, at 17.

from the debtor, to the claim of the other creditor.[54] Subordination is a voluntary act of the creditor to give away his statutory right in favour of another creditor. The creditor usually assumes higher risk when he is assured of a higher return on his investment. An important distinction between the equity-like capital and the debt-like capital relates to the right of recourse for repayment. Our legal system has provided recourse mechanism for debt in the form of Debt Recovery Tribunal. There is additional recourse under the Transfer of Property Act, Civil Procedure Code as well as the Companies Act. These provisions are provided because the right of repayment is a fundamental right of a debt holder. Under the Companies Act, contract for repayment of any debenture shall be enforced as a decree for specific performance.[55] The law gives the power to the creditor to initiate the winding up of the company in case the company is unable to repay its debts to the creditor.[56] Once the company is in the stage of liquidation, the assets of the company will be appropriated by the liquidator in accordance with the ranking of the claims laid down by law. As per section 325 of the Companies Act, 2013, the secured creditors shall have priority over the unsecured creditors. Once the debtors have been paid-off, preferential shareholders shall be repaid.[57] Thereafter, the equity shareholders will get their share *pari pasu* and any residual amount left after paying-off all the liabilities of the company.[58] Therefore, it can be concluded that the equity shareholders have to bear the highest amount of risk during the liquidation process of the company.

Risks and Liabilities of Shareholders

Shares are the assets of the company. The company is liable to pay the share capital to the shareholders at the time of winding up of the company only. In normal circumstances, the equity shareholders do not have the right to institute a suit for the recovery of their share capital. Therefore, equity shares are also referred to as the 'inside liability' of the company. On the other hand, debt is the liability of the company. The debt holder can not only institute the suit against the company for the recovery of the debt capital and also petition for winding up of the company on the ground of non-payment by the company. Therefore, debt capital is also popularly known as the 'outside liability' of the

54. Gullifer, at 17.
55. Section 71(12) of the Companies Act, 2013.
56. Section 271 of the Companies Act, 2013.
57. Section 325 of the Companies Act, 2013.
58. *Id.*

company. There is no certain return on equity shares of the company. The company is not bound to announce and distribute dividends on the regular basis. The company can pay the dividend in the company only out of the profits of the company for that year arrived at after providing for depreciation[59] or out of money provided by the Central Government or a State Government for the payment of dividend by the company.[60] Therefore, it can be concluded that the declaration of dividend is a voluntary act by the company and failure to provide for the same does not penalise the company in any way. There are times when the loan agreements bar the company from declaring the dividend during the pendency of the loan. On the other hand, the return on debt capital is in the form of interest. This interest can be either fixed or floating. The company is penalised under the loan agreement in the form of enforcement of security interest or creditors calling for voluntary winding up of the company if it fails to provide timely return on the same. Once the company is in public domain, any further issue of shares by the management can be an alarming signal. This is so because the company does not have to provide for any security interest and the ordinary shareholders do not normally have the resources to conduct the due-diligence on the company that debtors of the company have.[61] Therefore, it had been observed that the rights issue had increased during the recent economic recession period.

Exit Option from Various Form of Capital

Since equity capital represents the ownership of the company, there is no fixed timeline within which the investment shall be returned to the shareholder. Therefore, the shareholder, on dissolution, will receive the nominal value of the share and any other residual value left in the company. Debt creates a borrower-lender relationship and usually has a fixed maturity period. In India, shares are regarded as 'goods' of the company.[62] This is evident from the fact that as per the law, the shares in the public company are freely transferrable through the trade on the stock market. On the other hand, in a private company, since there is a maximum limit on the number of shareholders, therefore, the shareholders have the right to put certain share transfer restrictions popularly known as pre-emption rights. The main rights are right to first

59. Section 123(1)(a) of the Companies Act, 2013.
60. Section 123(1)(b) of the Companies Act, 2013.
61. Aswath Damodaran, Applied Corporate Finance, 26 (3rd Edn. 2010).
62. Majumdar, at 158.

offer (RoFO), right to first refusal (RoFR), drag along and tag along rights. In case of RoFO, the party who wants to sell its shares in the company is bound to offer the shares to the existing shareholders before approaching the third party. Similarly, in case of RoFR, the seller of the shares needs to offer the shares to the existing shareholder at the price offered by the third party. Tag along right is a provision for the protection of minority shareholders of the company. As per this right, if the majority shareholders decide to sell their shares to the third party, then the third party will also be obliged to buy the shares from minority shareholders on the similar terms. Many private equity investors insist on such provisions in the agreement as they invest in a company primarily based on their trust in the promoters of the company. If the promoter exists the company, then these investors too would like to exit. In case of drag along right, the majority shareholders will have the right to force the minority shareholders to sell their shares to the third party on similar terms and conditions when the majority shareholders plan to exit the company. Another manner in which the equity shareholders of the company can receive their investment back is when the company buys back its own shares.[63] The statute gives company the power to reduce its share capital by passing a special resolution to that effect and after subsequent confirmation by the Tribunal for the same.[64] The Tribunal shall give notice for any objection to the same by the creditors of the company.[65] But the buy-back of the shares needs to be authorised by the Articles of Association of the company and a special resolution needs to be passed at the general meeting to that effect.[66] The law has further prohibited the company from buying back its own shares when the company is defaulting in its obligation on repayment of loans or the payment of dividend to the shareholders.[67] On the other hand, if the company plans on reducing its debt liability, then it can prepay the loans before their maturity date. The company may have to bear a pre-payment penalty in certain cases but the company does not need to seek the approval at its general meeting for reducing its debt liability.

Evaluation of Fund Raising

In a nutshell, the firm enjoys several advantages from equity such as flexibility in issue and low cost of finance. Moreover, the shares of

63. Section 68 of the Companies Act, 2013.
64. Section 66 (1) of the Companies Act, 2013.
65. Section 66 (2) of the Companies Act, 2013.
66. Section 68 of the Companies Act, 2013.
67. Section 70 (1) of the Companies Act, 2013.

public listed companies are mainly brought based on its reputation in the market. The long maturity period of shares and fewer statutory regulations with respect to repayment makes shares a desirable form of capital in its early stage. On the other hand, debt provides tax benefits to the company as interest payment on debt is tax deductible while cash flow on repayment on equity is not.[68] Moreover, there is predictability in the rate and time of return on investment in case of debt which makes it an attractive option for investors with lower risk appetite. In practise, it has been observed that proprietors of company where the shareholding is concentrated in the hands of few individuals may favour borrowing money rather than issuing shares to new investors as this avoids the dilution of their control that they can exert through the medium of voting rights attached to their shares. There was an empirical study conducted for the period 1999-2000 to 2007-08 (majorly a pre-recession period) that studied three hundred Indian public listed companies over the last decade. This study concluded that the average debt-equity ratios of manufacturing companies were more than double of the average debt-equity ratio of service sector companies.[69] It indicates that service sector companies rely more on the equity and less on the debt, and *vice-versa* in case of manufacturing companies.[70] This is so because manufacturing businesses are relatively less risky compared to a service start-up and therefore, the financial institutions will prefer to give debt to manufacturing industry compared to a service sector start up.

Conclusion

In pure legal theory there is a very slight difference, if any, between equity and debt. The emergence of various kinds of hybrid instruments has given a shareholder and debenture holder almost similar rights and liabilities. Therefore, it can be appropriately concluded that the distinction between these two forms primarily stems from the fact that our law treats them differently. Thus, our law tends to create the fiction called the share capital and the debt capital.

68. Damodaran, at 72.
69. Dr. Jagannath Panda and Dr. Ashok Kumar Panigrahi, Determinants of Capital Structure: An Empirical Study of Indian Companies, *International Journal of Research in Commerce & Management*, Vol. 1, Issue 8 (2010).
70. *Id.*

21

Section 185 and Section 186 of the Companies Act, 2013: Danger Ahoy!

SHREYASH SHAH

SECTION 185 OF COMPANY ACT, 2013: LOAN TO DIRECTORS

Section 185 in the Companies Act, 2013 (hereinafter "the Act") was one of the few sections to be notified as early as on September 12, 2013 and the same is legally enforceable. Before going into the nitty-gritty of the provision, it would be appropriate to examine its legislative intent.

Legislative Intent

The legislative intent of the provision in the Act has not been expressly stated, contrary to normal convention particularly when a new provision or a statute is introduced. Be that as it may, it is obvious that the objective of the Section is to impose fetters on the provision of loans/Guarantees to directors/companies in which they are interested in the manner contemplated in the Section, which was earlier permissible under Section 295 of the Companies Act, 1956 (hereinafter "the old Act") albeit, with the approval of the Central Government. It must be understood that the Section intends to regulate only provision of loans to directors or persons/companies and other non-corporate entities in which the directors of the lending company are interested both directly and through their relatives. Its purpose is to ensure that the directors do not misuse their position to benefit themselves by facilitating provision of loans/financial guarantees from the Companies with which they are associated either to themselves or to entities in which they are interested. The underlying objective of Section 185 is to ensure that the instrumentality of the Company is not perpetrated to any form of abuse by the Directors. The Section is intended to evidently avoid a conflict of interest and can thus be termed as a "conflict of interest provision". It is pertinent to note that the intent of Section 185 is not to regulate inter-corporate loans. Section 186 in the Act is intended to regulate Inter-corporate loans and investments. This Section acts as a composite code by itself and is therefore independent of section 185.

Section 185 Dissected

Section 185 commences with the words, "Save as otherwise provided in the Act". The meaning of the above expression needs to be firstly understood. It contemplates that except where it is otherwise permitted under the Act, the fetter imposed by Section 185 as far as grant of loans to Directors will prevail, given the fact that the provision is in the nature of a specific provision. The Section universally applies to all types of Companies, be it private or public. This is perfectly justified, considering its objective.

Application to Loans given Both "Directly and Indirectly"

The Section puts an embargo on loans or other kinds of accommodation provided whether directly or indirectly under some kind of a subterfuge. Therefore, any form of "round tripping" to circumvent the provision is strictly to be abhorred.

Loan includes "Book Debt" also

The term "loan" is being given an extended connotation in the Section to cover any book debts due from a Director. This suggests that if any amount is due from a Director say, by way of rent against accommodation taken by him from the Company or against the value of goods supplied to him by the company on credit, it would tantamount to a "loan" and the outstanding will have to be necessarily squared off by the Director to ensure that it does not come within the ambit of the Section. Any "Book Debts" of the genre stated above which pre-existed prior to the coming into force of the Section has also been effectively drawn into the vortex of the Section, effective September 12, 2013.

Provision of Guarantee or Security Barred

The Section also comes in the way of the company providing any guarantee or any security in respect of a loan obtained by the Director from any other person.

Exceptions Carved out by the Proviso to the Section

Proviso under sub-section (1) lays down the exemption clause of the Section. The provision of any loan to the Managing Director or whole time director is insulated from the rigors of the section provided the same has been given as part of the conditions of service extended to all the employees of the company or is pursuant to any scheme approved by the members by special resolution. It follows from the above that the company cannot extend any loan to a non-executive Director and further the loan facility should be extendable to all the employees of the Company. Alternatively, the loan should be extended pursuant to any scheme which has the approval of the members by special resolution. The second limb of the proviso exonerates a company which, in the ordinary course of its business, provides loans or guarantees subject to the condition that the interest charged on the loan is at a rate which is not less than the bank rate declared by the RBI. The question that springs to mind from the above is whether a company belonging to the above category can provide loans to its directors under the shelter of this proviso. The answer would appear to be "yes" as long as the interest charged is in keeping with the rate stipulated above. Secondly, it would indeed be in the ordinary course of it business to lend to any entity including its Directors subject to their credit worthiness being satisfactory. It should be ensured however that if loans are provided to its Directors, the same terms as applicable to other borrowers should be applied, lest the company should fall foul of section 185.

Coverage of the Section

Explanation under Section 185(1) provides the canvas to the provision and amplifies the expression "*to any other person in whom director is interested*" to mean:

(a) Any director of the lending company, of a company which is its holding company or any partner or relative of any such director;
(b) Any firm in which such director or relative is a partner;
(c) Any private company of which any such director is a director or member;
(d) Any Body Corporate at a general meeting of which not less than 25% of the total voting power maybe exercised or

controlled by any such director or two or more of such directors, together; and

(e) Any Body Corporate, the Board of directors, managing director or manager, whereof is accustomed to act in accordance with the directions or instructions of the Board, or of any director or directors, of the lending company.

As may be observed from the above Explanation, its tentacles are intended to extend far and wide. Its ramifications therefore run deep. A plain reading of Clauses (a) and (b) above suggests that these clauses put fetters on the provision of any loan to the director of a lending company, the Director of its Holding company or to any partner or relatives of such a director as also to any firm in which such a Director, namely the director of the lending company or the Director of the holding company or his relative is a partner. Thus, the conflict of interest in the above two clauses can arise either through the direct interest of the concerned Director or through his relatives. The term "Relative" shall carry the meaning given to it by Section by 2(77) in the Act. The extension to the term "Relative" as provided in clause (iii) in section 2(77) may be found in Rule 4 of the Companies (Specification of Definitions Details) Rules, 2014. Clause (c), in the Explanation *ibid.*, envisages only a situation where the Director is involved directly in his individual capacity. Therefore, the provision of any loan to a private company in which such a director is a Director or member would be hit by clause (c), if the interest of the Director in the Private company is in the capacity of a member. Even if his shareholding in the private company is minuscule, the above Clause (c) shall become applicable. Clause (d) contemplates that where any loan is to be provided to a company in which 25% or more of the total voting power in General meeting is exercisable or controlled by such a director either individually by himself or together by two or more directors of the lending company, the provision of the loan or security shall be barred. It is pertinent to note that clause (d) considers control or exercise of voting power over 25% of the total voting power of the borrower company in General Meeting. Such control over the voting power can be through the direct holding of the Director himself or may be by two or more directors of the lending company. In either situation the exercise of voting power should be by the directors in their individual capacity and not indirectly. Control over voting power indirectly through relatives, partners, etc. does not fall within the ambit of clause (d). It would be also appropriate at this juncture to draw a distinction between the use of the expression "control" as contained in Section 2(27) of the Act and in clause (d) to the Explanation in Section 185. The definition of "control" in section 2(27) is much wider and it encapsulates exercise of control over the Management of a company, by exercise of the authority to appoint majority of directors or to control the management or policy decisions, exercise of shareholding rights in the company. The usage of the word "controlled" in clause (d) above is in an altogether different context. Further clause (d) above is restricted in application only to the extent of exercise of control over 25% or more of the total voting power exercisable in General Meeting. The word 'controlled' in Clause (d) is used in the form of a verb with reference to 25% of the voting rights of a company at general meeting, as against which 'control' in Section 2(27) is used in the form of a noun to connote control over a company, be it through exercise of voting rights or management rights or shareholders' agreement or in any other manner. Thus, the term "control" as used in section 2(27) and in the above clause (d) are not to be considered as synonymous with each other. As conventionally, only Equity shares of a company carry voting rights, the reference to the total voting power as stated in clause (d) should be only to Equity shares. It is common knowledge that in a General Meeting, voting power is exercisable only by the holders of Equity shares. Therefore, unless the circumstances laid down in Section 87(2) in the 1956 Act which corresponds to Section 47 in the Act come into play, voting rights bestowed through holding of preference shares are not to be taken into consideration in determining the threshold voting power laid down in clause (d). It is again reiterated that the voting rights in Clause (d) will have to be considered only on the basis of the direct holding of the directors of the concerned company or its holding company. Indirect holdings through relative, firms, etc. shall not be considered as the above Clause (d) clearly states that the voting power shall be exercised by "such director" or by "such directors". The Supreme Court in *Ombalika Das and another vs. Hulisa Shaw*[1] had occasion to explain the intent in the usage of the adjective "such" in legal parlance. The Apex Court opined that the adjective "such" when prefixed to a noun has to be read in the same sense as is attributable to it in the preceding part of the sentence. Going by this analogy, it may be stated that a company cannot advance loan or provide security or guarantee to a company limited by shares, in which more than 25% of the voting rights is exercised by the director(s) of the lending company or either singly or together with two or more Directors. Clause (e) in the Explanation to section 185 comes into play

1. (2002) 4SCC 539.

where the Body corporate, the Board of directors, the Managing Director or Manager of the company seeking the borrowing are accustomed to act in accordance with the directions or instructions of the Board or of any director or directors of the Lending company. The expression "Accustomed to act in accordance with the directions or instructions of the Board or of any Director or Directors of the lending company" clearly suggests that it has to be circumstantially proved or established by a series of events or as may be explicitly provided by any agreement or documents, that the directors have acted in accordance with the directions or instructions of any director or directors or the Board of the lender company.

In order to prove the above, it must be established that the directors of the borrower company do not exercise any discretion or judgment of their own, but act in accordance with the directions of the director(s)/Board of the Lender Company. It would be appropriate at this juncture to refer to a decision in *Hydrodam (Corby) Ltd. Re*[2] where it was held that where a parent company gave its sanction to a subsidiary for the disposal of the subsidiary's assets, this would not make the parent company a shadow director of the subsidiary. The sanction was given by the holding company in the capacity of a majority shareholder and not a controller from behind. As long as the decision was made by the directors of the subsidiary, exercising their own independent discretion and judgment, and the parent company only approved or authorized the decision, the parent company would not be considered as a shadow director. Evidence such as the existence of an agreement between the lender and the borrower companies in terms of which there is an express assertion that the Borrower company shall abide by the directions of the Directors of the Lender company would be pointer in that direction. The decision of the Bench in case of *Secretary of State for Trade and Industry vs. Becker*[3] has held that to show that a person is a shadow director; it must be proved that *de jure* directors followed a consistent pattern of compliance with the instructions of the shadow director makes interesting reading. It must however be borne in mind that in this case, the Board was found to be working at the behest of a person who though not being part of the Board had all the trappings of being a *de facto* Director. We must point out that Clause (e) is restricted in application to only those who are *de jure* Directors and not *de facto* Directors which shadow directors are.

2. (1994) 2 BCLC 180.
3. (2003) 1 BCLC 555.

Clauses (d) and (e) in Explanation Cover Companies Incorporated Outside India

It is also pertinent to point out that in both clauses (d) and (e) in the Explanation cited above, the expression "Body Corporate" has been used in contrast to the earlier clauses (a), (b) and (c) where the reference is to a "company". The term "body corporate" or "corporation" has been defined in Section 2(11) of the Act to include a company incorporated outside India. A co-operative society registered under any law relating to co-operative Societies and any other body corporate which is not a company as defined in the Act which the Central Government may by notification specify in this behalf do not come within the framework of a "body corporate". Thus, the provision of loans and guarantees to companies incorporated outside India will also come within the ambit of the Section if the circumstances contemplated in clauses (d) and (e) exist.

Head Note to the Section does not Tell the Full Story

Section 185 carries on the Statute Book, the head note "Loans to Directors, etc." As one can see from the discussion above, this head note is somewhat misleading in that the fetter imposed by the Section extends not only to loans and guarantees extended to directors but also to companies and bodies corporate in which the circumstances enumerated in clauses (c), (d) and (e) in the Explanation exist. Viewed from this perspective, the provision overlaps in a limited sense with Section 186 of the Act which is a composite code for regulating Inter-corporate loans and Investments.

Penalties for Contravention

Any contravention of the Section 185 of the Act is intended to be dealt with very severely with cash penalties on both the company and the errant Directors and other persons to whom the loan/guarantee has been provided which is extendable up to Rs. 25 lacs, apart from imprisonment which may extend to six months or both. In case of imprisonment, the errant Director will also invite disqualification and vacation of office under Sections 164 and 167 respectively.

If a Company Lends through Intermediary to the Persons who are otherwise Related with the Lending Company

Under sub-section (1) of section 185 a company does not advance a loan directly or indirectly. Indirect is interpreted in case of *Dr. Fredie*

Ardeshir Mehta vs. Union of India[4] as: "When section 295 refers to an indirect loan to a director, what it means is that the company shall not give a loan to a director through the agency of one or more intermediaries. The word 'indirectly' in section 295 cannot be read as converting what is not a loan into a loan." For example, if a company (A) borrow the fund from company (B) and lend the money to Company (C) and loan from (B) to (C) is covered by section 185. In this case section 185 also applicable in case of lending from company (A) to (C) because it also included directly or indirectly.

Understand the Section with the help of practical examples

Example 1: Company A has two Directors, Mr. X and Mr. Y. Both holds 50% share each of Company. Company A wishes to give loan to following and have asked for views on same.

Sr No	*Loan To*	*Whether Company Can*	*Reason*
1.	Loan to Director X.	No	Included in definition
2.	Loan to a relative of Director Y.	No	Included in definition
3.	Director of company D which is the holding company of A.	No	Included in definition
4.	A partner of Director of Holding Company.	Yes	A partner of Director of Holding Co. is not included.
5.	A partner of Director of company A.	No	Included in definition
6.	To a firm in which Mr. X is a partner.	No	Included in definition
7.	To a firm in which relative of Mr. Y is a Partner.	No	Included in definition

4. [1991] 70 Comp. Cas. 210 (Bom.)

Example 2: Private Ltd. Co. with Common Director.
Company B wishes to avail loan from Company A, Whether Possible?

Particulars	*Company A (Pvt. Ltd. or Ltd.)*	*Company B (Pvt. Ltd.)*
Directors-*cum*-share holder	A (shareholding 60%) B (shareholding 40%)	B (shareholding 75%) D (shareholding 25%)
Only Share holder	Nil	Nil

**A and B are Husband and wife. D is their Son.*

Company A cannot give loan to company B as it would be in contravention of Section 185 and would attract penalty.

Planning

1. Mr. B should resign from the post of Director of Company A and gift his shares to Mr. A (gift of shares is tax free). They shall appoint another Director in the company.
   As B resigns and transfer the shares then the provisions of section 185 wont apply and company A would be able to give loan to company B.

OR

2. Converting Company A into a LLP.

OR

3. Converting Company B into a Public Limited Company and Mr B reducing his shareholding in Company B to less than 25%.

Example 3: Private Ltd. Co. to Public Ltd. Co.
Company B wishes to avail loan from Company A, Whether Possible?

Particulars	*Company A (Pvt. Ltd. or Ltd.)*	*Company B (Ltd.)*
Directors-*cum*-share holder	A (shareholding 60%) B (shareholding 20%) C (shareholding 15%)	A (shareholding 10%) B (shareholding 10%) C (shareholding 5%)
Only Share holder	D (shareholding 15%)	Others (shareholding 75%)

No it is not possible to advance loan to company B as Directors A, B and C collectively are holding 25% of shares of Company B. And hence get covered under the clause 4 of interested party to Director.

Planning

1. Either Mr. A or Mr. B or Mr. C should resign from the post of Director of Company A. This would bring down the holding of shares to less than 25% and will enable the borrowing between two Companies.

OR

2. Converting Company A into a LLP.

OR

3. Either Mr. A or Mr. B or Mr. C should give up at least 1% of their share held in Company B to bring down the holding under 25%.

Impact of the Clarificatory General Circular No.03/2014 by Ministry

- It is to noted that section 372A is not applicable to private limited companies.
- There is no exemption provided to private limited companies.
- The exemption has been provided only to guarantee given or security provided by a holding company (not for loans given by a holding company to its subsidiary company).
- The exemption with regard to guarantee or security given by a holding company to its subsidiary company is only available in respect of loans made by a bank or financial institution.
- The other condition is that the loans obtained by the subsidiary company is exclusively utilised by the subsidiary company for its principal business activities.
- There is a typo error (it seems) in the second para—should have been section 186 and not 185.
- Even earlier to this circular, the prohibition was not relevant to holding-subsidiary if there were no common directors and other conditions given in section 185 getting satisfied.
- The point on exercise of not less than 25% voting power was also with regard to directors not the company. It is worthwhile to mention here that in case of holding subsidiary the exercise of voting is done by the company and not the directors.
- The circular draws reference to that sub-section of section 372A which mentions about wholly owned subsidiary. On a further reading of the circular, there is mention of holding company to its subsidiary company (not wholly owned subsidiary). One has to take a call on this. In my opinion it will be only for wholly owned will be only for wholly owned subsidiary.

Example: ABC Private Limited is a wholly owned subsidiary of XYZ Private Limited. The principal business activity of ABC Private Limited is manufacturing of cement. ABC Private Limited borrows money from State Bank of India. It seeks corporate guarantee from XYZ Private Limited. Mr. R is a director of ABC Private Limited and also a director of XYZ Private Limited. Prior to the clarification dated 14.02.2014, this would have attracted the provisions of section 185 because of common directorship. Post the clarification dated 14.02.2014, the corporate guarantee can be extended by XYZ Private Limited to ABC Private Limited provided the loan amount is utilised solely for its principal business activity.

Example: There are 4 private limited companies, all of which are giving corporate guarantee to the 1 company. The 4 companies have directors in common. There is this 1 public limited company which is taking the corporate guarantee. There is no common director between the givers and the taker. In this case, the corporate guarantee can be given.

Loan given by Holding Co. to Subsidiary Co. does not Always Attract Section 185

There is a general conception that if subsidiary Co. do not utilize loan given by its holding Co. for its principal business, provisions of Sec. 185 is attracted each and every time. In other words, if loan given or guarantee given or security provided by holding Co. to its subsidiary is not exempted by the Rule 10 of the Companies (Meetings of Board and its Powers) Rules, 2014, Sec. 185 is violated. The above view is not correct. One should first examine whether the provision of 185 is attracted by examining shareholding and directorship of holding and subsidiary company. There can be many instances when the basic provision of Sec. 185 is not attracted, if any loan is given by Holding Co. to its Subsidiary Co.

Example: H Ltd. has given a loan of Rs. 10 crores to S Ltd. There is neither any common director nor any common shareholder in between these two companies. Examine applicability of Sec. 185.

Assuming that there is neither any common shareholder nor any common director in holding Co. and subsidiary company, Sec. 185 is not attracted.

Such Loan will not be covered by Clauses (a), (b), (c), (d) and (e)

- Clause (a) (as applicable for individual),
- Clause (b) (as applicable for Firm),

- Clause (c) (for Private Ltd. Co., only if director is a director or member),
- Clause (d) (only if the director either by himself or two or more such directors hold 25% or more of total voting power in the borrowing company,
- Clause (e) (only if borrowing company/its Board/Directors are accustomed to act as per the Directors of the Board/Directors of the lending company. It is very difficult to prove that the board of subsidiary Co. has not only actually acted, but also accustomed to act as per the Directors of the Board/Directors of the lending company.

Any interest of director (or other person) in his "personal capacity (not holding as nominee of company)" is relevant to attract Sec. 185. Interest of holding Co. in subsidiary is not relevant.

Specific Exemptions Provided to Loan given by Holding Co. to Subsidiaries

There can be many instances when the loan or security provided by holding company to subsidiary is attracted by the provisions of Sec. 185. Let us illustrate such situations:

Example 1: When subsidiary company is a Private Ltd. Co. and some shares of subsidiary Co. is held by one or more director(s) of holding Co.

Example 2: When subsidiary company is a Private Ltd. Co. and One of the director of holding Co. is also a director in subsidiary Co.

Example 3: When one or more of such directors hold 25% or more of total voting power in the subsidiary company in such cases, Rule 10 provides specific exemptions from attractions of Section 185 provisions subject to some conditions mentioned in the said Rule. Rule 10 of the Companies (Meetings of Board and its Powers) Rules, 2014 states that (1) Any loan made by a holding Co. to its wholly owned subsidiary Co. or any guarantee given or security provided by a holding Co. in respect of any loan made to its wholly owned subsidiary Co. is exempted from the requirements under this section; and

(2) Any guarantee given or security provided by a holding company in respect of loan made by any bank or financial institution to its subsidiary company is exempted from the requirements under this section: Provided that such loans made under sub-rules (1) and (2) are utilised by the subsidiary company for its principle business activities. Every loan by holding Co. to its subsidiary company is not attracted by

section 185 even if money is not utilized for principal business activities. One should first examine whether the basic provision of 185 is attracted by examining shareholding and directorship pattern of holding and subsidiary company. If provision of Sec. 185 is attracted, then one should examine whether such loan is exempted under Rule 10 of the Companies (Meetings of Board and its Powers) Rules, 2014 and if it is not exempted under Rule 10, then only there will be violation of Sec. 185.

Conclusion

Section 185 of the Act applies to every company as opposed to Section 295 which did not apply to a private company unless it happened to be a subsidiary of a public company. The new section also includes "pseudo loans" in that it ropes in book debts due from a Director. Private companies which were profligate in the matter of providing loans to their Directors under the previous regime should be extremely wary of the pitfalls that lie ahead!

SECTION 186 OF COMPANY ACT, 2013: LOAN AND INVESTMENT BY COMPANY

Section 186 in the Companies Act, 2013 corresponds to Section 372A in the erstwhile 1956 Act. Section 186 of the Companies Act, 2013 is more rigorous law than Section 372A in the erstwhile 1956 Act. The intention of both the provisions is by and large identical namely to regulate primarily Inter-corporate Investments and loans. Although the provisions are substantially the same in spirit, there are certain subtle differences between the two in content which make Section 186 a much more rigorous and potent regime as compared to its predecessor in the 1956 Act.

Types of Specified Transactions are Covered under the Section

Section 186 covers 3 types of specified transactions entered into by a company directly or indirectly; Loans to any person or other body corporate; Guarantee or security given in connection with a loan to any other body corporate or person; and Acquisition by way of subscription, purchase or otherwise, the securities of any other body corporate. Section 186 is applicable from 1.4.2014. All transactions entered into up to 31.3.2014 will be covered by corresponding Section 372A of Companies Act, 1956 which is not in force now. This section is applicable to all Companies either private Companies or public Companies and Considering the sub-section (11) of Section 186 of the

Act, whole section except sub-section (1) shall be applicable on Private Company as well as Public Company also. But the Section 186 (Except Section (186 (1)) of the Companies Act, 2013 does not apply in Banking Company, Insurance Company, Housing Finance Company, etc. and any company whose main business of acquisition of shares or securities, etc. Investment under section 186 (1) means a company may not make investment its money more than Two Layer. The limit has been fixed. It is showing a good sign for transparency. The provisions of Section 186 (1) shall not be make compulsion on a company acquires any company which is incorporated outside India. (Such company has Investment Subsidiary beyond Two layers as per the law of host country) and a subsidiary company from having any investment subsidiary for the purpose of meeting of the requirement under any law framed under any law for the time being in force.

Limits for Investment and Guarantee under Section 186(2)

The Limit is fixed in the Section 186 (2) that 60% of Paid up capital + Free Reserve + Security Premium or 100% of Free Reserve + Security Premium; whichever is more. In this Section, the company cannot give loan, guarantee or provide any security or acquisition as per fixed limit. This sub-section restricts within limit.

Approvals for Investment and Guarantee, etc. under Section 186(3)

The sub-section (2) of Section 186 makes restriction, but Section 186(3), gives power to the company, that it may give loan, guarantee or provide any security or acquisition beyond the limit but before taking prioı approval from Shareholder in the General Meeting. It means once approval is taken from Shareholder in the General Meeting, thereafter investment may be made beyond the limit. It is duty of the Company to disclose in the Financial Statement the full particulars of the loan given, security provided and guarantee given. The Company shall also disclose in its Report about its utilization. The company must take 100% consent from Board to give loan and guarantee and provided security. In case of Company has already taken loan, etc. from any financial institutions, banks, etc. Then, it is mandatory to take prior approval also from public Financial Institution, banks, etc. The approval from Public Financial Institution shall not be required where the company has not been make default to pay interest and comply the limits and provisions of section 186(2).

Companies Registered with SEBI under Section 186(6)

Those companies or prescribed companies which are registered under SEBI can take inter corporate loans or deposited exceeding the prescribed limit. The intention of government is clear, if the company is registered under SEBI, this section is not applicable for the part of limit. But, simultaneously, it is prescribed a condition in Section i.e. at the end of the Financial Year, such companies shall furnish details of loans or deposit in its Financial Statement. So, the company can utilize the benefit mentioning the information and details in the Financial Statement of the Company. The Company must maintain a register under this section and it shall be kept at the registered office of the Company which shall be prescribed. This register shall be opened for inspection and in case of any member, if demand its extract, the company shall provide them as per prescribed fee. If company contravenes this provision, the company shall be penalized with fine which shall not be less than Rs. 25,000 but which may extend to Rs. 5 lacs and officer of the Company who is default shall be punishable with imprisonment for a term which may extend to Two Years and find which shall not be less than Rs. 25,000 but which may extend to Rs. 5 lacs.

Differences between Section 186 of the 2013 Act and Section 372A of the 1956 Act

Section 186 is applicable without prejudice to the provisions in the Act. There was no similar provision in Section 372A. Section 186 has been so worded with a view to isolate it from Section 185 which carries a blanket embargo on loans to Directors and their relatives. Section 186 imposes embargo on multi-layered Investments and Section 186(1) restrains a company from making investments beyond two layers of subsidiary companies subject to certain exceptions as provided under the Section which are as follows:

(a) Where an Indian company is seeking to acquire any other company incorporated outside India, if such other company has investment subsidiaries beyond two layers as per the laws of the concerned Country.

(b) A subsidiary company is not restrained from having any investment subsidiary for the purposes of meeting the requirements of any law for the time being in force.

(c) The above restriction did not apply under the erstwhile regime of Section 372A. The fact that investments could be made through multi-layered structures gave the investor company the much needed flexibility in the process of planning and structuring the investments. Sub-section (1) in Section 186 is therefore constrictive in its approach.

Section 186 Restrains Loans to Non-corporate Entities as Well

Whereas Section 372A regulated only inter-corporate loans and investments, Section 186 applies also to the provision of loans, guarantees, to non-corporate bodies. Clause (a) under sub-section (2) introduces this fetter by making the Section applicable to any person or other body corporate. Therefore, by a strange quirk of logic or lack of it, if you may, a company cannot provide loans to a non-corporate entity such as a partnership firm or a sole proprietor without approvals section 186. For that matter, even a loan given to an employee of a company will come within the ambit of the collective wisdom of the Board which will have to, willy-nilly, sit in pompous judgment on this triviality and approve of an innocuous application for financial support at a duly convened meeting. Having said this, the new Act, to its credit, does have some novel characteristics which are laudable. However, the flip side is that the contents of clause (a) in sub-section (2) above pushes its quality or the lack of it to a nadir. Surely there could not be anything more archaic and retrograde than this provision, in a legislation which is supposed to be contemporary and which seeks to supplant the 1956 Act which was considered as an anachronism and well past its useful shelf life. To be fair to the law-makers, there is a surmise is that this was an unintended aberration in drafting, the consequence of which they had not comprehended. Now that the MCA has set in motion the process of mitigating the hardships caused to stakeholders by some of the impractical provisions in the new Act through a slew of circulars to ease the rigours of several provisions, there is optimism that MCA will soon rectify the anomalous situation arising out of the above as well.

Section 186 only Regulates Inter-corporate Investments

Where it comes to investments, Section 186 regulates only investments made by a Company into any other body corporate. The term "body corporate" has to be given the meaning provided by Section 2(11) of the Act and includes a company incorporated outside India. It follows from the above that investments made by companies into non-corporate avenues such as mutual funds will not be subject to compliance with the procedure of Section 186.

Section 186 Exemptions are Less Liberal than its Predecessor Section 372A

The other major difference is that the provisions of Section 372A were in totality inapplicable to certain categories of Companies including companies, involved *inter alia*, in providing infrastructural facilities. As against this, as stated in sub-section (11) of section 186, the section does not apply only to loans made, guarantees given or securities provided, *inter alia*, by a Company engaged in providing infrastructural facilities. The expression "infrastructural facilities" refers to the facilities specified in Schedule VI to the Act. Therefore, if such a company makes an acquisition by subscription, purchase or otherwise, in the securities of any other body corporate, the limits laid down in section 186 shall apply. In the same vein, NBFCs registered with RBI whose principal business shall be in respect of its investment and lending activities will not have to seek approvals for making investments. In their case, the provision of loan and guarantees will come under the radar of the Board and in applicable cases, involve approval of the members as well.

Section 186 Considers "Securities Premium" for Determining Thresholds for Loans and Investments

For computing the aggregate value of investments/loans that can be made, the lender/Investor company is allowed to include the amount of "Securities premium" standing to the credit of its Books, in addition to its paid up capital and Free Reserves. By contrast under Section 372A one could consider only the aggregate of the paid-up share capital and free reserves. It is pertinent to note that in the 1956 Act, the term "free Reserves" was not specifically defined except by way of a passing reference in Section 293(1)(d) wherein the term has been referred to as "Reserves not set apart for any specific purpose". In contrast, Section 2(43) in the Act, provides a restricted "means" definition to the expression "Free Reserves" by describing it as "such reserves which as per the latest audited Balance Sheet of a company are available for distribution as dividend". In the light of the above, it is perhaps appropriate to allow the "Securities Premium" as a concomitant to the aggregate threshold for investments and loans.

Can Loans be Extended at Subsidized Rates of Interest?

Sub-section (7) to Section 186 which corresponds to sub-section (3) in Section 372A provides that no loans can be provided to a body corporate at a rate of interest which is lower than the prevailing bank rate being the standard rate made public under Section 49 of the RBI

Act,1934. This throws up a pertinent question as to whether a Holding Company can provide to its 100% Subsidiary loans at either zero or subsidized rates of interest for business exigencies. The answer to this question would be an emphatic "No" as appears from a plain reading of Rule 11 (1) of the Companies (Meetings of Board and its powers) Rules, 2014. The above Rule merely clarifies that where a loan or guarantee is given or an investment is made in the securities of a wholly owned Subsidiary or a joint venture company, the requirement of sub-section (3) of Section 186 shall not apply. Sub-section (3) calls for the passing of a special resolution where the limits contemplated in sub-section (2) are proposed to be exceeded. Hence, only the procedure of a special resolution can be dispensed with. All other requirements of section 186 will have to be met. On the other hand, in as much as clause (c) in sub-section (8) of Section 372A exonerated a Holding Company from complying with Section 372A for loans made to its wholly owned Subsidiary, it was possible under the previous regime to provide interest-free loans to a wholly owned subsidiary. The above is yet another fetter in the new law which is perhaps oblivious to the realities of business. In many circumstances it may be necessary for a Holding Company to nurse back an ailing wholly owned Subsidiary to good health through the provision of subsidized loans. By denying this benefit the new law could push many a subsidiary to the throes of an unprecedented financial crisis. This anomalous position needs to be addressed urgently in the interest of business.

Conflict between Sections 179 and 186

The new law also throws up a conflict as between Sections 179 and 186 in the matter of precedence very similar to the question which was raised between Section 292 and Section 372A in the 1956 Act once the latter provision was introduced in the Statute Book by the Companies (Amendment) Act, 1999 with effect from 31.10.1998. Section 179(3) in the Act, lists out the powers that are exercisable by the Board by means of resolutions passed at its meetings. Some of the powers listed out can be delegated by the Board to a Committee of Directors, the Managing Director, the Manager or any other principal officer of the company. The following powers can thus be delegated:

(a) the power to borrow monies;
(b) to invest the funds of the company; and
(c) to grant loans or give guarantee or provide security in respect of loans.

Whereas Section 186 provides that any decision to make investments or to make loans, extend guarantees has to be approved unanimously by the Board at a duly convened Meeting even if the investments proposed or loans to be made are within the limits of the Board's authority. The question therefore arises whether the power to invest the funds or to grant loans or guarantees can be exercised through the scope of delegated authority as envisaged in Section 179 by bypassing the rigmarole stipulated in Section 186. Section 186 is a specific and composite code to rein in inter-corporate investments and loans, if there is a conflict, competition between Sections 179 and 186, having regard to the settled principles of judicial interpretation, Section 179 being a general provision will have to yield place to Section 186 since the latter is a specific provision. Ceiling sub-section (2) of Section 186 provides that no company shall directly or indirectly if a Company subscribes to the securities of any other body corporate, the following limits shall apply:

(a) give any loan to any person or other body corporate;
(b) give any guarantee or provide security in connection with a loan to any other body corporate or person; and
(c) acquire by way of subscription, purchase or otherwise, the securities of any other body corporate.

Unanimous Approval of the Board Required

Where the value of investment does not exceed 60% of the Company's paid up share capital, free reserves and securities premium account or where the investment does not exceed 100% of its free reserves and securities premium account whichever is more; Approval of Board has to be at a Meeting and if the Company has obtained loans from any public financial institutions which are outstanding, prior approval of the institution would also be needed. If the above limits are exceeded, approval of members by special resolution will be needed. Rule 11 in the Companies (Meetings of Board) Rules, 2014 provides that where the loans or guarantees or securities have been given to a wholly owned subsidiary or a joint venture Company or where the investment is made by holding Company in its wholly owned subsidiary it will not be necessary to obtain shareholders' approval by special resolution under section 186(3). It is pertinent to note that where any Company subscribes to the shares of another Company under a Rights issue which is covered by Section 62, Section 186 shall not apply. In other words, if shares are acquired pursuant to a rights issue, the ceiling laid down under section 186 as stated above shall not apply. In view of the above, the applicability of section 186 to Companies is restricted to the Provision of loans, guarantees or securities can be made without any ceiling and without requiring compliance with Section 186. Investment in securities of non-corporate bodies such as mutual funds can be made without the regulation of the above provision. The ceiling laid down in Section 186(1) shall apply for any acquisition of the securities of any other Company. Whenever any investment is proposed by a Company into the securities of any other body corporate, approval of the Board should be obtained at a duly held meeting with the unanimous consent of the members, provided the investment is within the limits prescribed. If the investment exceeds the limits prescribed, approval of the shareholders has to be taken. The best strategy to get away the above from rigours of compliance is to make investments in the securities of another Company pursuant to a Rights issue made by it. In such a case the above section shall not apply. Therefore, whenever investments are made into any subsidiaries, it should make sure that the subsidiary is raising subscription through the rights issue. Otherwise the ceiling laid down in Section 186 shall apply.

Tabular Comparison of Companies Act, 1956 and Companies Act, 2013

Sl. No.	*The Companies Act, 1956*	*The Companies Act, 2013*
1.	The limit prescribed was 60% of Paid-up share capital and Free Reserve or 100% of Free Reserves whichever is more.	The limit prescribed is 60% of its paid-up share capital, free reserves and securities premium account or 100% of its free reserves and securities premium account, whichever is more
2.	Rate of interest should be in respect of bank rate under RBI Act.	Rate of interest should be in respect of dated government security.
3.	Loans or investments by holding company to its WOS company were exempted.	There is no exemption for these loans/investments.
4.	Private Companies were totally exempted from the provisions of Section 372A.	Even Private companies will be subject to strict compliance.
5.	One could escape from the punishment of imprisonment by fully repaying the inter-corporate loan contravening Sec. 372A.	This is not possible.
6.	For the purpose of Sec. 372A, loan includes debentures.	This is not so under Sec.186.

Conclusion

The new Act demonstrates the systemic move towards greater regulation of corporate transactions in India with a view to facilitate increased accountability. The Act has introduced greater disclosure and compliance requirements in regulating access of capital by companies via loans and borrowings. The enhanced standards aim at protecting the rights of the all stakeholders, specifically by facilitating greater shareholder participation when companies obtain/provide loans. However, the move towards increased regulation of corporate loans and borrowings under the new Act shall significantly affect the ability of companies (specifically private companies) to access funds. In the above discussion, it is endeavoured to capture the nuances of the new provision Sections 185 and 186 and bring home the differences between the same and its predecessor 1956 Act both in terms of their forcefulness and subtlety. Without doubt Sections 185 and 186 comes off as a more potent and rigid law. There exists still considerable headroom for making the law more pliable and friendly to companies.

CHAPTER X

New Challenges

22

Uniform Financial System: An Achievable Objective or a Myth

NAVTIKA SINGH AND SHUCHITA AGARWAL

Introduction

One of the most significant modifications that new Companies Act, 2013 has conveyed in comparison to Companies Act, 1956, is to have a uniform financial year ending. Section 2(41) of new Companies Act has very evidently demarcated the term financial year. This modification to Companies Act, 2013 has carried in to align with the requirements of Income Tax Laws.[1] According to the New Act, the move which is in conformity with universal accounting standards and global finest practices, would craft a room for uniformity in their reporting timelines. Various reasons for such directives are:

(a) To align commercial actions in India with modern fashions within the global financial marketplaces.
(b) To permit for easy assessment of the financials.
(c) To foster cognizant competition amongst performers.
(d) To lessen the misperception usually faced by investors and stakeholders regarding various Financial year endings.
(e) To make it consistent with the Income-tax Act.
(f) To make Companies in industries with cyclical/seasonal

1. Income Tax Act, 1961 (43 of 1961).

businesses, e.g., sugar industry, able to reflect the results of one production cycle in a single set of financial statements.

At present, the Fiscal Year End (FYE)[2] of Indian companies ranges from April to March or July to June, or January to December or October to September, which often creates confusion and makes it difficult to compare results across the sector. As a result of the development, we expect that companies to adjust their FYE. There are various companies which report Financial Year results with periods less than 12 months (range of 8-10 months) while some companies report for periods in excess of 12 months (range of 15-18 months). Consequently, estimations across the segment become a challenge in the months ahead as the new policies lead to substantial distortion.

Definition of Uniform Financial Year

Financial year defined long back with the 1956 legislation, the exhaustive definition under Section 2(17) of Companies Act, 1956 describes as "financial year" means, in relation to a body corporate, the period in respect of which any profit and loss account of the body corporate laid before it in annual general meeting is made up, whether that period is a year or not: Provided that, in relation to an insurance company, "financial year" shall mean the calendar year referred to in sub-section (1) of section 11 of the Insurance Act, 1938. It is apparent from the definition that a financial year might not consist of a full year and no corporation is authorized to finalize its financial year at any cost. Does it signify that the corporation can finalize any period to be its financial year? Undoubtedly not. However, the provision of Section 210 of the Act says that the profit and loss account shall relate: (a) in the case of the first annual general meeting of the company, to the period beginning with the incorporation of the company and ending with a day which shall not precede the day of the meeting by more than nine months; and (b) in the case of any subsequent annual general meeting of the company, to the period beginning with the day immediately after the period for which the account was last submitted and ending with a day which shall not precede the day of the meeting by more than six months, or in cases where an extension of time has been granted for holding the meeting under the second proviso to sub-section (1) of

2. Fiscal year end means the completion of a one-year, or 12-month, accounting period. A firm's fiscal year-end does not necessarily need to fall on December 31, and can actually fall on any day throughout the year.

section 166, by more than six months and the extension so granted. The period to which the account aforesaid relates is referred to in this Act as a "financial year"; and it may be less or more than a calendar year, but it shall not exceed fifteen months. Provided that, it may extend to a period of 18 months and where a special permission has been granted in that behalf by the Registrar. Section 3(21) of the General Clauses Act, 1897 describes financial year as "financial year" shall mean the year commencing on the first day of April. Though, for the Companies Act, 1956 definition specified in the Companies Act will succeed over the definition specified in General Clauses Act. Additionally, it is also appropriate to go through Section 166(1) of the Companies Act, 1956 which states as: (1) Every company shall in each year hold in addition to any other meetings a general meeting as its annual general meeting and shall specify the meeting as such in the notices calling it; and not more than fifteen months shall elapse between the date of one annual general meeting of a company and that of the next; Provided that a company may hold its first annual general meeting within a period of not more than eighteen months from the date of its incorporation; and if such general meeting is held within that period, it shall not be necessary for the company to hold any annual general meeting in the year of its incorporation or in the following year. Provided further that the Registrar may, for any special reason, extend the time within which any annual general meeting (not being the first annual general meeting) shall be held, by a period not exceeding three months.

Essential Provisions for Financial Year

On going from beginning to end of the above provisions we locate that the Act offers for the following essential rules:

(i) At the time of first AGM, gap among last day of the financial year and the date of AGM must not go beyond nine months.

(ii) In the case of any consequent AGM, gap among last day of the financial year and the date of AGM ought not to exceed six months without the authorization of the ROC and nine months with the authorization of the ROC.

(iii) The upper limit period of financial year can be fifteen months. Though, with the consent of the ROC it can go up to eighteen months.

One has to act in accordance with both the Sections and cannot disregard one Section at the same time as following another one. Therefore, AGM can happen on a date which is prior of the two deadlines; one as according to Section 166 and another as according to Section 210.

The word 'Financial year' has been termed in section 2(17) of the Companies Act, 1956. According to this Section the term 'Financial year' in respect to any company means, the duration in respect of which any profit and loss account of the company laid before it in Annual General Meeting is made up, whether that period is a year or not. Hence, a company was at its liberty to follow any financial year whether or not it ends on 31st March. However, for the purpose of Income Tax, accounts will have to be made on 31st March. In simple terms the period to which the balance sheet and profit and loss account to be laid before a company in Annual General Meeting relate is called a "financial year". It is pertinent to quote Section 210(4) of 2013 Act, where a financial year may be more or less than a calendar year, but it shall not exceed fifteen months and the proviso[3] of the same section furthermore held that the financial year may extend to eighteen months where special permission has been granted in this connection by the concerned Registrar of Companies. Thus, annual accounts may be prepared for a period up to eighteen months with the special permission of the Registrar on the application submitted in the Form 61. The position in the New Companies Act, 2013, needless to mention that in terms of the Income-tax Act, 1961, it is mandatory for companies to follow uniform accounting year, i.e., ending 31st March. Hence, to align with the provisions of the Income tax Act, companies to have a uniform financial year ending on 31st March each year. In this regard the section 2(41) of the Companies Act, 2013 which is reproduced as "financial year" in relation to any company or body corporate, means the period ending on the 31st day of March every year, and where it has been incorporated on or after the 1st day of January of a year, the period ending on the 31st day of March of the following year, in respect whereof financial statement of the company or body corporate is made up. Provided that on an application made by a company or body corporate, which is a holding company or a subsidiary of a company incorporated outside India and is required to follow a different financial year for consolidation of its accounts outside India, the Tribunal may, if it is satisfied, allow any period as its financial year, whether or not that period is a year. Provided further that a company or body corporate, existing on the commencement of this Act, shall, within a period of two

3. The Companies Act, 1956, Proviso of Section 210(4).

years from such commencement, align its financial year as per the provisions of this clause. As is evident from the reading of second proviso to section 2(41), a company or body corporate, existing on the commencement of Companies Act, 2013, not having financial year ending on the 31st day of March every year, shall, within a period of two years from such commencement, must ensure its financial year will be the period ending on 31st March every year. The 2013 Act also requires all companies to adopt a uniform financial year of 1st April to 31st March with limited exception to a company which is a holding company or subsidiary of a company incorporated outside which may be required to follow a different financial year for consolidation outside India. All exceptions would however require the approval of the National Company Law Tribunal (the Tribunal). As part of transition provisions, Companies would be given a period of 2 years to change their accounting year to 1st April to 31st March. Only holding or subsidiary companies of a company incorporated outside India would be entitled to the exception of having a different accounting year. However, these companies have to seek specific approval from the Tribunal to avail the exception which might be administratively burdensome. Further, it appears that associates/joint ventures are not covered under the exception.

Definition of Financial Year in Companies Bill, 2011

It was proposed to introduce concept of uniform financial year in new Companies Act also. Clause 2(41) as introduced in Lok Sabha defines financial year as; "financial year", in relation to any company or body corporate, means the period ending on the 31st day of March every year, and where it has been incorporated on or after the 1st day of January of a year, the period ending on the 31st day of March of the following year, in respect whereof financial statement of the company or body corporate is made up. Provided that on an application made by a company or body corporate, which is a holding company or a subsidiary of a company incorporated outside India and is required to follow a different financial year for consolidation of its accounts outside India, the Tribunal may, if it is satisfied, allow any period as its financial year, whether or not that period is a year. Provided further that a company or body corporate, existing on the commencement of this Act, shall, within a period of two years from such commencement, align its financial year as per the provisions of this clause.

Definition in the New Act of 2013

According to section 2(41) of Companies Act, 2013, in respect of any enterprise or body corporate, signifies the period ending on the 31st day of March each year, and wherever it has been incorporated on or after the 1st day of January of a year, the period ending on the 31st day of March of the following year, in respect whereof financial statement of the company or body corporate is made up. Uniform financial year should end on 31st March—the Companies Act, 2013. Now businesses in India should have uniform financial year. This signifies a company's financial year must start from 1st of April of a year to 31st March of another year. If it's a recently incorporated company then we need to look into the date of its beginning. If incorporation date is earlier than 1st January then financial year finishes on coming 31st March else it will be period completing on the 31st day of March of the subsequent year. For illustration: if an establishment is incorporated on 2nd January 2012 then financial year according to section 2(41) would be beginning from 2nd January 2012 to 31st March 2013. As an alternative of 2nd January 2012, if it's incorporated on 28th December 2011 then financial year will be beginning from 28th December 2011 to 31st March 2012. Section 2(41) additionally specifies that if an establishment or Corporation is a holding or subsidiary of a foreign concern and in lieu of this purpose they are obligatory to follow a different financial year for association of its financial declaration outside India, then tribunal if contented, may agree for any other period as company's financial year, not being a full year compulsorily. Establishments or body corporate which are in existence at the commencement of Companies Act, 2013, intend to act in accordance with this section within a span of 2 years from such commencement and bring into line with the new financial year ending of the 31st day of March. Enterprises incorporated afterwards 1st January can consider subsequent year's 31st March as their comprehensive financial year and subsequently they can take financial year beginning from 1st April to 31st March. Because of this amendment, numerous large Indian corporations like HCL technologies and Ranbaxy Laboratories have to amend their financial year. Transnational companies like Glaxo Smith line, Thomas Cook, Proctor and Gamble, Siemens, Nestle India, Ambuja cements, Bosch, are also obligated to act in accordance with this provision.

The Maximum Period of First Financial Year

Section 210 of 1956 Act provides that in general a financial year can consist of not more than 15 months. Though, with the authorization of the Registrar it is allowed to get extended up to 18 months. It is correct for first financial year also. But it is tough to decide the duration of first financial year of a company. Therefore, for the same, we need to do to the following:

Decide Year-end Date of Financial Year of the Company

The Companies Act, 1956 does not authorize a company to follow a uniform financial year as has been mandatory in the provisions of Income Tax Act, 1961 which states that a company has to get its financial records prepared and audited as at the conclusion of 31st March every year. On the other hand, under the Companies Act, 1956, the corporation is free to pursue any accounting year of its preference. Most of the companies finalize their books of accounts on 31st March every year to fulfil the requirements of both the Acts. Nevertheless, some companies due to a variety of reasons still close their books of accounts on 30th June or 31st December and so on.

Work out Alternatives Presented Considering Requirements of Sections 166 and 210

All corporations can use the duration from date of incorporation of the corporation to the immediately next year-end date as the initial financial year of the corporation without getting involved into more details. However, if such financial year is too small, corporation may not want to get the financial statement audited for such undersized period. In such circumstances one has to locate whether the corporation can decide to have next succeeding year end date as the last date of the first financial year taking into consideration the provisions of Sections 166 and 210 of the Act.

Power of ROC to Extend Time for Holding AGM

On a collective reading of both 166 and 210 it become apparent that the first Annual General Meeting of the company must held within 18 months from the date of its incorporation and within 9 months from the date of close of the financial year. An Annual General Meeting other than the first Annual General Meeting is supposed to be held on the most primitive of the following dates:

(a) 15 months of the date of last AGM;
(b) 6 months from the close of the financial year; and
(c) The last day of the calendar year.

Though, the ROC can provide extension of time for holding Annual General Meeting under section 166(1) up to 3 months. Now the question is whether ROC has authority to provide extension for holding successive Annual General Meeting under section 210 within 9 months from the closure of the financial year or not because the words of Section indicates that extension can only be given under section 166 and not under section 210. But it has been elucidated by the Ministry of Corporate Affairs that where the corporation faces genuine complicatedness in holding its Annual General Meeting within 6 months of the closure of the financial year while it could hold it within the time limit agreed under section 166, the ROC can on merits of each issue, permit extension under section 166, even if the period agreed under section 166 are not probably to be exceeded, so that the corporation can take benefit of the extension and is permitted to hold its AGM beyond the duration of 6 months agreed under section 210 and up to 9 months of the financial year. Here the words "month" and "year" used in the Act must be clear as to what is actually meant by these terms. Different forms of calendars are being used in the state which carries diverse meanings of these terms. These terms have not been described in the Companies Act and as such therefore, as per general philosophy of interpretation we need to refer General Clauses Act, 1897.[4] Therefore, we have to follow British calendar for the clear definition of the words "month" and "year" to be used in the Companies Act, 1956.

Impacts of Uniform Financial Year

On the whole, a standardized and uniform year end for corporations could have the following outcome on the segment and its stakeholders:

(a) Requires preparation for transition and alignment with Auditors and other stakeholders.
(b) The price of banking stocks will have a predetermined behavior as they churn out performance results and announce corporate actions almost at the same time.
(c) We expect the CBN to subsequently introduce a policy framework that would compel all banks to conform to a unique financial reporting standard.

---

4. General Clauses Act, supra note under Section 3 describes these words as: "(35) "month" shall mean a month reckoned according to the British calendar; (66) "year" shall mean a year reckoned according to the British calendar."

(d) Given observed trend in the industry, which shows that most banks usually headhunt towards their financial year end, we expect immense competitive pressure on human resource recruitment in the industry around December and a consequent jump in staff costs.

(e) The timing for the release of results could improve as it would serve as a means of assessing performance and corporate governance.

(f) It could result in fierce but healthy competition amongst sector players.

(g) Regulators can easily identify poor reporting standards and clamp down policy defaulters more easily.

(h) As reporting accountants and auditors come under pressure, induced by the need for timely delivery of financial reports and statement of accounts, there is the risk of shoddiness in the preparation of banks' results, at least in the near term. However, this risk could be mitigated by an urgent increase in existing capacity among these stakeholders.

(i) We expect industry analysis to become more objective and less complicated. Industry groupings would also become easier and valuations more realistic.

In 2012, infrastructure firm IVRCL was going through a restructuring process and awaiting a court nod for the merger or demerger. Hence, to avoid cumbersome accounting with respect to the merger/demerger and to have the merged balance sheet in place, the company decided to extend the accounting year up to June 2012. For the next year, the company reverted to the usual April-March period. Thus, while the Financial Year 12 profit and revenue numbers were for a 15 months period, Financial Year 13 numbers were for a truncated, nine-month period.[5] Several Indian companies make such alterations. Till now, they had the scope to alter the accounting year, depending on in-house reasons such as profitability, productivity and external actions such as court orders. Conversely, the Companies Act, 2013, has hold tightly on this. It has detached the provisions that permitted companies to reduce or extend financial years as they require, making way for

5. N. Sundaresha Subramanian & Sudipto Dey, 226 firms to march to a new accounting year New Companies Act gives two years for all firms to shift to year ending March 31, http://www.business-standard.com/article/companies/226-firms-to-march-to-a-new-accounting-year-113100300666_1.html (last updated Oct. 3, 2013).

uniform reporting by corporate India. The Act has described financial year as "the duration ending on the 31st day of March each year, and wherever it has been incorporated on or later than the first day of January of a year, the duration ending on the 31st day of March of the subsequent year, in regards where of financial statement of the corporation or corporate body is made up. It stated all existing companies are supposed to, within a time slab of two years; align their financial year with the provisions of this section. This means various companies, together with large ones such as HCL Technologies (which follows the year ending June) and Ranbaxy Laboratories (which follows the calendar year) have to regulate their accounting sequence in coming days.[6] According to data provided by advisory firm Corporate Professionals, as many as 226 listed companies don't follow financial years ending March. Of these, 74 follow the calendar year for accounting; 58 follow the year ending September, while 89 follow the July-to-June financial year. A few listed companies follow the financial year ending April, August and October as well.[7] One of the most important reasons for diverse accounting years is the cyclicality of the industry. Saurabh Agarwal, Director of Kennis Consultancy, cites the example of the sugar industry. "Most companies in the sugar industry follow the July-June year because typically, the sugar season starts in September. In March, most of these have stocks in their books. By June, all the stocks are sold and the books look very good. This practice would come to an end."[8] The Ministry of Corporate Affairs move to carry uniformity in the corporate segment could be the initial step towards harmonizing various sectors in the financial system. Today, diverse accounting years are pursued within different government organizations. Despite the fact that the Union government keeps on to follow the April-March year, the Reserve Bank of India (RBI) follows the July-June financial year. Agricultural products such as wheat, sugar and paddy have different crop years, associated to their relevant harvest seasons.[9] Sometime ago, the government had well thought of the July-June financial year so that whilst building the Union Budget, the finance minister had an enhanced idea of the monsoons, a chief factor influencing the agriculture-based economy. Pranab Mukherjee, in his first stint as finance minister, had even set-up a committee under former

6. *Ibid.*
7. *Ibid.*
8. *Ibid.*
9. *Ibid.*

RBI Governor L.K. Jha to study and make recommendations in this regard. However, the idea was dropped.[10] However, another reason for having different accounting years is combination of accounts with an overseas parent or a subsidiary. Numerous multinational companies like Nestle India, Glaxo Smithkline, Ambuja Cements, Bosch, Thomas Cook, operating in India follow the financial year of July-June year for accounting, and on the other hand Siemens closed its books in September, whereas Procter & Gamble and Gillette ended the financial year in June itself. However, the new companies Act, made it apparent that there should be a uniform financial year, which should be followed by each and every company, it will try to give a different kind of transparency, although the new provision will bring more transparency and uniformity and will be in harmony with other steps such as implementation of IFRS (International Financial Reporting Standards) and XBRL (Extensible Business Reporting Language). The Uniform System will give benefit to officials in companies that don't pursue the year ending March said their workings would now be easier, as they had to preserve different books for tax purposes, as according to the country's tax rules where the date of year closure is 31st March. In this way an IVRCL representative recalled how the company had to plan and maintain two sets of accounts. Generally financial year of a corporation is of 12 months. Still, in some cases it may possibly not be so. In the context of newly incorporated company, financial accounts should be made starting from the date of incorporation of the corporation till the year-end day of the financial year which could or could not be of 12 months. Correspondingly in case of consequent amendment of financial year by the corporation, the financial year in the same year of such alteration may not essentially be of 12 months. In such cases, there is a need to vigilantly explore provisions of the Companies Act, 1956 and after that decide exact duration of the financial year depending upon particulars of each case.

Comparative Analysis of Two Financial Years

The permissible provisions could be without doubt understood with the help of a few illustrations. *Illustration-1*: Company having 31st March as its year-end date; It can be explained in the form of Table 1:

10. *Ibid.*

Table 1

No.	Date of incorporation falls between	Financial year-end date without the approval of ROC (within 15 months of incorporation)		Extended financial year-end date with the approval of ROC (within 18 months of incorporation)	Last date of first AGM as per various options of financial year if not a public holiday (being earlier of two dates as per Sections 166 and 210)		
		Option-I	*Option-II*	*Option-III*	*Option-I*	*Option-II*	*Option-III*
1.	1/1/2012 to 31/3/2012	31/3/2012	31/3/2013	N.A.	31/12/2012 [Sec. 210]	18 months from incorporation [Sec. 166]	N.A.
2.	1/4/2012 to 30/6/2012	31/3/2013	N.A.	N.A.	18 months from incorpor-ation [Sec. 166]	N.A.	N.A.
3.	1/7/2012 to 30/9/2012	31/3/2013	N.A.	N.A.	31/12/2013 [Sec. 210]	N.A.	N.A.
4.	1/10/2012 to 31/12/2012	31/3/2013	N.A.	31/3/2014	31/12/2013 [Sec. 210]	N.A.	18 months from incorporation [Sec. 166] *(See Note-1 below)*

Thus it is evident from the above discussed table that a company incorporated in the first part (quarter) of the year 2012 and willing to close its books on 31st March can seal the books either on 31st March 2013 or on 31st March 2012 since both dates fall within approved period of 15 months from date of incorporation. But a company built-in in any other quarter (part) of the year can seal its books only on 31st March 2013, however, the third arrangement where a company incorporated in the last quarter of the year can seal its books on 31st March 2014 but with special permission of ROC while this date will fall within extensive period of 18 months from the date of assimilation of the company. Nevertheless where a company incorporated in first phase can close its accounts in appropriate ending, but in second or third quarter of the year the companies does not have any other option as the next probable date, i.e. 31st March 2014 will be outside 18 months of date of incorporation. *Illustration-2*: Company having 30th June as its year-end date; It can be explained in the form of Table 2.

Table 2

No.	*Date of incorporation falls between*	*Financial year-end date without the approval of ROC (within 15 months of incorporation)*		*Extended financial year-end date with the approval of ROC (within 18 months of incorporation)*	*Last date of first AGM as per various options of financial year if not a public holiday (being earlier of two dates as per Sections 166 and 210)*		
		Option-I	*Option-II*	*Option-III*	*Option-I*	*Option-II*	*Option-III*
1.	1/1/2012 to 31/3/2012	30/6/2012	N.A.	30/6/2013	31/3/2013 [Sec. 210]	N.A.	18 months from incorporation [Sec. 166] *(See Note-1 below)*
2.	1/4/2012 to 30/6/2012	30/6/2012	30/6/2013	N.A.	31/3/2013 [Sec. 210]	18 months from incorporation [Sec. 166]	N.A.
3.	1/7/2012 to 30/9/2012	30/6/2013	N.A.	N.A.	18 months from incorporation [Sec. 166]	N.A.	N.A.
4.	1/10/2012 to 31/12/2012	30/6/2013	N.A.	N.A.	31/3/2014 [Sec. 210]	N.A.	N.A.

Thus it is clear from the above table that a company incorporated in the second quarter of the year 2012 and wishing to close its books on 30th June can close the books either on 30th June 2012 or on 30th June 2013 since both dates fall within prescribed period of 15 months from date of incorporation. A company incorporated in first quarter of the year can close its books only on 30th June 2012. Similarly, a company incorporated in third or fourth quarter can close its books only on 30th June 2013. Only a company incorporated in the first quarter of the year can close its books on 30th June 2013 with special permission of ROC since this date will fall within extended period of 18 months from the date of incorporation of the company. A company incorporated in third or fourth quarter of the year does not have any other option since next possible date, i.e. 30th June 2014 will be beyond 18 months of date of incorporation. In the instances where financial year is enlarged to 18 months with the endorsement of ROC, first Annual General Meeting will have to be held within the period of 18 months of incorporation of the company. If in case the company is incorporated in the beginning days of the quarter and the company might not be in a condition to give 21 clear days notice for summoning the AGM. In such a circumstance, subject to the conditions of the Articles of Association (AOA) of the company, AGM shall have to be convened at an immediate notice with the consent of member's under section 171(2) of the Act.

Conclusion

The Company is probably face prosecution in the cases/provisions under Sections 166 and 210 of the Act if not complied with true spirit. Company Secretary plays a distinguish role in counseling the Board of Directors of the company appropriately in fascination of financial year, particularly in the first financial year thereby avoiding examination for unintentional default. Companies in the Other Financial Institutions sub-sector must conform to uniform accounting year-end policy. The Ministry of Corporate Affairs and Reserve Bank of India has directed companies in the other Financial Institutions sub-sector which include; microfinance banks, primary mortgage institutions and finance companies to adopt a uniform accounting system. The directive, according to the authorities is targeted at ensuring that companies, financial institutions, microfinance banks alongside other financial banks align with standards. The inference, according to analysts, is that temporal right to use funds for other financial institutions to cover up little shortfalls in their financial statements or to meet some regulatory requirements will no longer be feasible as all the companies will be likely to hold their annual general meetings at the conclusion of every year. The move is to avoid authoritarian arbitrage and supply a level playing field for all employers in the commercial and financial sector. For the avoidance of doubt, all primary companies and finance companies are obligatory to adopt 31st March as their accounting year-end. Accordingly, directors of all companies are hereby advised, as a first step, to pass a resolution to that effect and inform the relevant agencies in line with Section 2(41) of the Companies Act, 2013. It states that upper limit of accounting period is of 18 months and a minimum of nine months were permissible in line with established accounting practice during the phase of transition. The proper audited financial statements inclusive of Profit and Loss Accounts, Balance sheets, Cash Flow Statements with Board of Directors Report and Corporate Governance Report should be submitted to the portal of Ministry of Corporate Affairs in the duly prescribed time limit as according to Section 210 and

166 of the Companies Act, 1956 because the corresponding sections of Companies Act, 2013 are yet not notified. Companies whose accounting year ends on 31st March should as usual, forward their full year's accounts to MCA for approval not later than one month after the Annual General Meeting for that financial year. It also pointed out that the audited statements for the pro-rated duration should likewise be submitted not later than one month after the period-end for MCA approval and subsequent publication, in accordance with Companies Act, as amended. The Ministry of Corporate Affairs has put certain penalized action against the companies who do not follow their financial years and are not holding the Annual General Meeting in line with the requirements of the Companies Act, 1956. This concept of fixing financial year has been described as a good initiative intended at salvaging the financial sector. It was stated that before commencement of 31st March uniform accounting year-end for all companies, there were strong indications that they were rotating funds among themselves to shore up their balance sheets at financial year end. Also the Income-tax Act necessitates all companies to follow 1 April to 31st March as their previous year, for tax reporting purposes. The obligation of the Companies Act, 2013 is consistent with Income-tax Act and will abolish the requirement to arrange separate tax financial statements. And companies in businesses with cyclical/seasonal industries, e.g., sugar industry, will not be able to reproduce the effects of one production cycle in an only set of financial statements. As a result, a better synchronization will be conceivable with uniformity of financial year; however, it will escalate the workload of the authorities due to completion of work under same closing dates for various acts. The policy if well managed in the corporate sector which will bring transparency and accountability as it has capability to curtail bad corporate governance. It is a truth that regulators and other stakeholders are concerned in their performance and consequently efforts are on to safeguard that each company rewards its diverse stakeholders adequately. Moreover, this will give chance to the investing public and shareholders to evaluate the performance of their establishments as this will usher in an era of opposition. The Adoption of a uniform financial year-end will allow for proper evaluation of corporations.

23

Statutory Remedies and Shareholder Oppression: Is there a Need to Re-Define Judicial Boundaries?

DEVARSHI MUKHOPADHYAY

Re-formulating Foss *vs.* Harbottle: Establishing the Need for the Balancing Act

Striking the appropriate balance and drawing the fine line between excessive or uncalled for judicial intervention in a Company democracy on one hand and shareholder protection on the other, has found a significant position in the core debate surrounding the evolving corporate jurisprudence relating to statutory remedies in the face of minority oppression.[1] While on one hand, a significant section of the corporate arena stand strictly by the view that interfering with a Company's majority rule would tantamount to excessive jurisdictional exercise and interference in the Company's internal affairs, a distinct section also posit, that the rule of the majority cannot be allowed to outrun the interests of the very constituents of the Company, which are its shareholders in general.[2] The moot point therefore, is to adequately

1. Editorial Board, "Right of Equitable Owner of Stock to Bring Derivative Action," *The Virginia Law Review*, Vol. 40, 1952.
2. Editorial Board, "Statute of Limitations and Shareholder's Derivative Actions," *The Columbia Law Review*, Vol. 56, 1956.

define the boundaries of judicial investigation and remedy, in order to fulfil the larger objective of drawing and maintaining the fine line between excessive and necessary *"interference"*. Having acknowledged the changing face of derivative action as well as individual oppression applications, the author argues that given the general trend to relax the division between the two, there is a need to increase the subject matter jurisdiction of Section 402(g)[3] of the Companies Act 1956, which currently is 242(2)(m) of the 2013 Act.[4] The argument in this regard revolves around the fact that the general scope of an equitable shareholder remedy has been drastically re-defined in order to accommodate a much wider scope of investigation into the Company's affairs. In the face of such redefinition, and the rigid categorization of the exceptions to the rule in *Foss* vs. *Harbottle*[5], the scope of the *"just and equitable remedy"* within Section 242 (2)(m) must be read widely and in deviation from the settled principle that the scope of the Tribunal's order is strictly controlled by the general scheme of Section 241 of the 2013 Act (not yet in force). Given the fact that the corporate jurisprudence of common-law jurisdictions across the globe have given birth to statutory remedies in order to overcome the shortfalls of the rule in *Foss* vs. *Harbottle,* the argument of the author is for the purposes of asserting the need to expand the current judicial boundaries, in order to afford greater scope of accountability and relief for the shareholder in the face of controller actions in a Company.

The English Position on Derivative Action

At a very preliminary level, it becomes pertinent to note that in matters of corporate recovery, the established principle of law is that the Company is the "proper plaintiff".[6] In fact, a representative suit brought by the shareholders against persons in control of the Company and accused to have perpetrated a wrong on the Company, has been strictly restricted to certain judicially carved out exceptions to the general norm, as was laid down in the classic 1843 case of *Foss* vs. *Harbottle* (in distinction from the rule in *Attorney General* vs. *Wilson*[7]). In the factual scenario specific to this case, a legal proceeding was initiated by two

3. Section 402(g), the Companies Act 1956 (India).
4. This section is not yet in force.
5. (1843) 67 E.R. 189.
6. The test of the "proper plaintiff" was laid down in the case of *Foss* vs. *Harbottle* in order to precisely outline the scope of derivative action and corporate recovery.
7. (1840) Cr. and Ph.

shareholders against the promoters and directors of the Company, alleging an improper mortgage. The strict standard that was laid down in the matter, also now known as the "rule in *Foss* vs. *Harbottle*", was that in such matters, where a wrong is alleged to have been committed against the Company, the "proper plaintiff" was the Company itself, and not the two individual shareholders in question. Having derived this general legal position from the two settled principles of separate corporate personality and limited interference by the Court in the internal affairs of a Company democracy, the rigid application of this rule subsequently found four judicially carved out exceptions.[8] The first exception, namely that of *ultra vires* or illegality found reflection in the 1915 case of *Cockburn* vs. *Newbridge Laundry Co.*[9] as well as in the 1988 case of *Smith* vs. *Croft*,[10] while the 1950 case of *Edwards* vs. *Halliwell*[11] carved out the second exception for actions statutorily requiring a special majority. A third exception was created for cases where the individual right of the shareholder was being infringed, as was observed in the 1877 case of *Pender* vs. *Lushington*.[12] However, the judicial exception most commonly resorted to, for derivative claims, is the fourth and final "fraud on the minority" exception which is intended to cover those situations where (a) the majority has obtained a definite benefit (*Pavlides* vs. *Jensen*,[13] in 1956), (b) the aforementioned benefit must have accrued to the majority at the cost of the Company's interests (*Regal Hastings Limited* vs. *Gulliver*,[14] in 1967), and (c) the majority used the "control" exercised by them on the Company in order to prevent an action being brought against them (the average position in the abovementioned cases). As Gower and Davies observe, the strict standard set by the rule in *Foss* vs. *Harbottle*, and the generally unclear position of law in the exceptions carved out therein, significantly narrowed the shareholder's avenues of recourse under common law. As a result of this, a need was felt for creating avenues for separate statutory remedies for individual cases of oppression. Given the fact that shareholders are generally at a disadvantageous position with respect to derivative claims, because of (a) informational disadvantages which disable an alleging shareholder

---

8. Ralph Carson, "Current Phases of Derivative Actions against Directors," *The Michigan Law Review*, Vol. 40, 1942.
9. (1915) I I.R. 237.
10. (1988) Ch. 114.
11. (1950) 2 All E.R. 1064.
12. (1877) 6 Ch.D. 70.
13. (1956) 2 All E.R. 518.
14. (1967) 2 A.C. 134.

from adequately assessing the strength of their claim, and (b) the costs and time of initiating the proceeding, the separate statutory remedies afforded to shareholders provided for the much needed avenue for recourse in separation from common law.[15] Now, one of the more noted distinctions which one draws between a derivative action and an oppression application is that while the former is brought in certain specific situations in the name of the Company, which necessarily requires a much higher burden to be discharged (a derivative action usually requires proof of a legal wrong while a claim for oppression can be made credibly so long as a legitimate expectation of the shareholder has been unfairly prejudiced), an individual application of oppression requires the discharge of a particular instance of damage caused to the complainant. The author argues that this distinction is one which has been significantly diluted in the modern context, where there may very well be the possibility of a credible claim for a derivative action as well as an individual application, but the shareholder may decide to take recourse under the second option because of a lesser standard of proof and a lesser possibility of an informational disadvantage.

The Canadian Position on Derivative Claims

For instance, as Newbury, J. observes in the landmark decision of *Furry Timber Corporation* vs. *Laad Ventures Ltd.*,[16] the two categories cannot said to be mutually exclusive and that there is always a distinct possibility that the wrong in question, affects both the interests of the Company in general, and the shareholders, either directly or even indirectly.[17] As a result of this particular dictum, the doctrine of separate corporate personality stood diluted to the extent that the court recognized that if the interests of the Company were being adversely affected by the rule of the majority, it certainly affected the overall interests of the shareholders as well. To that extent, it would lead to a miscarriage of justice, if the two entities were seen as strictly separate. Further, the opinion of Justice LaForest in the matter between *Hercules Management* vs. *Ernst and Young*[18] is of critical importance where his Lordship opines that there may be a situation of co-existence of the corporation's claims along with that of the shareholder. Relying on

15. G.R Sullivan, "Restating the Scope of Derivative Action," *The Cambridge Law Journal,* Vol. 44, 1985.
16. (1992) 75 B.C.L.R. 246.
17. *Ibid.*
18. (1997) 2 S.C.R. 165.

clarifying the scope of the 1974 case of *Goldex Mines* vs. *Revill*,[19] where the Court had drawn the bare distinction between the two categories, the liberal position of law which was developed as a result of these cases found adequate reflection in the subsequent development of case law jurisprudence. For instance, in the 2007 matter between *Gopal* vs. *Burke*[20], it was established that the diversion of corporate opportunities in general was a wrong done to the Company and would attract a derivative claim, but when the same was done in the interest of the majority, then a separate claim for oppression would also lie. Therefore, an "indirect harm" caused to the shareholder in question, would also create a valid ground for a claim of oppression, in addition to the already existent scope for a derivative claim in the name of the Company.[21] Naturally, this position of law has been largely unclear and rebutted, as was observed previously in the 1978 cases of *Brunei* vs. *Irwin Industries Ltd.*,[22] as well as in the 2004 case of *Pasnak* vs. *Chura*,[23] where the Court was of the opinion that unless it was reasonably shown that a "unique harm"[24] has been caused to the shareholder in question, the appropriate remedy was derivative action and not a claim for oppression. However, the generally liberal position which emerges from the Canadian courts, is adequately reflected by Armstrong, J. in the 2008 matter between *Malata Group* vs. *Jung*,[25] where the honorable Judge explicitly stated that a "bright-line distinction"[26] could not be drawn between a derivative and an oppression claim, and therefore the correct way of interpreting a fact specific situation was to undertake a purposive reading of the very nature and aim of such shareholder remedies in matters of corporate recovery.

A Flittering Judiciary and a "Notoriously Vague Concept"

If one shifts the focus to the corporate jurisprudence in the United Kingdom, a similar trend is observed, with the exception that even for oppression claims, the Judiciary has flittered in its stand. However, despite this generally unclear position of law, the fact that the strict scrutiny standard with respect to the *Foss* vs. *Harbottle* exceptions has been diluted is now settled. For instance, if one takes a look at the

19. (1974) 7 O.R. 216 (C.A.).
20. (2007) B.C.S.C. 1930.
21. *Ibid.*
22. (2002) B.C.S.C. 757.
23. (2004) B.C.C.A. 221.
24. *Ibid.*
25. (2008) O.N.C.A. 111.
26. *Ibid.*

landmark opinion of Vinelott, J. in the 1981 matter between *Prudential Assurance Company Ltd.* vs. *Newman Industries Ltd.*,[27] the complete overhaul of the manner in which "fraud on the minority" was being interpreted, leads to the possibilities of a more liberal and pro-shareholder approach in the context of modern corporation law. Prior to this particular case, a fairly conservative definition of fraud was followed, whereby the definition was restricted only to those transactions which involved an element of dishonesty reflected in a breach of duty. As a result of this decision, however, it was subsequently expanded to also include those acts where the alleged act amounted to an "unconscionable act in addition to dishonesty" as was observed in the immediate aftermath of this decision, in *Estmanco Ltd.* vs. *Greater London Council*[28] in 1982. Although the definition of fraud had been significantly expanded since the early 1900s (*Burland* vs. *Earle*[29]), it did not find adequate application in case law, which is possibly a reason why the fourth exception to the rule in *Foss* vs. *Harbottle*, became a "notoriously vague concept" as observed by the Report of the Company Law Committee.[30] Now, this later judicial trend primarily came about as a result of the decision of the court in *Cook* vs. *Deeks*,[31] where the defendant directors were held to have committed fraud, on the basis of expropriation of the Company's property. Holding that such action was unratifiable, it is interesting to note that it was personal liability that was asked for and attributed in the facts of the case. The distinction between this particular factual scenario, and the ruling of the Court in *Regal Hastings Limited* vs. *Gulliver*,[32] where the breach was held to be ratifiable, was that in *Cook*,[33] the directors had acted in bad faith while in *Regal*[34] they had not. Therefore, profit in the latter case was held to be only incidental. Now, as both Goode and Professor Gower note, so long as an element of bad faith is present, the violation of a fiduciary duty was to be held as not capable of ratification. Accordingly, what one observes from this particular string of cases in British jurisprudence, is that the manner in which the scope of derivative action as a strict exception was interpreted, was significantly reformulated, to also

27. (1982) Ch. 204, Court of Appeal.
28. (1982) I W.L.R.
29. (1902) A.C. 83, 93.
30. Report of the Jenkins Company Law Committee, 1962.
31. (1916) 1 A.C. 554.
32. *Supra* note 17.
33. (1916) 1 A.C. 554.
34. (1967) 2 A.C. 134.

accommodate primarily the element of "bad faith".[35] As a natural consequence of this, acts such as the diversion of a commercial opportunity to the Company (*Industrial Development Ltd.* vs. *Cooley*[36]), or the negligent use of an authority to sell (*Daniel* vs. *Daniel*[37]), were also included within the ambit of the fourth exception to the rule in *Foss*. Naturally, this was a landmark judicial trend which allowed for a much wider base for judicial intervention even in the internal affairs of a Company, sometimes even going to the extent of making them unratifiable. Another pivotal trend which one may observe at a similar time is the changing definition of "*control*" for the purposes of casting a wider net of liability on persons taking major decisions within the corporation structure. The author has briefly discussed this in the following section of the paper. For instance, as Vinelott, J. observes, the operative question which one would have to ask was if the defendants had access to the "means of manipulation" to ultimately defraud the minority. While one may possibly criticize the indefinite extension of the term *control* to matters like monopoly over information or the use of managerial vetoes in the voting process, the interventionist stand of the Judge is adequately reflected when he sets the final question in terms of the futility of calling a general meeting to ratify a particular action of the majority, albeit a fraud on the minority, where either indirectly or directly, the influence of the majority was going to render the ratification a mere formality. Clearly, this particular string of cases marked a paradigm shift in terms of (a) an expanded ambit of fraud under common law and corporation structures, and (b) a reformulated definition of "control" in order to expand the liability net and afford greater minority protection.

In the context of claims of oppression however, one notices the lack of uniformly developing case law jurisprudence. In the first landmark case of *Scottish Co-operative Wholesale Society* vs. *Meyer*,[38] the opinion of Lord Denning significantly increased the subject matter jurisdiction of Section 210 of the English Companies Act, 1948, stating that the statutory remedy was to be made available even when the business of the Company had been halted. Therefore, the honorable Judge, attributing a wide meaning to the term "bring to an end the matters complained of (the alleged oppression)", significantly restated the original purpose of

35. *Ibid.*
36. (1972) 1 W.L.R. 443.
37. (1978) 2 All E.R. 89.
38. (1958) 3 All E.R. 66.

statutory remedies (Section 210 in this case) working in order to afford a greater coverage than derivative action under common law. However, in the same year, in 1958, the opinion of the Court in the matter between *In Re: H.R Harmer Ltd.*,[39] while narrowing the scope of Denning's opinion, also added to the confusion regarding the scope of the oppression remedy. While on one hand, the scope is restricted by virtue of the Court requiring a continuing act of oppression which can be attributed to particular members in that particular capacity, an unclear position of law also emerges when the Court while failing to define what constitutes "oppression" states with authority that a just and equitable remedy in favour of the shareholder would not apply in every case. In the 1973 opinion of the House of Lords however, in *Ebrahimi* vs. *Westbourne Galleries Ltd.*,[40] a relatively greater degree of clarity was observed, by virtue of the Court ruling that the removal of a person from the Board of Directors, by majority rule, did qualify as a valid pre-condition for a winding up order. Although the general scope of this remedy was recommended to be increased in 1962 by the Jenkin Committee on Company Law with the introduction of the terms "unfair prejudice", it wasn't until the introduction of Section 459 (which now stands as Section 994 of the 2006 Companies Act, U.K) in the 1985[41] Companies Act that such scope was widened. In fact, as J. Coffee notes in his 1989 essay in the Columbia Law Review, the true essence of such "looser form" of corporate statutes was to enable the Courts to "fill the gap" between common-law policy-making and the judicial role in resolving certain difficult and fact specific situations. Therefore, the author argues that the proper manner of interpreting the gradual change of case-law with the parallel change in the legislative provisions is to see the developments as allowing a broader base for shareholder protection. Despite this move, the opinion of Justice Peter Smith further diluted this liberal base in the 2004 matter between *Rock Nominees Ltd.* vs. *R.C.O. Holdings Ltd.*,[42] where his Lordship opined that on the question of undervaluation of Company assets, a high burden would have to be discharged to show that the expert body on the basis of which the assets were valued, were incorrect in terms of the market price of the assets which were sold and otherwise transferred. As such, the presumption of the Court would be that the best price had been achieved, unless

39. (1958) 3 All E.R. 689.
40. (1973) A.C. 360.
41. Section 459, Companies Act, 1985, U.K.
42. (2004) E.W.C.A. 118.

specifically and credibly rebutted to be otherwise. This view was also endorsed by Justice Jonathan Parker and Sir Swinton Thomas at the Court of Appeal. However, a liberal protection base was provided by the Privy Council in its 2007 decision in the matter between *Gamlestaden Fastigheter A.B* vs. *Baltic Partners Ltd.,*[43] where relief for unfairly prejudicial conduct was made available to a non-member as well, thereby specifically watering down the requirement in *Harmer's* case. In fact, in the words of Justice Warwick, so long as a benefit was in question, no further questions were to be asked regarding the membership status of the applicant. Therefore, a review of the development of British corporate jurisprudence makes it amply clear that (a) the development of the liberal base for greater shareholder/interested party protection has been fragmented and context specific, and (b) irrespective of the contrary opinion, if one notices the legislative trend, then a fair inference can be made about the fact that the intention of the legislature has been to provide the Courts with a greater chance to intervene in the internal affairs of the Company democracy. Considering that the Indian corporation law has borrowed and developed significantly in line with that of the United Kingdom, the two common law scenarios in Canada and the U.K. were provided in order to set sufficient context for the study of the law in India.

Indian Position on Minority Shareholder Interests

In the 1973 case of *Manmohan Singh* vs. *Balbir Singh,*[44] the High Court at Delhi held section 397 of the 1956 Companies Act in India to be analogous to Section 210 of the 1948 U.K. Companies Act, relying heavily on the reasoning of an alternative remedy provided by Palmer's Company Law (21st Edition). Relying on the decision of the Court in *Rajahmundry Electric Supply Corporation* vs. *A. Nageshwar Rao and Others*[45] in contrast with that of the case of *Shanti Prasad Jain* vs. *Kalinga Tubes,*[46] the Court went on to state that the essence of Section 397 as an alternative remedy to shareholders was that it remained independent of the qualification required as an exception to the rule in *Foss.* Further, in the matter between *Needle Industries (India) Ltd.* vs. *Needle Industries (Holding) Ltd.,*[47] the Court went on to observe that oppression

43. (2007) U.K.P.C. 26.
44. I.L.R. 1975 Delhi 427.
45. AIR 1956 213.
46. AIR 1962 Orissa 202.
47. 1981 S.C.R. (3) 698.

applications would be entertained so long as it could be credibly shown that the affairs of the Company were being conducted in a manner that was oppressive to the members or amounted to prejudice the interests of the public. However, although the strict scrutiny standard had been largely diluted as a result of the abovementioned judicial observations, the introduction of a high burden of proof significantly limited the scope of Section 397. For instance, the *prima facie* establishment of a lack of confidence or unfair Company dealings would not qualify the application as credible. What was required to be shown was an "unfair abuse of powers" and "an impairment of confidence in the probity", as was subsequently echoed by the Court in the cases of both *S.P. Jain* as well as *Needle Industries.*[48] On the question of coverage however, the Indian position has been liberal, by virtue of the echoing of judicial reasoning imported from the *Baltic Partners Case*[49], in the Indian cases of *Srikant Datta* vs. *Venkateshwara Real Estate Ltd.,*[50] whereby the Court held that although the applicants name did not appear in the Company's register of members, the concerned applicant could credibly make an individual oppression application under Section 397 of the 1956 Act. Therefore, although the standard of proof had been diluted previously in 1969, through the case of *Raghunath Mathur* vs. *Swarup Mathur*[51], to include a "reasonable probability of injury to the interests of the Company"[52], the later emergence of case law seem to indicate that a higher standard of proof would have to be discharged in terms of showing an individual cause of action. Further, under the 1956 regime and as was also observed in the abovementioned case, the oppression being complained of would have to be a continuing act of oppression, and single acts wouldn't afford a credible claim. In addition to the problem of standard of proof, one of the more vital issues of debate has been the discretionary scope of the Tribunal under 402(g) of the 1956 Act. While the 1964 case of *Seth Mohanlal Ganpatram* vs. *Jubilee Cotton Mills,*[53] observed that although the powers granted were very wide, an element of abundant caution would have to be exercise in interpretation, since the power was necessarily conditioned to only those matters contained within Section 397. Similarly, in the 1973 case of *Bennet*

48. *Supra* note 58.
49. *Supra* note 54.
50. (1990) 4 C.L.A. 3 (Karnataka).
51. (1967) 37 Comp Cas 802 (Allahabad).
52. *Ibid.*
53. (1964) 34 Comp Cas 777 (Gujarat).

Coleman and Co. and Maula Chand vs. *Union of India,*[54] a seemingly different yet liberal stand was endorsed by the Court when it laid down that so long as a reasonable nexus existed between the judicial order and the object of the Sections in question, the subject matter jurisdiction of the Court was not to be questioned. This particular line of reasoning was subsequently also endorsed in the 1977 matter between *Cosmosteels Pvt. Ltd.* vs. *Jairam Das Gupta.*[55] In a response that was significantly different from the liberal stand, the 1984 case of *V.J Thomas* vs. *Kuttanad Rubber Co. Ltd.,*[56] the Court stressed on the need to restrain itself when it came to questions of interfering in the internal affairs of the Company in question. The element of abundant caution was also stressed upon in the case of *Synchron Machine Tools Ltd.* vs. *Umesh Rao* (1992).[57] Meanwhile, in what was to be interpreted as the final limitation on the discretionary authority granted to the authority under Section 402(g) of the 1956 Act, the Court in the 1974 decision in the matter between *Prabhakaran* vs. *Selva Saroja,*[58] very clearly limited the scope of the "just and equitable" remedy by constraining its schematic application to those contemplated by Sections 397 and 398.

Concluding Remarks: Is there a Need to Redefine the Judicial Ambit?

The position which emerges from India is that although the initial string of case law clearly established that the statutory remedies were intended to afford greater coverage than the derivative action route, the subsequent case law clearly demonstrates an unusually high level of caution to be exercised by the Judiciary in "interfering" with the company's internal affairs. If one notices the manner in which statutory remedies were created in the first place, and the legislative trend therein, it becomes amply clear that the very purpose of these remedies was shareholder protection through greater "interference" in the Company's internal affairs. Initially, at the backdrop of the rule in *Foss*, this became increasingly difficult in the garb of avoiding frivolous litigation, since any caveat to the rule would have to be reflected in the form of judicial opinion. Given this general shortcoming, and the serious infirmities in derivative action proceedings, statutory remedies sought to increase the protection base by adopting a liberal stand and lowering the standard of proof. Evidently, the development of case law witnesses a movement of

54. MANU/MH/0134/1973.
55. 1978 AIR 375.
56. (1984) 56 Comp Cas 284 (Kerala).
57. I.L.R. 1992 Karnataka 3329.
58. (1978) 48 Comp Cas 503 (Madras).

law that is perhaps significantly different from what was contemplated. The Canadian and the British jurisprudence hint very clearly at a dilution of the exceptions to the rule in *Foss*, either by expanding the equitable scope of fraud or by redefining the definition of control or even by expanding the base of application to non-members. This expansion, coupled with the fact that the line of distinction between the two stands significantly diminished as a result of the general difficulty in drawing a strict line of difference, is indicative of the fact that derivative action in the modern context, has moved well beyond the rigid defines of the conservative common law approach. On the other hand, as India clearly observes, the remedy which was intended at compensating the strict recourse under common law derivative action, has constantly been greeted by a judicial cold shoulder, either through the lack of uniform precedent and acknowledgment, or through the general levels of caution exercised by it. Consequently, the author argues that the subject matter jurisdiction of Section 402(g) of the 1956 Act and Section 242(2) (m) of the 2013 Act must be expanded in terms of a lower level of caution and the lack of a strict constraining provision for the residual clause (402/242) considering that the very basis on which such remedies were to be made available, has been redefined significantly. Therefore, in the overall interests of the shareholder, the scope of the "just and equitable remedy" under the abovementioned Sections must be widened to include those acts of oppression which may afford a reasonable nexus between the judicial order and the intended coverage of the Sections.

Conclusion

Law is dynamic and being changed as per demand of society. Company law is the reflection of societal need as well as economic condition of the nation. It was enacted by the British several times for Indian economy since 1850 and after independence new law was enacted on the recommendation of Bhaba Committee in 1956 to adopt new industrial policy. The Companies Act, 1956 has been already amended as many as 24 times since 1956. The major amendments were Amendment Act, 1988 after considering the recommendations of the Sachar Committee and the Companies Amendment Act, 2002 on the basis of the report of the Eradi Committee. The new law of 2013 has been enacted for highly competitive globalised corporate sector of India through better protection for investors and greater flexibility for entrepreneur. But problems have not been solved completely. Presently, two Acts are in force and debates are going on. Again the term 'Corporate Social Responsibility' has not been properly defined and tax exemption for CSR has opened another debate. New experiments and researches are being continued for better transparency and fairness. Almost every month new Regulations with their amendments are coming on from Ministry of Corporate Affairs and SEBI. The Companies (Amendment) Act, 2015 inserted another new corporate crime[1] relating to public deposits. The Securities Laws Amendment of 2015 has been introduced 'Special Courts' in the SCR Act, 1956, the SEBI Act, 1992 and the Depositories Act, 1995 to deal with related matters. The forums are being transferred from the High Courts to Company Law Board to National Tribunal. Though constitutional validity of company tribunals of 2005 Amendment and 2013 Act has

1. Section 76A of the Companies Act, 2013.

been approved by the Supreme Court but overlapping of jurisdiction by too many forums under new law is still an issue. The new law has incorporated prohibition of insider trading under section 195 and at the same time in 2015, SEBI has introduced new regulations on Insider Trading repealing 1992 regulations. Too many regulatory agencies may complicate the case. The Damodaran Committee[2] already pointed out that India's regulatory architecture is getting complex with the setting up of new regulatory bodies which are inadequately empowered and insufficiently manned in terms of both numbers and skills. We know, one of the main functions of company is to regulate conflicts of interest between directors and shareholders and historically it was the courts that played the major role in discharging that function by applying to directors a range of duties analogous to those they had developed in relation to trustees.[3] Now Indian judiciary has a great role to interpret the new company law in various upcoming cases to make it workable in present socio-economic condition. In the line of the Supreme Court of India, Overseas investments in Joint Ventures (JV) and Wholly Owned Subsidiaries (WOS) have been recognised as important avenues of global business in India. Potential users of off-shore finance are: international companies, individuals, investors and others and capital flows through FDI, Portfolio Debt Investment and Foreign Portfolio Equity Investment and so on. Demand for off-shore facilities has considerably increased owing to high growth rates of cross-border investments and a number of rich global investors have come forward to use high technology and communication infrastructures. Removal of barriers to cross-border trade, the liberalisation of financial markets and new communication technologies have had positive effects on global economic growth and India has also been greatly benefited.[4] Now it is a challenge before the nation to combat with present economic problems within globalised and liberalised Indian market through the Companies Act, 2013.

2. Report of the Committee for Reforming the Regulatory Environment for doing Business in India, Ministry of Corporate Affairs, September 2013, p. 29.
3. Eilis Ferran, *Principles of Corporate Finance Law*, Oxford University Press, 1st edition 2008, p. 10.
4. *Vodafone International Holdings B.V.* vs. *Union of India*, Civil Appeal No. 733 of 2012 (Arising out of SLP (C)) No. 26529 of 2010, pp. 96-97.

Index